Peter Harrison's
PC CRASH COURSE SERIES

 *British authors!*

Microsoft Word 2000
Beginners Course

 *You are not allowed to copy any part of this publication in any format without the written permission of the publisher.*

Microsoft Word 2000
Beginners Course

227 ~ ISBN: 1873005695 ~ 25/06/99

Welcome!

Thank you for choosing this book. A team of authors and editors at **PC Productions** has worked together to develop the course to the highest standards. We continually monitor the style of writing and check that instructions and exercises work properly. Our aim is to provide course material that is easy to understand and use - it should also be an effective learning tool for the user. We hope that you will be fully satisfied with this course.

PC Productions publishes a large range of computer books and training courseware with over 150 titles in all. More information is available through your local book shop or dealer.

GLASGOW CITY COUNCIL LIBRARIES/ARCHIVE	
C002645892	
SM	Cypher
22.10.01	£22.95
005.369 20	CW

Microsoft, MS-DOS, PivotTable, PowerPoint, TipWizard, Windows and Wingdings are registered trademarks, and AutoSum and IntelliSense are trademarks of Microsoft Corporation in the USA and other countries. Word Pro is a trademark and 1-2-3, Approach, Freelance Graphics and Lotus are registered trademarks of Lotus Development Corporation. WordPerfect is a registered trademark of Corel, Inc. Paradox is a registered trademark of Ansa Software, a Borland Company, and Quattro Pro is a trademark of Borland International, Inc. IBM is a registered trademark of International Business Machines Corporation. Hewlett-Packard, HP, LaserJet and PCL are registered trademarks of Hewlett-Packard Company. Arial and Times New Roman are registered trademarks of The Monotype Corporation. Avery is a registered trademark of Avery Dennison Corporation. All other brand or product names are trademarks or registered trademarks of their respective companies.

Companies, names and data used in screen shots and examples are fictitious, unless otherwise stated.

PC Productions Limited cannot accept any responsibility for loss, disruption or damage to your data or your computer system that may occur while using our courseware.

© Copyright PC Productions Limited, all rights reserved.

PC Productions Limited
Dudbridge Road
Stroud
GL5 3HT
England

Published by
PC Productions Limited

Printed and bound
in England

Quick Reference

Chapter 1 ~ Introduction 11
Chapter 2 ~ Getting Started 16
Chapter 3 ~ Your First Document 47
Chapter 4 ~ Your Second Document 67
Chapter 5 ~ Open, Close, New & Save As 81
Chapter 6 ~ Views, Toolbars & Options 97
Chapter 7 ~ Selecting Text for Editing 121
Chapter 8 ~ Simple Text Formatting.............................. 137
Chapter 9 ~ Simple Paragraph Formatting 153
Chapter 10 ~ Undo & Redo 175
Chapter 11 ~ The Spelling and Grammar Checker 185
Chapter 12 ~ Printing & Print Preview.......................... 205
Chapter 13 ~ Page Layout 219
Chapter 14 ~ Headers & Footers 233
Chapter 15 ~ Addressing Envelopes & Labels.............. 249
Chapter 16 ~ A Final Exercise 261
Appendix A ~ Windows Basics....................................... 267

Study instructions

Items with a round bullet are instructions that you should follow. For example:

- `Open the` **`File`** `menu and choose` **`Close.`**

Other indented, bulleted items are information only - they should <u>not</u> be treated as instructions. For example:

- ✋ To close a document, open the **File** menu and choose **Close**

Running text may contain explanations or supplementary information.

Using the mouse

Most application programs these days make extensive use of the mouse. There are a few mouse operations that you should be familiar with:

Operation	Description
Point	To point using the mouse, simply move your mouse across your desk or mouse mat. The mouse pointer on the screen will follow the movement. If you run out of space, just lift the mouse, move it and put it down again, then carry on moving it.
Click	To click an object means that you should point at the desired object and press the LEFT-HAND mouse button ONCE.
Right-click	As for Click above, but using the RIGHT-HAND mouse button instead.
Double-click	As for Click above, but press the LEFT-HAND mouse button TWICE in quick succession. If you do this too slowly, your computer will interpret this as two single clicks.
Drag	First position the mouse pointer over an object, then press the left-hand mouse button down and hold it down while you move the mouse around. The object will be dragged around until you release the mouse button.

Table of Contents

Chapter 1 ~ Introduction 11
   What is a word processor? 11
   Course objectives 13
   The insertion point and mouse pointer 14

Chapter 2 ~ Getting Started 16
   Starting Word 17
   The Office Assistant 19
   The Word window 20
   The Minimize, Maximize, Restore and Close buttons 22
      The Minimize button 22
      The Maximize button 22
      The Restore button 22
      The Close buttons 23
      Re-sizing and moving a window 23
   The insertion point 24
   The mouse pointer 25
   Using the menu system 25
      Using the mouse 26
      Using the toolbar buttons 29
      The More Buttons palette 29
      Using the keyboard 31
      Usage data 32
   Shortcut key combinations 33
   The shortcut menu 34
   Using the Office Assistant 35
      Showing the Office Assistant 36
      Using the Office Assistant 37
      Resetting the tips 38
      Hiding the Office Assistant 39
   Closing a document 39
   Exiting Word 41
   Summary ~ Getting Started 42

Chapter 3 ~ Your First Document 47
   Typing text 48
   Automatic spelling & grammar checking 48
      Turning on automatic spelling & grammar checking 50
      Correcting a word 51
      Correcting mistakes as you type 52
      Word wrap and the Enter key 53
   Typing more text 53
   Moving the insertion point 56
   Changing text 58
   Saving your document 58
   Printing your document 60
      Using the Print button in the toolbar 61
   A few more changes 61
      Saving the document again 61
   Turning off automatic spelling & grammar checking 62
   Summary ~ Your First Document 63

Chapter 4 ~ Your Second Document 67
   Typing text 68
   Saving your document 69

Print Preview 70
Adding more text 72
  Closing the document 73
Exercise 4a 74
Exercise 4b 74
Exercise 4c 75
Summary ~ Your Second Document 77

Chapter 5 ~ Open, Close, New & Save As 81
Opening and closing a document 81
Open - using the Look in box 83
Clearing the screen 84
  New or Close? 84
Starting a new document 85
  Using the menu option File, New 85
  Using the New Blank Document button or Ctrl+N 86
Working with two Word document windows 87
  Closing without saving 88
Save As 88
Recently opened files 90
Exercise 5a 91
Exercise 5b 92
Summary ~ Open, Close, New & Save As 93

Chapter 6 ~ Views, Toolbars & Options 97
The different views 98
  The Document Map 101
  Web Layout view 102
Zooming a document 103
Showing formatting marks 105
Toolbars 106
  Resetting a toolbar 107
  Changing the length of a toolbar 107
  Other toolbars 108
Hiding and showing the ruler 111
Options for customising Word 112
Changing the units of measurement 113
Exercise 6a 115
Summary ~ Views, Toolbars & Options 116

Chapter 7 ~ Selecting Text for Editing 121
Scrolling a document 122
  ScreenTips 123
  Using the mouse and keyboard 124
  Scrolling with the Microsoft IntelliMouse 125
About selecting text 126
Selecting text using the mouse 126
  Selecting a phrase 127
  Selecting a single word 128
  Selecting a sentence 128
  Selecting a line of text 129
  Selecting a paragraph 129
  Selecting a whole document 129
  Shift & click - selecting large sections of text 130
Selecting text using the keyboard 130
  Selecting a phrase 130
  Selecting a single word 131
  Selecting a sentence 132
  Selecting a paragraph 132
  Selecting a whole document 132
Extending selected text 133
Summary ~ Selecting Text for Editing 133

Chapter 8 ~ Simple Text Formatting 137
- Applying bold, italic and underlining to selected text 138
    - Undoing changes 138
    - Bold 139
    - Underlining text 140
    - Italic 141
- Combining features 141
    - Removing a feature 141
- Applying the features as you type 142
- Changing the font and font size 143
- Printing the document 145
- Exercise 8a 146
- Exercise 8b 147
- Exercise 8c 148
- Summary ~ Simple Text Formatting 150

Chapter 9 ~ Simple Paragraph Formatting 153
- Paragraph alignment 154
- Indents 156
- Click and Type 157
- Bullets 160
    - Automatic bullets as you type 161
    - Removing bullets 162
- Lists of numbered points 162
    - Automatic numbering as you type 163
- Aligning text as type 164
- Using default tab stops 166
    - Showing tab characters in text 166
    - Adding some more entries 167
- Exercise 9a 167
- Exercise 9b 169
- Summary ~ Simple Paragraph Formatting 170

Chapter 10 ~ Undo & Redo 175
- Immediate undos 176
    - Repeated undos 177
- Using the Undo and Redo lists 178
    - Using Undo 178
    - Using Redo 179
- Exercise 10a 181
- Summary ~ Undo & Redo 182

Chapter 11 ~ The Spelling and Grammar Checker 185
- Using the Spelling and Grammar Checker 186
- Checking spelling and grammar as you type 187
- Spelling & grammar checking on demand 188
    - Changing and ignoring suggestions 190
    - Correcting grammar problems 191
    - Adding words to AutoCorrect 193
- Spelling and grammar checking options 194
    - Custom dictionaries 196
- Word count 197
- Exercise 11a 198
- Exercise 11b 199
- Summary ~ The Spelling & Grammar Checker 200

Chapter 12 ~ Printing & Print Preview 205
- Choosing a printer 206
- Using the Print button in the toolbar 208
- Choosing what to print 208
    - Printing the current page only 210
    - Printing specific pages 210
    - Printing selected text 210

How many copies?.. 211
Previewing a document 211
Exercise 12a 214
Summary ~ Printing & Print Preview.. 215

Chapter 13 ~ Page Layout 219
The general layout of the page 220
Margins 221
Paper size options 224
Paper source options... 225
Layout options 226
Inserting manual page breaks 227
    Page breaks in Normal view 228
Exercise 13a 229
Summary ~ Page Layout 230

Chapter 14 ~ Headers & Footers.. 233
Using headers and footers... 234
Adding a header 235
Adding a footer 235
    Inserting a page number 236
Changing the header and footer 236
Different on odd and even pages.. 237
    Header and footer AutoText 239
Different on the first page 241
Formatting headers and footers.. 242
Exercise 14a 243
Summary ~ Headers & Footers 245

Chapter 15 ~ Addressing Envelopes & Labels 249
Addressing envelopes 250
    Changing the delivery address... 251
    Envelope options 251
    The return address.. 253
    Printing the envelope 253
Labels 254
    Label options... 254
Exercise 15a 256
Exercise 15b 257
Exercise 15c 258
Summary ~ Addressing Envelopes & Labels....................................... 258

Chapter 16 ~ A Final Exercise 261
Creating the letter 261
    Adding the header and footer.. 263
    Entering the text 263
Saving the letter... 264
Addressing the envelope 265
Printing the document 265

Appendix A ~ Windows Basics 267
DOS.. 267
The arrival of Windows 268
Windows 95 & 98.. 269
    Pnp – plug and play 270
    Long file names... 270
    Windows 98 271
Starting Windows 95.. 271
    Logging on 271
    The Welcome screen 272
The Desktop 274
The Start button 275
The Taskbar 277
Closing programs 278

Shutting Down 279

Chapter 1 ~ Introduction

Welcome to the *Microsoft Word 2000 Beginners Course*.

The sheer volume of original documentation supplied with any major software application these days can be rather daunting. It is not intended that this course should simply replace that original documentation. It has been designed to guide you through the most important features of the program, using language that is easy to understand and examples that are easy to follow.

In this chapter you can read about:

- What is a word processor?
- The course objectives
- Using the mouse to point, click, double-click and drag
- The insertion point and mouse pointer

What is a word processor?

Your word processing system - program plus computer - could be considered to be a typewriter equipped with built-in scissors, paste and correction fluid. Although a word processing program functions in the same way as a highly sophisticated typewriter, there are important differences:

- You can write letters, reports, memoranda, invoices and much, much more, quickly and efficiently
- You can print them out and store them for future use
- You do not have to interrupt your work in any way when a line fills up, or at the end of a page - the word processor will automatically advance your text onto a new line or a new page
- You will never have to re-write a page if you make a mistake - just correct the mistake and carry on

- It will recognise typing errors and correct them for you

- Using the available fonts and font sizes, you can dramatically improve the look of your documents

- You can send the same letter to a number of different people by copying the letter as many times as required and inserting the different names and addresses

The following pictures show a document in the making.

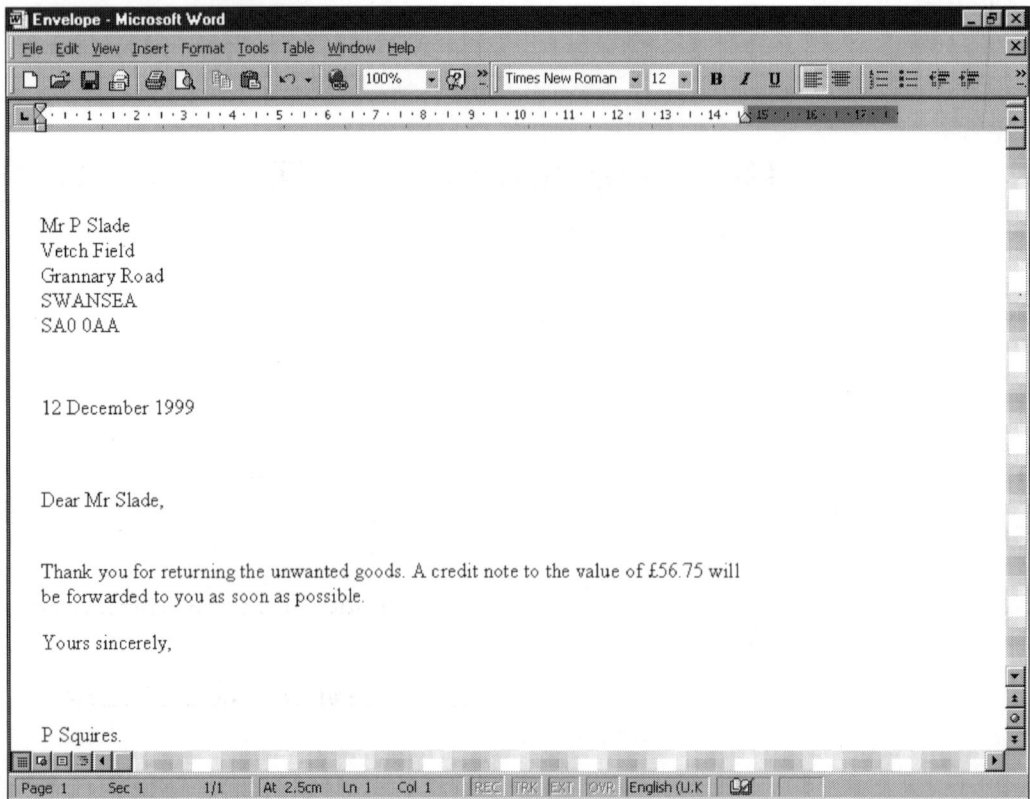

You can edit the document and apply different styles before printing it.

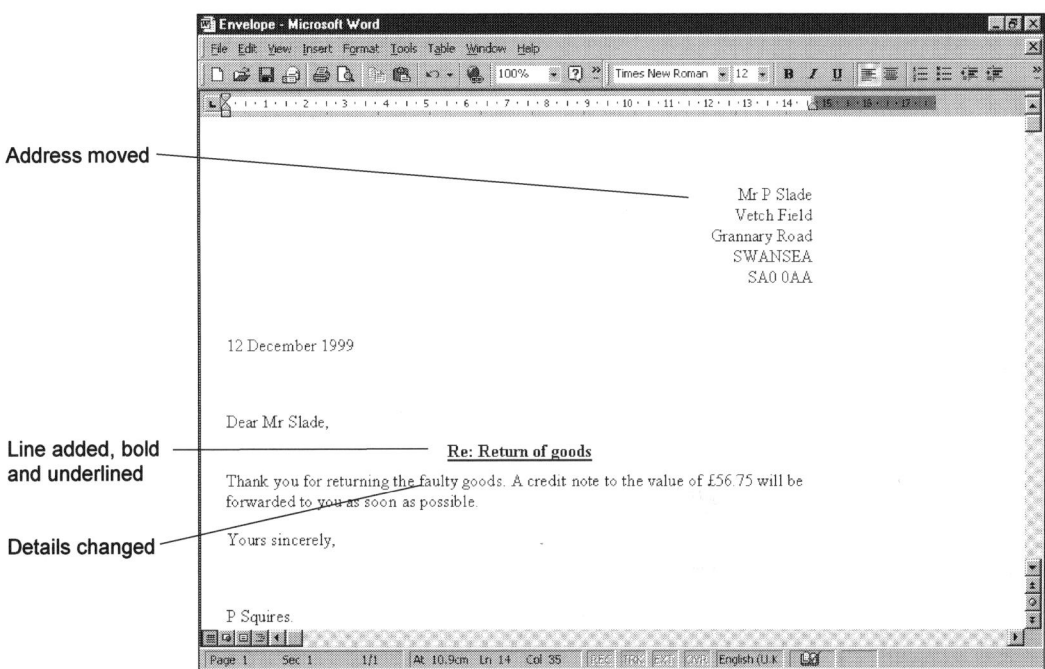

Address moved

Line added, bold and underlined

Details changed

The document can be saved, re-used and printed as many times as you like!

Course objectives

By the end of this course you will be able to:

- Start and exit Word.

- Use the menus, toolbar buttons and shortcut key combinations.

- Change and zoom the view; hide and show toolbars.

- Create new documents; type text making use of word wrap; correct mistakes using the Spelling and Grammar Checker.

- Use Undo and Redo.

- Open, close, save and print documents; use Print Preview to view a document on screen as it will be printed.

- Select words, sentences and phrases; apply various fonts, font sizes and font styles; align paragraphs.

- Use the Page Setup options to set margins, paper size and orientation.
- Add headers and footers to your documents.
- Print envelopes and labels.

Having learnt all of the above, you will be able to produce professional documents and letters, address envelopes and save the document files for future use.

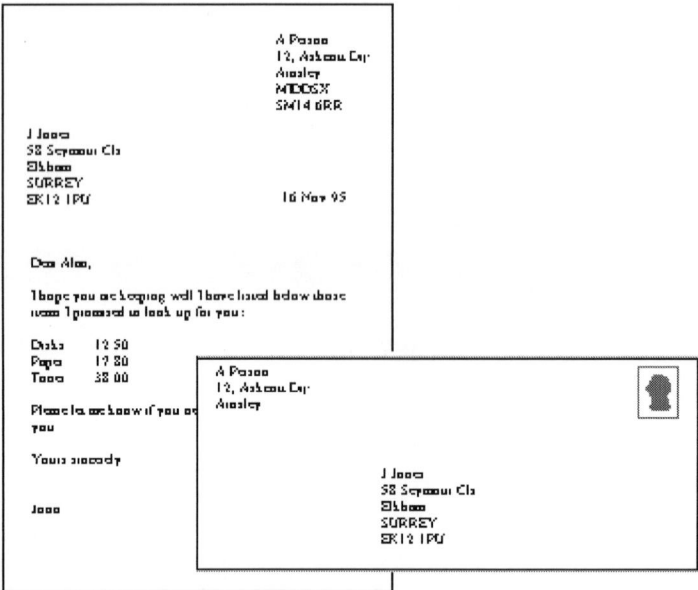

The insertion point and mouse pointer

If you are working with text, or have to enter text in an input box, you will see a flashing bar - this is known as the *insertion point*. Whenever you type anything, the text is always inserted at the *insertion point*.

- The mouse pointer is the small picture that moves around on your screen when you move your mouse.
- Most often the mouse pointer will be an arrow when positioned over a menu option, toolbar button, the Status bar or a scroll bar.

- When positioned over a text area it will be an I-beam. Clicking the mouse on the text area moves the insertion point to that position.

- When positioned over the borders of a window, or other object that can be re-sized, it will change to a double-headed arrow.

The mouse pointer may take other shapes at other times.

With so much to learn, it's time to get started! ***GOOD LUCK!***

Notes

Use this page to make notes of your own.

Page #   Notes

Chapter 2 ~ Getting Started

In this chapter you will learn about:

- Starting Word
- The Word window
- The **Minimize**, **Maximize**, **Restore** and **Close** buttons
- The Office Assistant
- The insertion point and mouse pointer
- Using the menu system
- Using the mouse and keyboard to choose menu options
- Buttons in the toolbars
- Shortcut key combinations
- Closing a document
- Exiting Word

It is assumed that:

- Word is installed correctly on your system
- You know the basics about using Windows
- You know how to *click*, *double-click* and *right-click* with the mouse

Starting Word

- If necessary, switch on your computer and printer – Windows should start automatically.
- In the Taskbar, click the **Start** button to open the Start menu.
- In the Start menu, point to **Programs**.

Microsoft Word 2000 ~ Beginners Course

Your menus may differ from those shown here

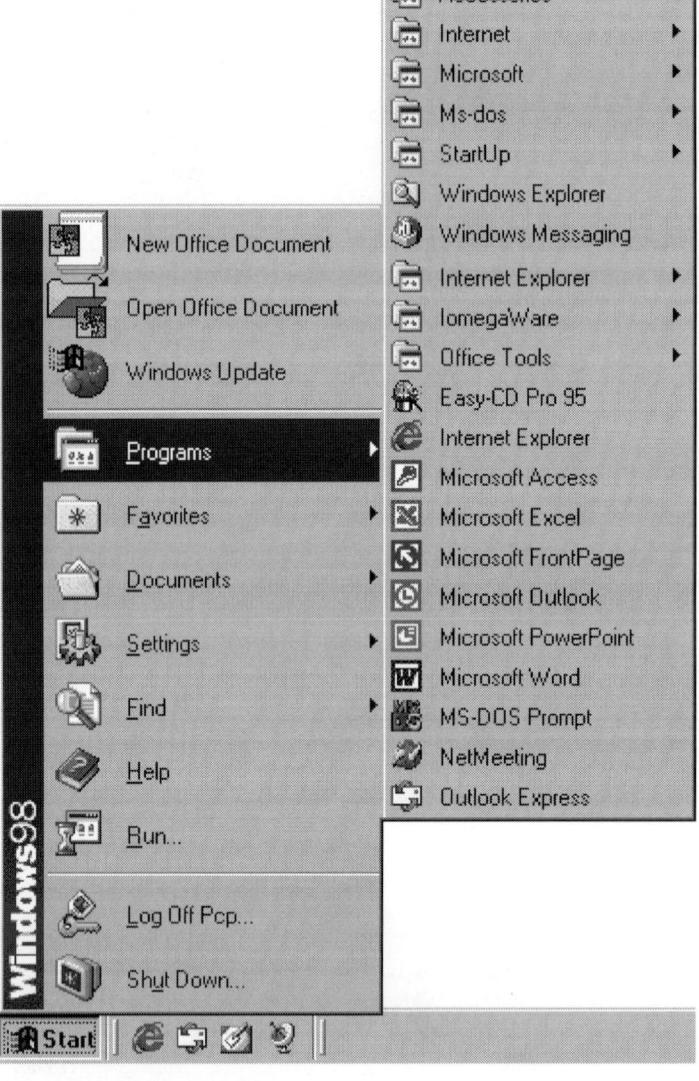

- In the Programs menu, click **Microsoft Word**.

> ✋ *It is possible that the **Microsoft Word** icon is in a different menu, for example, Microsoft Office.*

After a few seconds the Microsoft Word window will be displayed. The Office Assistant may also appear.

> ✋ *All the pictures in this course are taken from a system showing 800 x 600 pixels. Your screen displays may differ slightly from the pictures shown, but the important details will be the same.*

The Office Assistant

The Office Assistant is a small character that is displayed on your screen - there are eight different characters to choose from. It offers help and advice as you work with applications in the Microsoft Office suite. If this is the first time Word has been opened on your computer, the Office Assistant will be there to greet you. It will display the welcome message shown in the next picture.

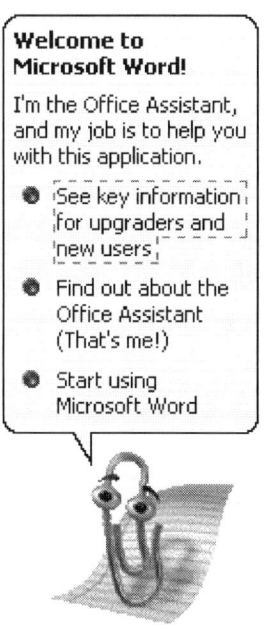

If the Welcome to Microsoft Word message is displayed:

- Click **Start using Microsoft Word.**

If the Office Assistant is not displayed:

- In the toolbar at the top of your screen, click the **Microsoft Word Help** button - it's near the middle. Then click outside the Office Assistant speech bubble to close it.

The Office Assistant is displayed and Microsoft Word will be ready with a new document.

The Word window

In Word 2000, when you have only one document open, it is the Word window that you see. This is what is shown in the next picture - the main components are indicated in the picture, and explained in the table that follows it.

If you have more than one document open, each document has its own Word document window. Each of these windows has the main components of the Word window - Menu bar, toolbars, Status bar and so on. The key difference is that a Word document window only has one set of Window buttons - these operate on the document window. To switch between open documents, you can use the buttons in the Windows Taskbar.

At present you have only one document open so the Word window is displayed. Note that this has one set of Window buttons and an extra **Close** button - this closes the document but not the Word window.

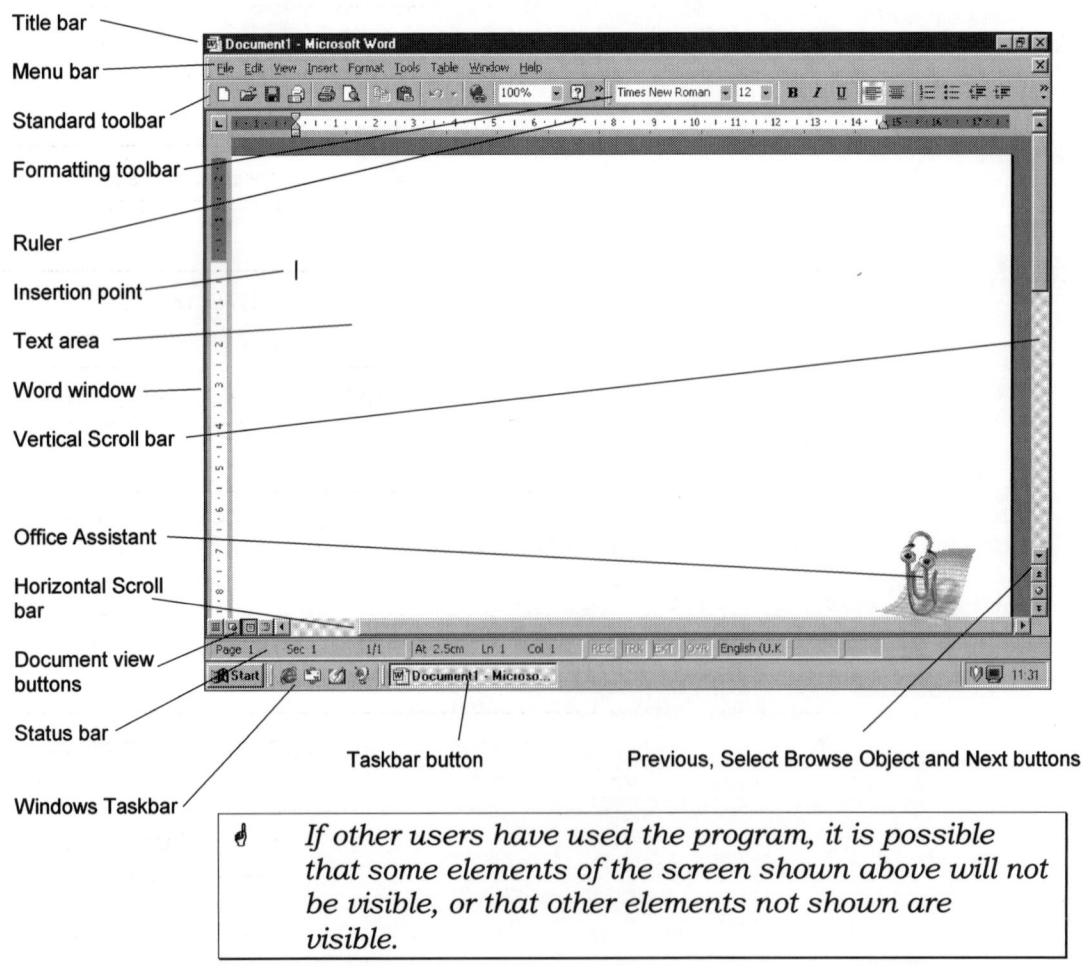

If other users have used the program, it is possible that some elements of the screen shown above will not be visible, or that other elements not shown are visible.

The Word window may fill the whole of your screen. The following table explains the main components of this window:

Component	Description
Word window	If you have only one document open, the Word window is displayed. The window may be maximised to fill the screen. If you have more than one document open, each is displayed in a separate Word document window - more about this later.
Title bar	Displays Microsoft Word and the current document name.
Menu bar	Consists of a list of menus that can be opened to choose features and functions.
Standard toolbar	Shortcut buttons to access some features quickly by clicking the button.
Formatting toolbar	Shortcut buttons to help you quickly change the format of the text.
Ruler	Ruler to help you judge positions and quickly set tabs, etc.
Text area	Area for typing your document.
Scroll bars	Show you where in the document you are working, relative to its start and finish, and allow you to move to other parts of the document.
Document View buttons	These buttons let you change the view of the document.
Select Browse Object button	Displays the Select Browse Object menu, where you can choose the type of object you want to browse through the document.
Previous and Next buttons	These buttons let you show the next or previous object in the document, based on your choice in the Select Browse Object menu.
Status bar	Displays information about the active document or selected feature.
The Office Assistant	A small character that offers help and advice as you work with programs in Microsoft Office.
Windows Taskbar	The Taskbar is not part of the Word program; it belongs to the Windows system. If it is not visible, point at the very bottom of the screen and it may appear.

Before continuing, you will hide the Office Assistant. But don't worry, he will pop up again later. He is never far away!

- Right-click the Office Assistant and choose **Hide**.

The Minimize, Maximize, Restore and Close buttons

The Word window has a **Minimize**, **Maximize**, **Restore** and **Close** button in the top right-hand corner. If you have more than one document open, these buttons minimise, maximise, restore and close the Word document window. If you have only one document open, there will also be a **Close Window** button for the document beneath the Window buttons for the Word window.

> *The **Minimize**, **Maximize**, **Restore**, **Close** and **Close Window** buttons have ScreenTips. If you forget which button is which, just point the mouse at a particular button and a ScreenTip will appear telling you the name of the button.*

The Minimize button

 ✧ If you minimise a window, it is reduced to a button in the Taskbar - click the button to show the window again

The Maximize button

 ✧ If you maximise a window, it expands to fill the whole screen

The Restore button

 ✧ If you have maximised a window, you can click its **Restore** button to reduce its size again

The Close buttons

↳ When you have more than one document open, if you click the **Close** button, only that particular document will be closed

↳ When you have only one document open, if you click the **Close** button for the Word window, the whole program is closed down

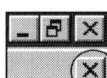

↳ When you have only one document open, if you click the **Close Window** button, only the document is closed - the Word window remains open with no document displayed

Re-sizing and moving a window

Using the buttons mentioned, you can quickly re-size a window. Try this now.

- In the top right-hand corner of the Word window, click the **Minimize** button.

The window is reduced to a button in the Windows Taskbar. If you don't have any other programs running, you will see the Windows Desktop.

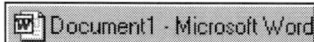

- In the Taskbar, click the **Document1 - Microsoft Word** button.

The window fills the screen once again.

- In the top right-hand corner of the Word window, click the **Restore** button.

The window is reduced in size. You can also re-size a window by dragging any of its borders in or out.

- Position the mouse pointer over any border of the Word window.

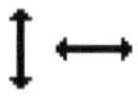

The mouse pointer will change to a double-headed arrow.

- Use the mouse to drag the border in or out a little.

You can move the window around your screen by dragging its Title bar.

- Position the mouse pointer over the Title bar of the Word window and drag the window left, right, up or down a little.

- To finish off, maximise the window again.

The insertion point

At the start of the text area you will see a flashing bar - this is known as the *insertion point*. Whenever you type text, the text is always inserted into your document at the insertion point.

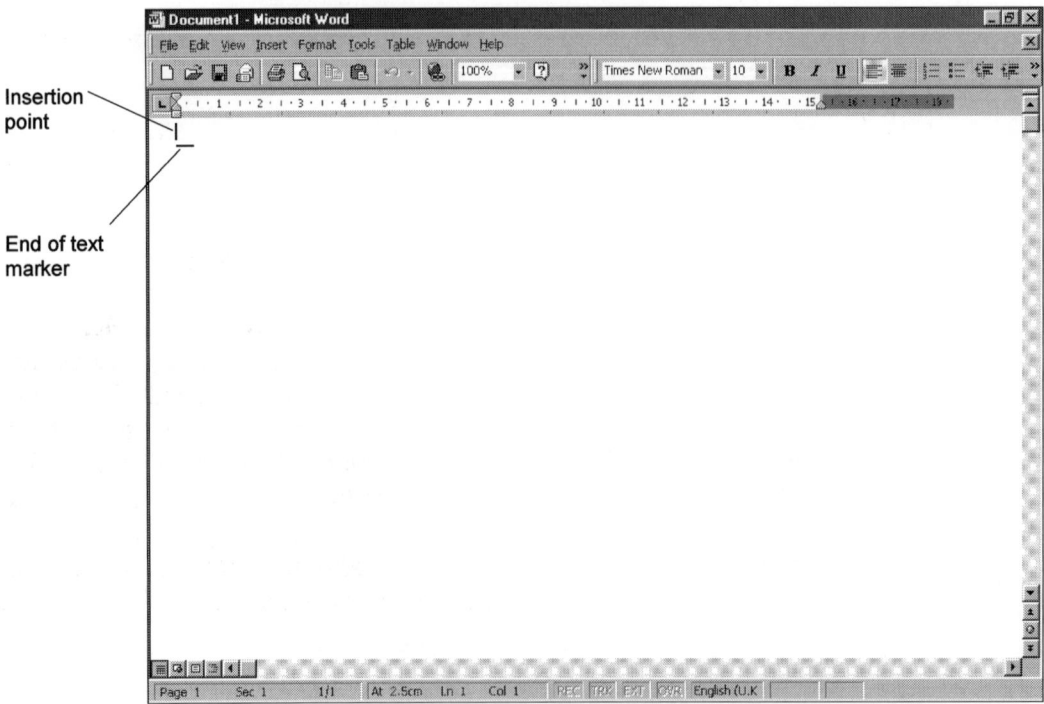

Insertion point

End of text marker

The end of text marker (_) shows the end of the document. This may or may not be shown just now, depending on which view is displayed - as you will learn later on, Word has several different views.

The mouse pointer

The *mouse pointer* is the small picture that moves around on your screen when you move your mouse. The mouse pointer will change its appearance depending on its position.

Most often the mouse pointer will be an arrow when positioned over a menu option, the Status bar, Taskbar or a scroll bar.

When positioned over the text area the mouse pointer will be an *I-beam*. Clicking the mouse on the text area moves the insertion point to that position.

In Print Layout view - which you will learn about later - the mouse takes on other shapes when it is pointed below the text area. If you double-click the page with one of these mouse pointers you can then start typing at that position on the page. The alignment of the text you type will depend on which pointer was displayed when you double-clicked - more about this in a later chapter.

Using the menu system

Word has a *pull-down* menu system. There is a Menu bar along the top of the screen. The first three menu headings are: File, Edit, and View. Choosing one of these headings will open up that menu to show a list of options. At first, only a few options will be displayed. However, if you wait a short while, or click the double-arrow button at the bottom of the menu, several other options will be displayed. These options are shown with a paler grey background. Some options in the menus will produce dialog boxes with more options in.

There are many ways of choosing options:

- Use the mouse to click the desired choice in the Menu bar. The menu will then open and you can click the desired option.

- Each menu heading in the Menu bar has one letter underlined. You can use the **Alt** key together with this letter to open the menu. The **File** menu heading has the letter F underlined. By pressing **Alt+F** you would open the **File** menu. Each option can then be chosen by pressing the corresponding underlined letter for that option.

- Some options have a shortcut key combination, such as **Ctrl+S** to save the current document. You will learn some of these combinations as you work through the course.

- Some options have a button in one of the toolbars which allows you to choose the option quickly with a single click. If you position the mouse pointer over a button in a toolbar, the button will pop up from the toolbar, and a small box will be shown below the button to tell you what it does. The small box is called a ScreenTip.

- In a dialog box, you will often see that one option is active because it has a dotted line around it. This means that pressing **Enter** will cause the active option to be chosen. You can use the **Tab** key to move between the various options on display.

The method you eventually choose will be a personal decision. Most people will combine the different methods as they find most convenient.

Using the mouse

Try choosing one of the menu options using the mouse.

- ```
  In the Menu bar, click View to open the
  View menu.
  ```
  ```

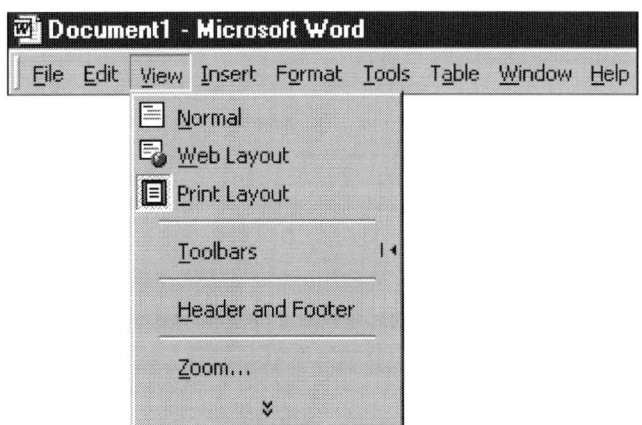

If you wait a few seconds, the menu will probably expand to show more options.

- If the menu does not expand to show more options, click the double-arrow button at the bottom of the menu.

The full menu is now displayed.

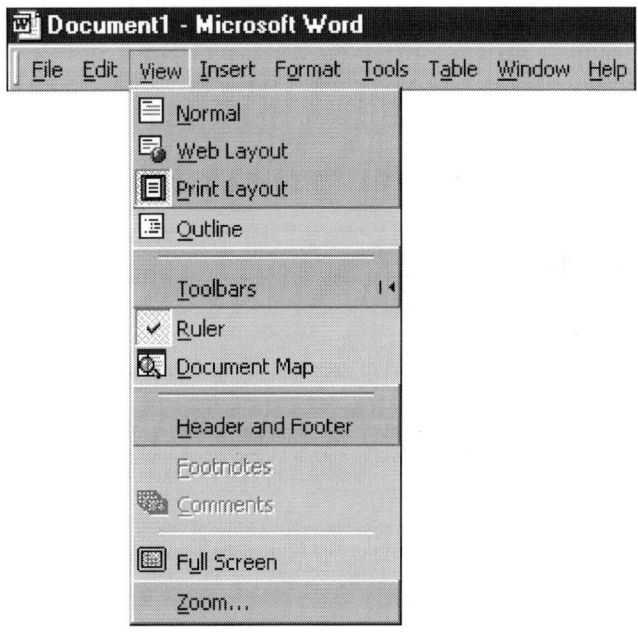

There are a few points to note about menu options:

- The options shown with a pale grey background are those you are likely to use less often. If you choose one of these options, the next time you open the menu it will be displayed in the first list of options you see - as you work with Word, it customises your menus.

- The options shown in the same colour as the background are not available at the present moment and cannot be chosen, for example, **Footnotes** and **Comments**.

- Some options have three dots after them, for example, **Zoom...**. This means that choosing the option will open a dialog box.

- Some options will have a tick to their left, for example, the **Ruler** option. This is used for options that can be turned on or off by choosing the option. A tick means that the option is on, or active.

- Some options will have a depressed symbol to their left, for example, the **Print Layout** option. This is used to show which option from a group of options is chosen, or active.

- Other options have a picture to their left, for example the **Document Map** option. The picture corresponds to a shortcut button that may be found in one of the many toolbars.

- Some options will have an arrow to their right, for example,
Toolbars. This is used to show that this option opens a sub-menu if you choose it.

- Some options will have a shortcut key combination to their right, for example, **Save Ctrl+S** (in the **File** menu). These key combinations can be used without first having to open a menu.

Try one of the options.

- `Click the Zoom option.`

The Zoom dialog box is now displayed. Don't worry about what it all means for now, you will just close it again.

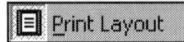

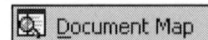

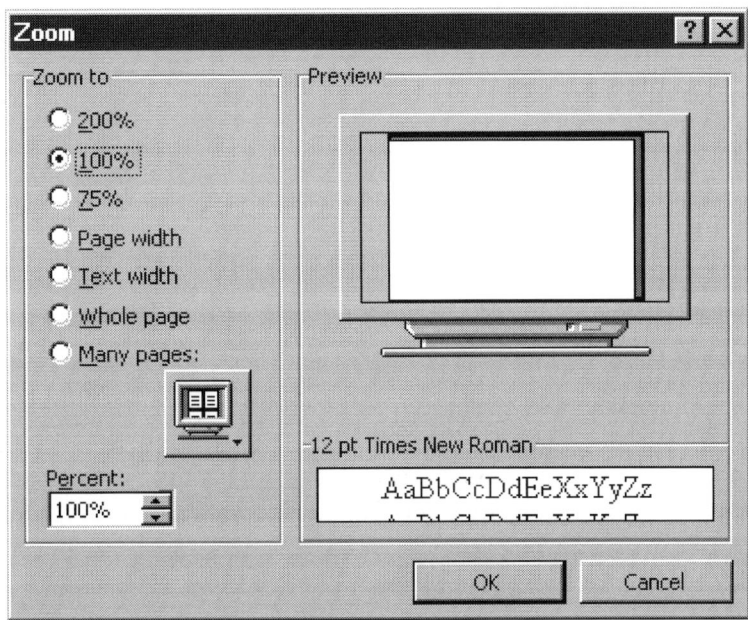

- Click **Cancel** to close the dialog box without making any changes.

Using the toolbar buttons

Some of the menu options have a shortcut button in one of the toolbars. The example in the margin is the toolbar button for saving a document.

- Position the mouse pointer over the **Save** button, without clicking it, and wait a second.

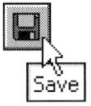

The button pops up and a ScreenTip that names the button shows that you are pointing at the **Save** button.

The More Buttons palette

If your toolbars are arranged side by side, you will not be able to see all the buttons in each toolbar. Buttons that you use less often can be found in the More Buttons palette of a particular toolbar. To display a More Buttons palette:

⇨ Click the **More Buttons** button at the right-hand end of the appropriate toolbar

Microsoft Word 2000 ~ Beginners Course

You will look at the More Buttons palette of the Standard toolbar.

- Move the mouse pointer over the **More Buttons** button in the centre of your screen - you will see the ScreenTip <u>More Buttons</u>.

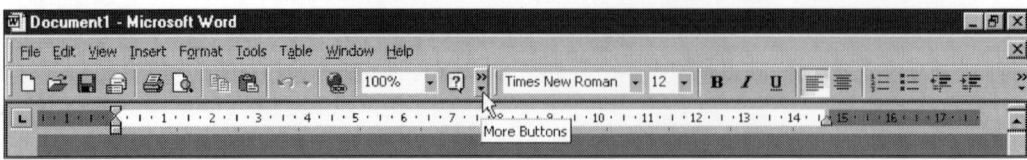

- Click the **More Buttons** button.

A palette of extra buttons is displayed.

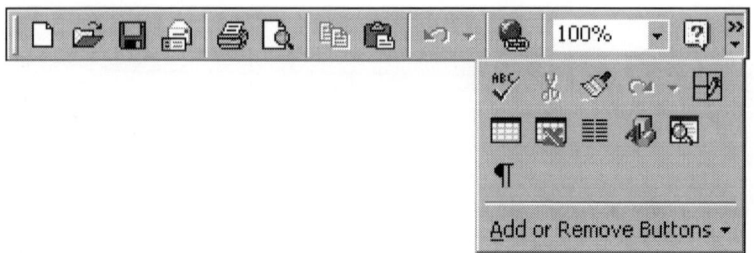

You can now see all the buttons that make up the Standard toolbar. If you stacked the toolbars one above the other, all these buttons would be displayed on your screen all the time. The Formatting toolbar to the right of the Standard toolbar also has a hidden palette of buttons that can be displayed in the same way.

- In the Standard toolbar, click the **Spelling and Grammar** button.

Because the document is empty, the spelling check will be completed straight away.

- Click **OK** to close the message box.

The Spelling message box is closed again.

> ☝ *Just in case!*
> *If, for some reason, you have typed some text and the spelling checker has found a mistake, you will need to click **Cancel** to close the Spelling and Grammar dialog box.*

Note that the **Spelling and Grammar** button is now visible in the Standard toolbar across the top of your screen. Word customises your toolbars so that the buttons you use most often are displayed all the time. Don't worry about losing the buttons you don't use very often. You can find them in the More Buttons palette of that toolbar - just click the **More Buttons** button to display them.

Using the keyboard

This time, try using the keys to choose a menu option. In the Menu bar, the **F** in **File** is underlined and can be used together with the **Alt** key to open this menu.

- ```
  Press Alt+F to open the File menu.
  ```

Notice that the **A** in **Save As** is underlined.

- ```
  Press A to choose the Save As option.
  ```

The Save As dialog box is displayed - again, don't worry just now about what it all means.

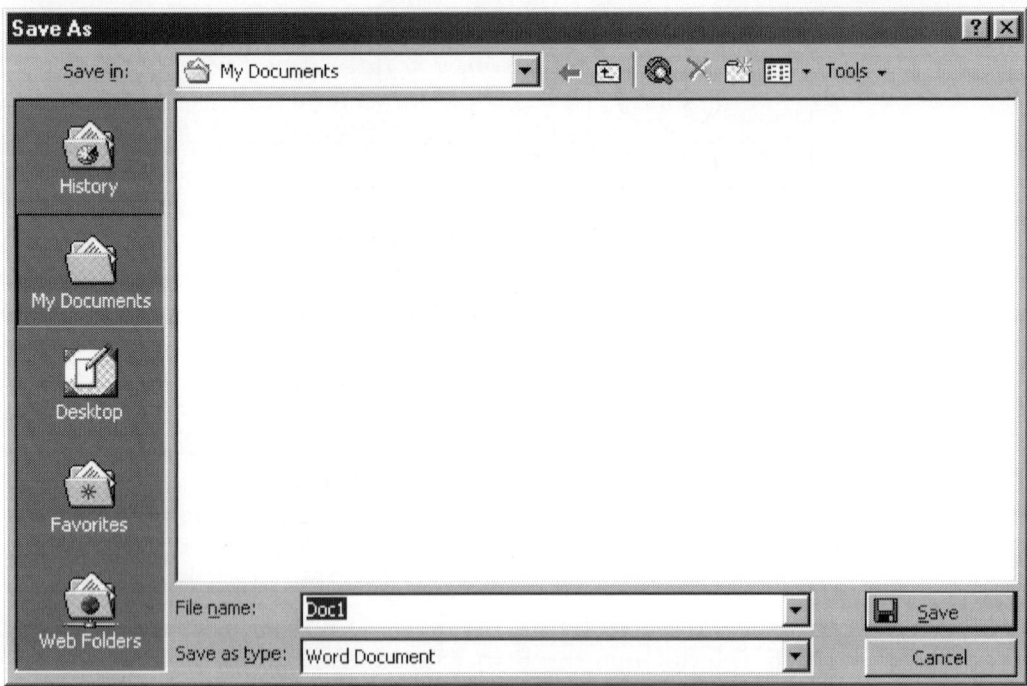

Notice that the **Cancel** button does not have any letter underlined. However, pressing the **Esc** key is the same as choosing **Cancel**.

- `Press Esc to close the Save As dialog box.`

The dialog box is closed and you are returned to the document again.

Usage data

As you have already learnt, Word customises your menus and toolbars so that the options and buttons that you use most frequently are readily available. If you want, you can reset your usage data so that the menus and toolbars are reset to their default settings. You will not do this in this course but you might like to know how to do it:

- Open the **Tools** menu and choose **Customize**
- Click the **Options** tab
- Click **Reset my usage data**
- Choose **Yes** to confirm that you want to restore the default settings for the menus and toolbars
- Click **Close** to close the Customize dialog box

Shortcut key combinations

Another way of choosing certain options is to use the shortcut key combinations that are shown beside some menu options. Some of the most common examples are:

	Ctrl+O	to open a document
	Ctrl+S	to save a document
	Ctrl+P	to print a document
	Ctrl+B	to apply bold font style
	Ctrl+U	to apply underlining
	Ctrl+I	to apply italic font style
	Ctrl+C	to copy to the Clipboard
	Ctrl+X	to cut selected text
	Ctrl+V	to paste from the Clipboard
	Ctrl+Z	to undo the last change
	F1	to open the Office Assistant

You don't need to learn these shortcut key combinations now, but you may find it useful to learn them as you go along. Try out **Ctrl+P** now.

- `Hold down the Ctrl key and press P.`

The Print dialog box is opened.

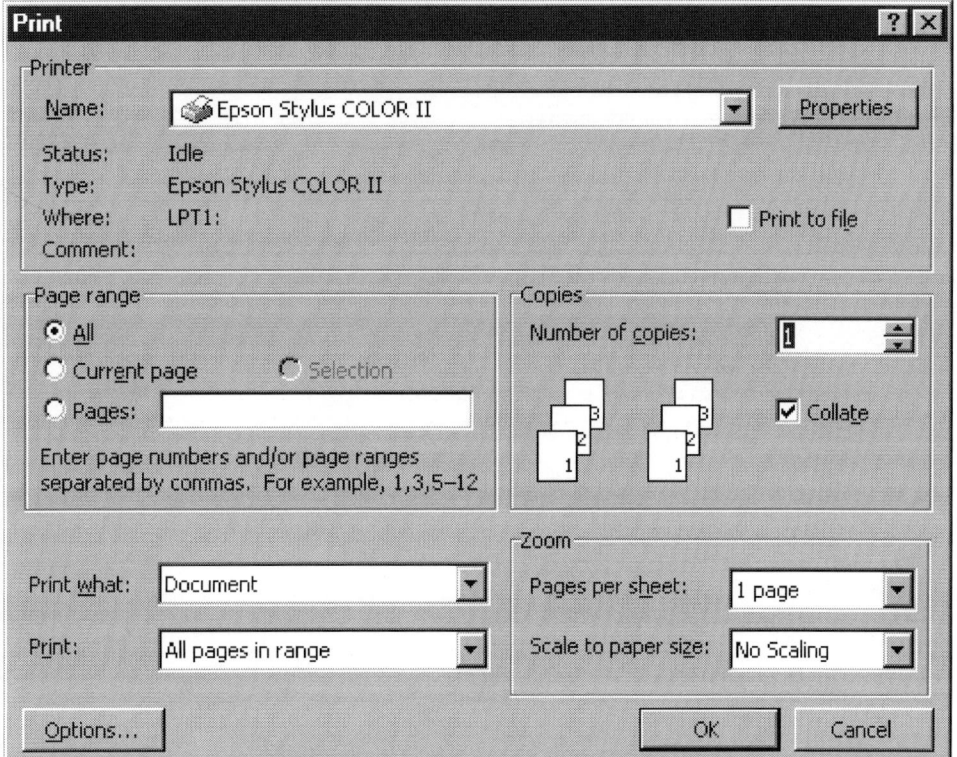

- Press **Esc** to close the Print dialog box.

The shortcut menu

Yet another way of choosing certain options is to use the special shortcut menu by clicking the right-hand mouse button. A list of useful menu options is then displayed.

- Move the mouse pointer over the text area and click the right-hand mouse button.

A shortcut menu is displayed.

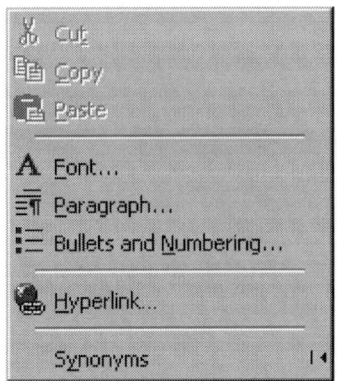

The options shown relate to formatting text. Any of the available options can be chosen by clicking them in the shortcut menu.

- Press **Esc** to remove the shortcut menu.

- Now move the mouse pointer over one of the toolbars and right-click.

A different shortcut menu is displayed.

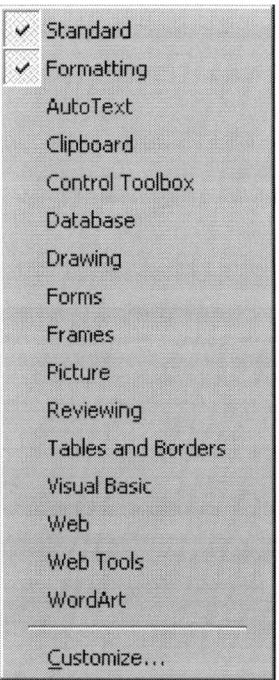

This particular menu allows you to choose which toolbars to display. Generally, the shortcut menu will offer options relevant to where the mouse pointer is positioned. It can be a useful way of speeding up certain actions.

- ```
  Click outside the shortcut menu with the
  left-hand mouse button, or press Esc, to
  remove the shortcut menu.
  ```

Using the Office Assistant

The Office Assistant offers you various tips on how to use Word more effectively. In general, it will try to give you tips that are relevant to the task you are currently undertaking. Some users find it quite helpful to have the Office Assistant displayed all the time. It enables them to 'soak in' information about working with Word. Others find it irritating.

The Office Assistant works in several ways, depending on whether it is displayed or hidden. When it is displayed all the time:

- It will display messages regarding saving documents, completing a spell check, etc.
  ```

- If it can see a more efficient way of doing a task that you are currently undertaking, a light bulb will appear above the Office Assistant. To view the tip, just click the light bulb.

- If you need help, just click anywhere on the Office Assistant. An input box will then be provided for your question. The Office Assistant may also provide a list of help topics that it considers relevant.

If the Office Assistant is hidden:

- When a tip is available, a light bulb will appear on the **Microsoft Word Help** button in the Standard toolbar. To view the tip, just click the **Microsoft Word Help** button.

- If you need help at any time, click the **Microsoft Word Help** button, or press **F1**. The Office Assistant will appear and provide an input box in which you can type your question.

Showing the Office Assistant

The Office Assistant is currently hidden. To display the Office Assistant, do one of the following:

- Click the **Microsoft Word Help** button

- Press the **F1** key

You will try this now. You should note that if the Office Assistant currently has a tip for you, the **Microsoft Word Help** button will have a light-bulb symbol on it.

- In the Standard toolbar, click the `Microsoft Word Help` button.

The Office Assistant appears. As you had the Print dialog box open earlier, it may display several help topics about printing.

If you had a question, you would type it in the box and then click **Search**. For now, you will just close the bubble.

- Click outside the Office Assistant bubble.

Using the Office Assistant

Now that the Office Assistant is open, it will display any messages that Microsoft Word has for you. To see this, you will run the spelling checker program again.

- Click the **Spelling and Grammar** button – if it is not displayed in the Standard toolbar, remember to use the **More Buttons** button.

After a short while the Office Assistant displays a message for you.

- Click outside the Office Assistant bubble to close it.

Microsoft Word 2000 ~ Beginners Course **37**

Resetting the tips

Once the Office Assistant has displayed a particular tip, it will not display it again unless you reset the tips. However, it will continue to give you Microsoft Word messages and new tips. To reset the tips, you need to open the Office Assistant dialog box. To do this:

> Right-click the Office Assistant and choose **Options** in the shortcut menu

Try this now.

- Right-click anywhere on the Office Assistant and choose **Options** in the shortcut menu.

The Office Assistant dialog box is displayed.

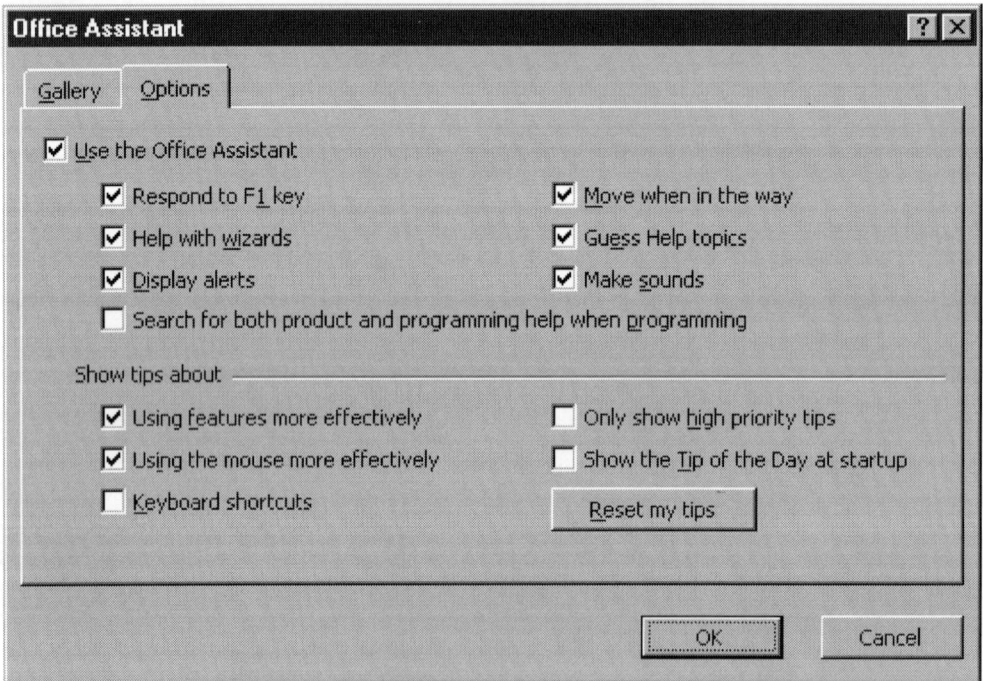

- Read through the options to see what is available.
- When you are ready, click the **Reset my tips** button.

The Office Assistant displays a message informing you that you may see tips that you have seen before.

> You have just reset your tips for this application. You may see tips you have seen before.

- In the Office Assistant dialog box, click **OK**.

The tips are now reset.

Hiding the Office Assistant

After a while, you may find the Office Assistant irritating. There are two ways to hide it:

- Open the **Help** menu and choose **Hide the Office Assistant**

- Right-click the Office Assistant and choose **Hide**

You will hide the Office Assistant now.

- Right-click the Office Assistant and choose **Hide**.

The Office Assistant is removed from your screen.

> *All the pictures and instructions throughout the remainder of this course make the assumption that the Office Assistant is hidden. If it does appear at any time, just read what it has to say and then right-click it and choose **Hide**.*

Closing a document

When you have finished working with a document, you should close it. There are several ways of closing a document, including:

- Open the **File** menu and choose **Close**

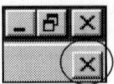

➥ If you have only one document open, click the **Close Window** button in the top right-hand corner of the window, just below the **Close** button for the Word window

➥ If you have more than one document open, there will only be one **Close** button displayed - this closes the document

➥ Press **Ctrl+W**

There are two points worth noting when you close a document:

➥ If you have not saved the document since making any changes, Word will ask you if you want to save it.

➥ You can choose to exit the program rather than closing a document. This closes the document automatically and gives you the chance to save any changes before the program is shut down.

You will now close the current document.

- `Open the` **File** `menu and choose` **Close.**

Word asks if you want to save the changes to the document.

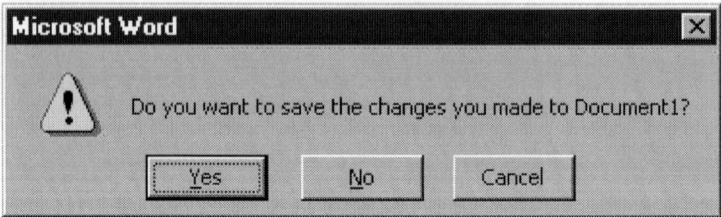

- `Click` **No** `to avoid saving the document.`

The document is closed. The Word window remains open with no document displayed.

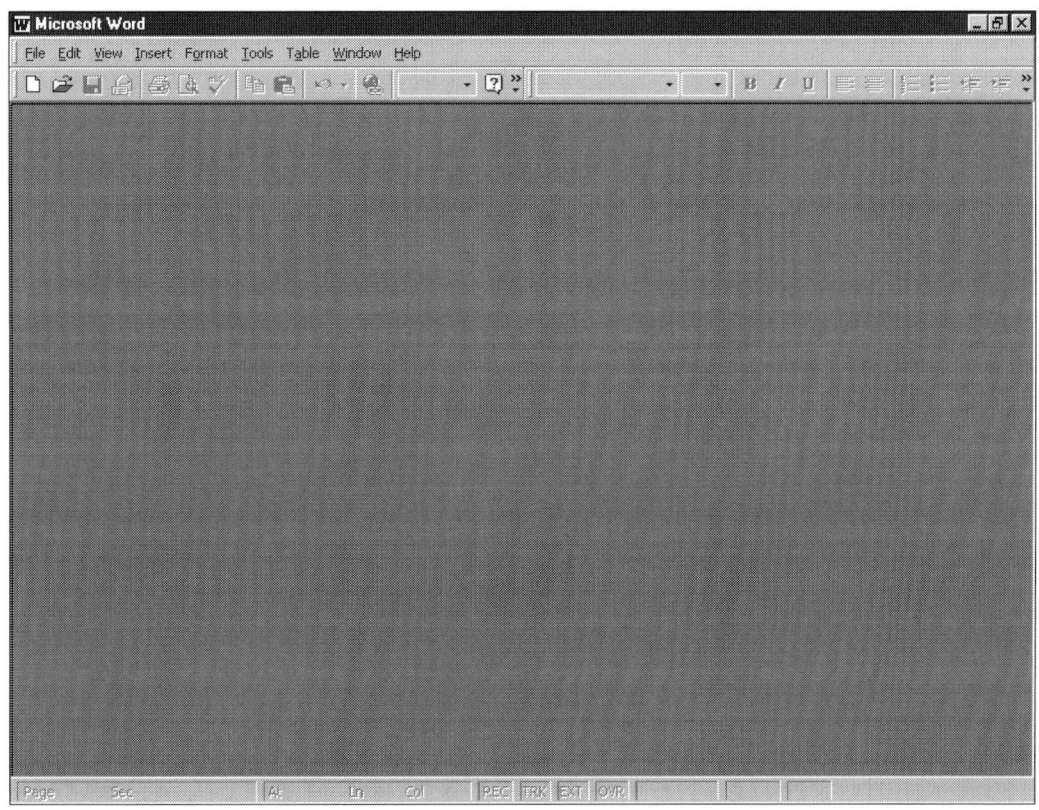

Exiting Word

You have now finished your short introduction to the Word environment and it is time to exit the program. As you will have understood by now there are several ways of doing the same thing. To exit Word, do one of the following:

- Open the **File** menu and choose **Exit**, either using the mouse or the keyboard (press **Alt+F** then **X**)

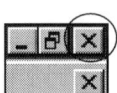

- If you have no documents open, or only one document open, you can click the **Close** button in the top right-hand corner of the Word window

- If you are an experienced Windows user, you may know that you can press **Alt+F4** to close the current application

✥   If you have no documents open, or only one document open, click the small icon in the top left-hand corner of the Word window and choose **Close**

    ✥   In the Taskbar, right-click the **Microsoft Word** button and choose **Close**

In this course you will always be instructed to open the **File** menu and choose **Exit**, but do use one of the other methods if you prefer.

- ```
  Open the File menu and choose Exit.
  ```
- ```
  If you are at all uncertain about how to
  start Word, or how to make menu selections,
  you should repeat this chapter now.
  ```

Summary ~ Getting Started

Starting Word

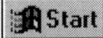

    ✥   Click the **Start** button

    ✥   In the Start menu, point to **Programs**

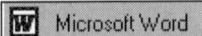

    ✥   In the Programs menu, click **Microsoft Word**

After a few seconds the Microsoft Word window will be displayed. The key elements of the Microsoft Word window are listed in the table on page 21.

The Office Assistant

The Office Assistant may, or may not be displayed, when you start Word. If the Office Assistant is displayed, read what it has to say, and then right-click it and choose **Hide** to remove it from your screen. If you want to display it at any time, click the **Microsoft Word Help** button in the Standard toolbar, or press **F1**.

Insertion point

The flashing bar seen at the start of a new document is known as the insertion point. Whenever you type text it is always inserted at the insertion point.

Mouse pointer

The mouse pointer is the small picture that moves around the screen when you move your mouse. It will change its appearance depending on where the mouse is pointing, for example: an arrow over the toolbars, or an *I-beam* over the text area.

Using the menu system

Word has a *pull-down* menu system. There is a Menu bar along the top of the screen. The first three menu headings are: File, Edit, and View. Choosing one of these headings will open up that menu to show a list of options. If you keep the menu open, or click the double-arrow button at the bottom of the menu, more options will be displayed. Some options will produce dialog boxes with more options in.

Toolbar buttons

The New Blank Document button

Some features can be accessed quickly using shortcut buttons in the toolbars. For example, the first button in the left-hand end of the Standard toolbar is used to open a new blank document. If you point the mouse at any button without clicking it, a ScreenTip will name the button.

As you work with Word, the toolbar buttons you use most often will be displayed in the toolbars on your screen; those you use infrequently will move to the More Buttons palette of the toolbar. If you cannot see the button you want, click the **More Buttons** button for the appropriate toolbar and locate the button in the More Buttons palette.

Shortcut key combinations

To access a menu option you can often use a shortcut key combination. For example, pressing the **Ctrl** key together with the letter **P** is the shortcut for printing a document. The main shortcut key combinations are listed on page 33.

Shortcut menu

Word also has shortcut menus, accessed by right-clicking the mouse. The menu content depends on where the mouse is pointed when you click it, and whether or not any text has been selected.

Closing a document

You can close a document in several ways, including:

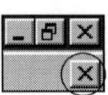

- Open the **File** menu and choose **Close**
- If you have only one document open, click the **Close Window** button in the top right-hand corner of the window, just below the **Close** button for the Word window

- If you have more than one document open, there will only be one **Close** button displayed - this closes the document
- Press **Ctrl+W**

If you have not saved the document since making any changes, Word will ask you if you want to save it.

You can choose to exit the program rather than closing the document. This closes the document automatically and gives you the chance to save any changes before the program is shut down.

Exiting Word

You can exit Word in several ways. Three simple methods are listed below:

- Open the **File** menu and choose **Exit**
- Use the shortcut key combination **Alt+F4**

 ✎ When you have only one document open, click the **Close** button in the top right-hand corner of the Word window

Notes

Use this page to make notes of your own.

Page #   Notes

Chapter 3 ~ Your First Document

In this chapter you will learn about:

- Typing text
- Automatic spell checking
- Deleting text when you make mistakes
- Word wrap
- Moving the insertion point
- Saving a document on your exercise diskette
- Printing your document

You will soon create your first document, save it, make a couple of changes and then print it. If you do not have a printer, then you will not, of course, be able to print your document, but you can follow all of the other instructions.

Getting started

To start you need to have a new blank document to work with. Follow one of the two instructions given below depending on whether or not Word is already started:

- If Word is already started: close any documents that are currently open (**File, Close**), then open a new document by clicking the **New Blank Document** button in the Standard toolbar, or by pressing **Ctrl+N**.

- If Word is not already started: start your Word program – a new document will be opened automatically.

You should now have a new blank document with the insertion point flashing at the top of the page.

Microsoft Word 2000 ~ Beginners Course   **47**

The Office Assistant

If the Office Assistant is displayed, you should hide it before continuing.

- `If necessary, right-click the Office Assistant and choose` **Hide**`.`

Typing text

You can now start to type.

- `Type:`

    What is a computer?

- `Press the` **Enter** `key to conclude the heading.`

- `Press the` **Enter** `key again to create an empty line after the heading.`

Automatic spelling & grammar checking

Word has a spelling checker that can automatically check your spelling as you type. If you type a word that Word does not recognise, and the automatic spelling checker is on, a red wavy line will appear underneath the word. Right-click the offending word and Word will suggest some alternatives.

Likewise, if you type a phrase which Word thinks is grammatically incorrect, and the automatic grammar checker is on, a green wavy line appears beneath the phrase. Right-click the phrase to display a shortcut menu and, if necessary, choose an alternative from the list provided.

First, try typing a spelling mistake.

- `Type:`

    This word is spelt rong.

- `Press the` **Enter** `key.`

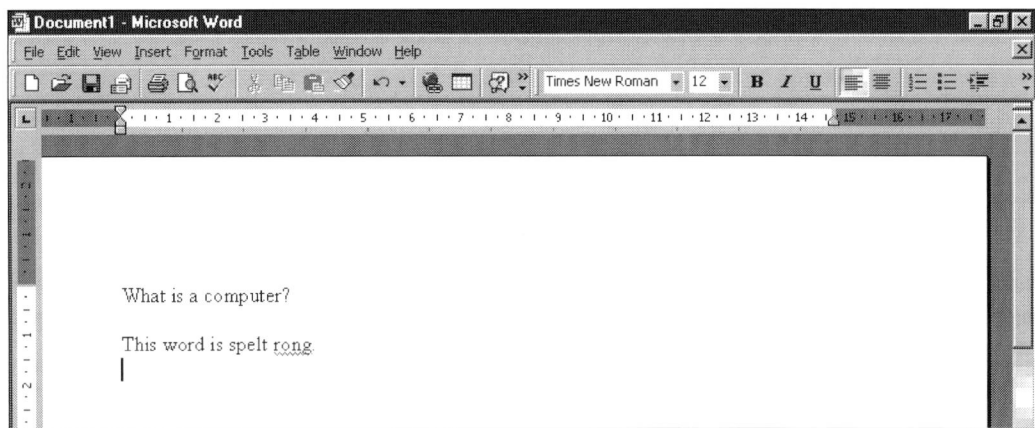

If you can see a red wavy line under the word rong, the automatic spell checker is on - you can then skip the next section about turning it on.

Now try a grammar mistake.

- Type:

    There computer is faster than mine.

- Press **Enter**.

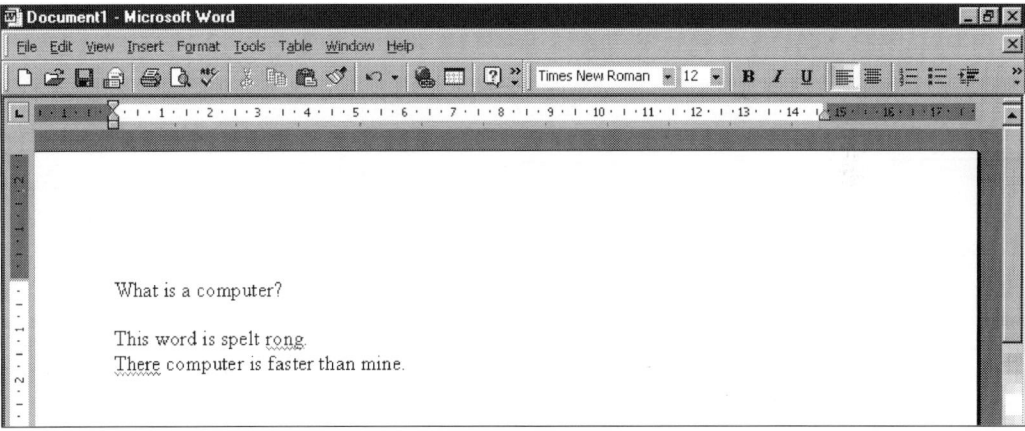

If you can see a green wavy line under the word There, the automatic grammar checker is on - you can then skip the next section about turning it on.

> *Note that Word will not check a word for a spelling mistake until it knows that you have finished it by pressing the **Spacebar** or the **Enter** key. Word will not check a sentence for a grammatical error until it knows you have finished it by typing a full stop and starting a new sentence, or by pressing the **Enter** key.*

Turning on automatic spelling & grammar checking

If the automatic spelling and grammar checker did not work, you can turn it on as follows:

- Open the **Tools** menu and choose **Options**.

The Options dialog box is displayed. It has ten sets of options, each of which has its own named tab.

- Click the **Spelling & Grammar** tab to show these options.

The Spelling & Grammar options are shown.

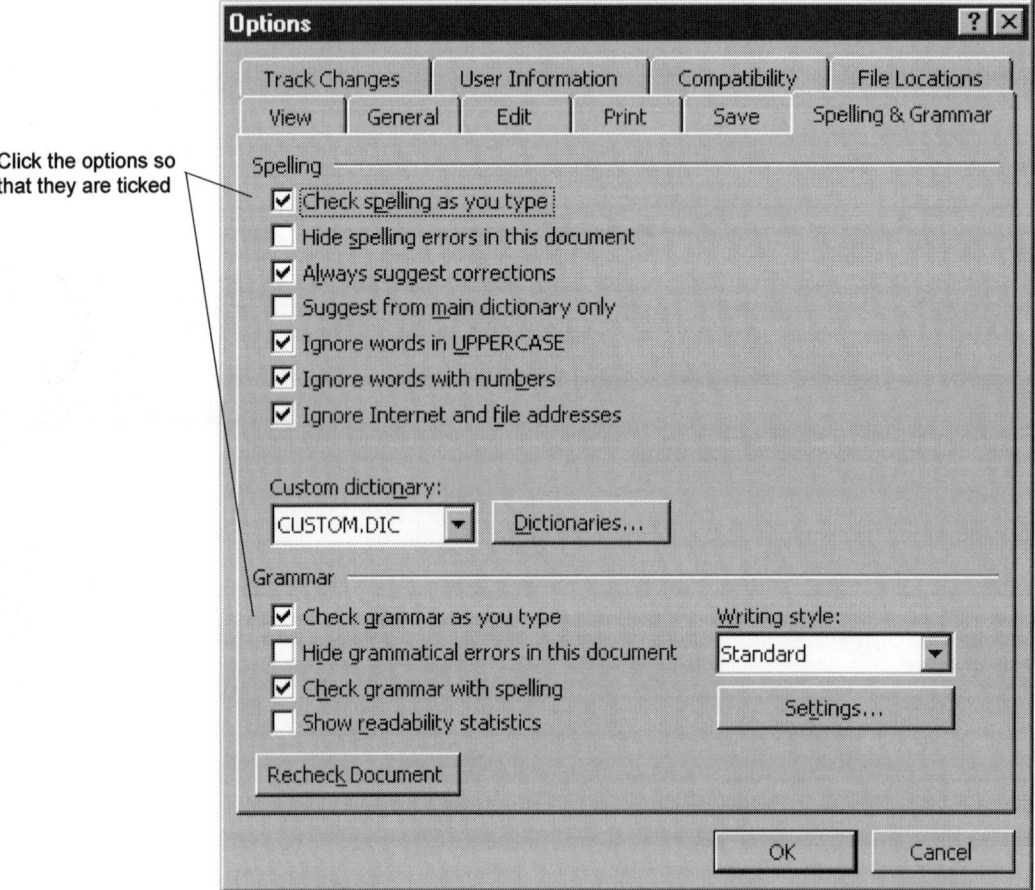

Click the options so that they are ticked

- In the Spelling options, click the **Check spelling as you type** option so that it is ticked.

- In the Grammar options, click the **Check grammar as you type** option so that it is ticked.

- Click **OK**.

The word rong in your document should now have a wavy red line underneath it, and the word There should now have a wavy green line underneath it.

Correcting a word

There is a **Spelling and Grammar Status** icon in the Status bar at the bottom of the Word window. A red tick means there are no errors in the current document; a red cross means there are.

You will try to correct a word using the right-hand mouse button.

- Right-click the word rong in your document.

A shortcut menu appears.

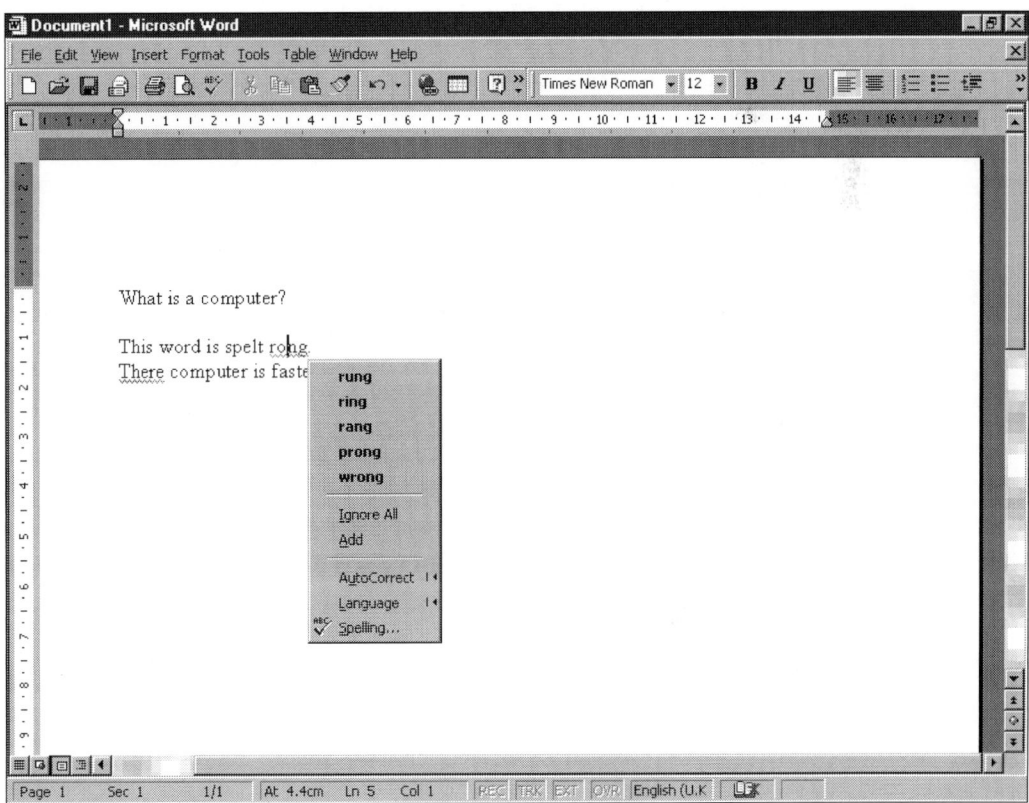

Microsoft Word 2000 ~ Beginners Course

The menu offers various options including ignoring all occurrences of the word, adding it to a dictionary and starting the Spelling Checker program. Word will also present a list of alternative spellings. In this case, you need to choose the alternative wrong.

- In the shortcut menu, choose **wrong**.

The word is corrected for you and the red line disappears. Now look at the shortcut menu for the word There.

- Right-click the word There in your document.

This time a smaller shortcut menu is displayed.

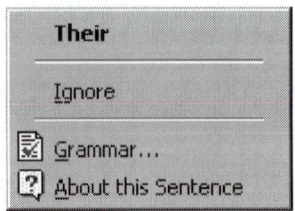

The menu offers the options to change the word to Their, ignore the sentence altogether, open the Grammar checking program, or ask the Office Assistant about the sentence. In this case you can accept the alternative Their.

- In the shortcut menu, choose **Their**.

The word is corrected for you and the green line disappears. The sentence is now complete.

 Notice that the **Spelling and Grammar Status** icon now has a red tick - there are no more errors in the document.

Correcting mistakes as you type

When you make mistakes, you don't have to use the spell checker; you can simply delete the error and re-type the correct word. There are two easy ways to correct mistakes as you type:

    ✎   Use the **Backspace** key to delete characters to the left of the insertion point

    ✎   Use the **Delete** key to delete characters to the right of the insertion point

52 Microsoft Word 2000 ~ Beginners Course

> ✐ *The easiest way to correct a small mistake as you type is to press the **Backspace** key to delete the mistake and then type the correct text.*

Delete the last sentence now.

- In the sentence `Their computer is faster than mine`, click just before the `T` -

The insertion point should now be flashing there.

- Press the **Delete** key repeatedly until the sentence is deleted.

- Click just after the full stop following the word `wrong` - the insertion point should flash there.

- Press the **Backspace** key repeatedly until the sentence is deleted.

Word wrap and the Enter key

Before typing more text, there is one important concept that you should be absolutely certain about. Unlike an ordinary typewriter, you should not press the carriage return, or **Enter** key, at the end of every line of text. The program adjusts the lines of text for you whenever the text reaches the right-hand margin. This feature is known as *word wrap*.

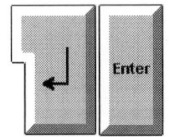

☞ You should only press the **Enter** key to conclude a paragraph, or to create an empty line

Typing more text

Now type some more text.

> ✐ *When typing this and subsequent text, the line breaks shown in the course will not necessarily match the line breaks shown on your screen. Do not worry about this - let the program take care of the line breaks with its word wrap feature.*

- Type, correcting mistakes as you go:

    In simple terms, a computer is no more than an electrical appliance. Like your television, or freezer, it has been developed to be able to perform certain tasks. For example, you can use your computer as a typewriter for writing letters, or as a pocket calculator to do your sums. You can also use it to store telephone numbers, play games, produce technical drawings and develop camera-ready documents for printing. Computers can even be used to run production lines.

- Press the **Enter** key to conclude the paragraph.

- Press the **Enter** key again to create an empty line.

- Type:

    Just like any other electrical appliance, computers can and do break down and cause problems. However, be very sceptical when a mistake is blamed "on the computer". In most cases it's a human error that causes you to receive that notice from British Telecom that says that unless you pay your outstanding bill for £4,567,333, your telephone will be disconnected.

- Press the **Enter** key twice to conclude the current paragraph and create an empty line.

Your document should now resemble the following picture.

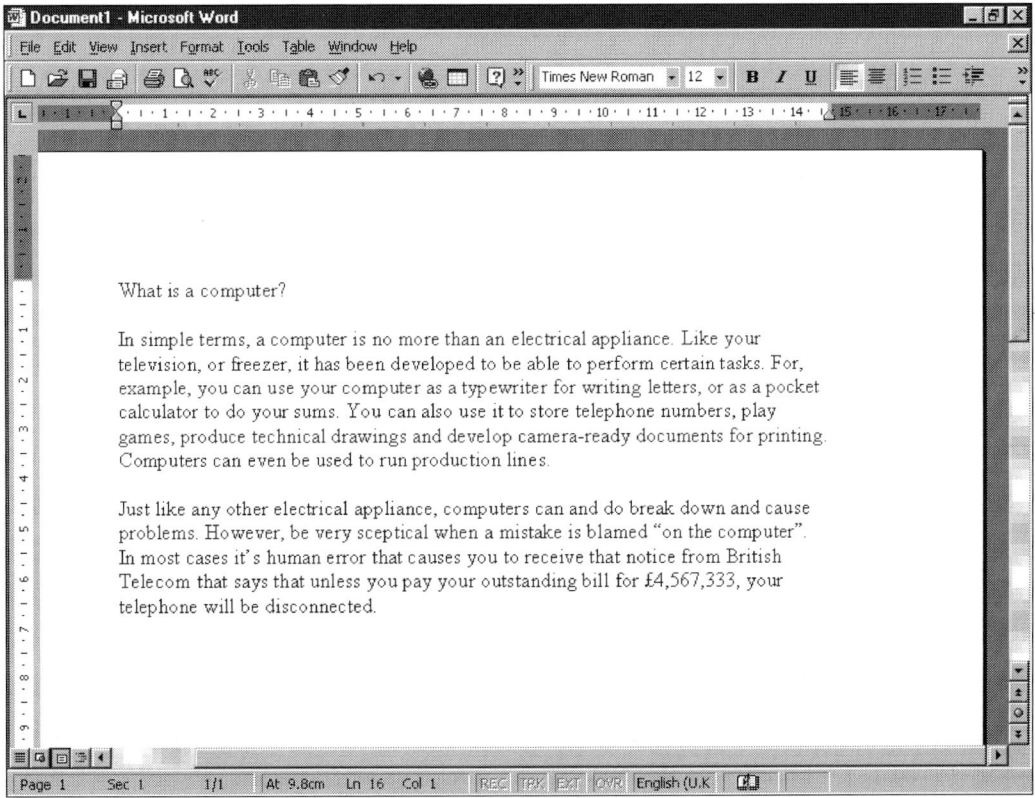

> ✋ *The next instruction asks you to type more text. You can ignore this instruction if you don't want to type more now.*

- Type:

    `A computer is not some sort of supernatural, super-intelligent, all-mighty machine, poised to take over the world. A computer cannot think for itself, it can only follow instructions. It is not capable of suddenly deciding that it would like to have an ice-cream cone, or of feeling the desire to take a long vacation on some sunny island beach.`

- Press the **Enter** key twice to conclude the current paragraph and create an empty line.

- Type:

    `A computer can, however, follow instructions and perform pre-defined tasks at an amazingly high rate: a million or so instructions per second.`

- Press the **Enter** key to conclude the paragraph.

Moving the insertion point

The insertion point can be moved in different ways:

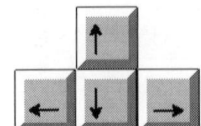

- Use the mouse to reposition the insertion point anywhere in your text. Simply move the mouse pointer to the desired position in the text and click the left-hand button. The insertion point moves to that position.

- Use the arrow keys (**ArrowUp ↑**, **ArrowDown ↓**, **ArrowLeft ←**, **ArrowRight →**) immediately to the right of the main keypad. The insertion point moves one character in the direction of the arrow.

- If you use the scroll bars to scroll the document, the insertion point is not moved automatically, but it will enable you to view a different part of the document and then click it.

Whether you use the arrow keys or the mouse will depend entirely on your own working habits and what you are used to. Many experienced typists prefer to have their fingers close to the "home keys" and therefore use keys rather than the mouse.

> *The home keys are **asdf jkl;** used by typists as a reference point for positioning their fingers.*

Other key combinations allow you to move the insertion point more quickly. The **Home**, **End**, **Page Up**, **Page Down** and **Arrow** keys are used as described in the following table.

To move the insertion point...	Use the key(s)
Left/Right one character	←→
One word to Left/Right	**Ctrl+←/Ctrl+→**
Up/Down one line at a time	↑/↓
Beginning/End of line	**Home/End**
Beginning/End of document	**Ctrl+Home/Ctrl+End**
One screen up/down	**Page Up/Page Down**
Top/bottom of screen	**Alt+Ctrl+Page Up/Alt+Ctrl+Page Down**

There are several more key combinations than those listed here. In the beginning, you may find it easier just to click at the desired location in the text if it is shown, and use **Page Up/Page Down** to move more quickly up and down the document if it is not shown.

> *When moving the insertion point downwards, you cannot position it past the end of document.*

Try using the mouse and key combinations now.

- In the second paragraph, click just before the word appliance.

- Press **Home** to move to the beginning of the line.

- Press ↑ seven times to move to the start of the previous paragraph.

- Press **Ctrl+→** five times to move to the start of the word computer.

- Press **Ctrl+Home** to move to the beginning of the document.

- Press **Page Down** to move down the page of text.

Changing text

In this section you will practise using the **Backspace** and **Delete** keys to change the text you have typed. Start off by changing freezer to video using the **Backspace** key.

- In the second sentence of the first paragraph, position the insertion point immediately after the word freezer - use the arrow keys or the mouse.

- Press the **Backspace** key seven times.

- Type:

    `video`

Now change British Telecom (towards the end of the second paragraph) to the phone company using the **Delete** key.

- In the second paragraph, position the insertion point immediately before the B of British Telecom.

- Press the **Delete** key 15 times.

- Type:

    `the phone company`

Saving your document

In order to save the text that you have typed, you must give your new document a name. Call it **Computer** and save it on your exercise diskette.

> ♪ *Word can accept long filenames; up to 255 characters for the drive letter, folder path and filename. By default, Word will use the first line of your document as the filename. You will change this.*

- Insert the exercise diskette provided in drive A.

- Open the **File** menu and choose **Save,** or click the **Save** button in the Standard toolbar, or press **Ctrl+S**.

Because you haven't previously saved this document, the Save As dialog box is displayed.

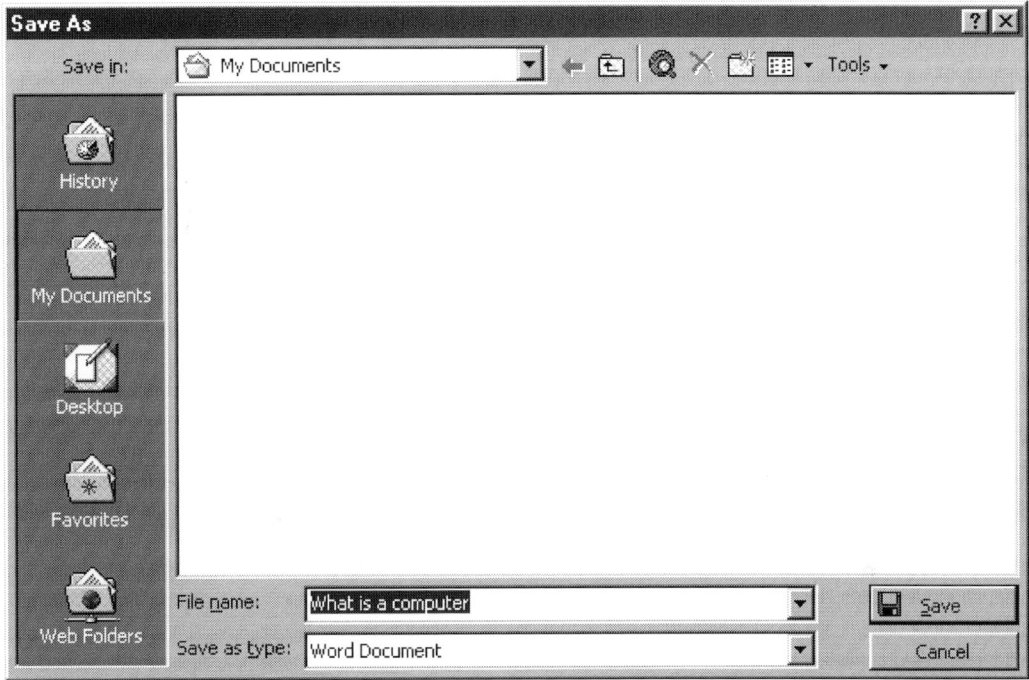

You can choose a drive, a folder and a filename for your document. First type the filename in the File name box. You can then use the Save in list box to choose a drive and a folder. However, when you are using a diskette, it is quicker to avoid choosing most of the information by typing the drive and filename directly in the File name box.

Notice also that the entry What is a computer in the File name box is highlighted. This means that anything you type now will replace that entry.

- Type:

    a:Computer

- Click **Save,** or press the **Enter** key.

> *Typing **a:** at the beginning of the filename instructs Word to save the document on the exercise disk in drive A - the letter A can be in upper or lower case, but a colon must be entered after it.*

The name of the document is now shown in the Title bar as Computer.

Microsoft Word 2000 ~ Beginners Course

Printing your document

It is time to see what your document looks like on paper. If you use the **File**, **Print** menu option, or press **Ctrl+P**, the Print dialog box is displayed.

- ```
  If you have a printer, make sure it is
  switched on and ready to use.
  ```

- ```
  Open the File menu and choose Print, or
  press Ctrl+P.
  ```

The Print dialog box is displayed.

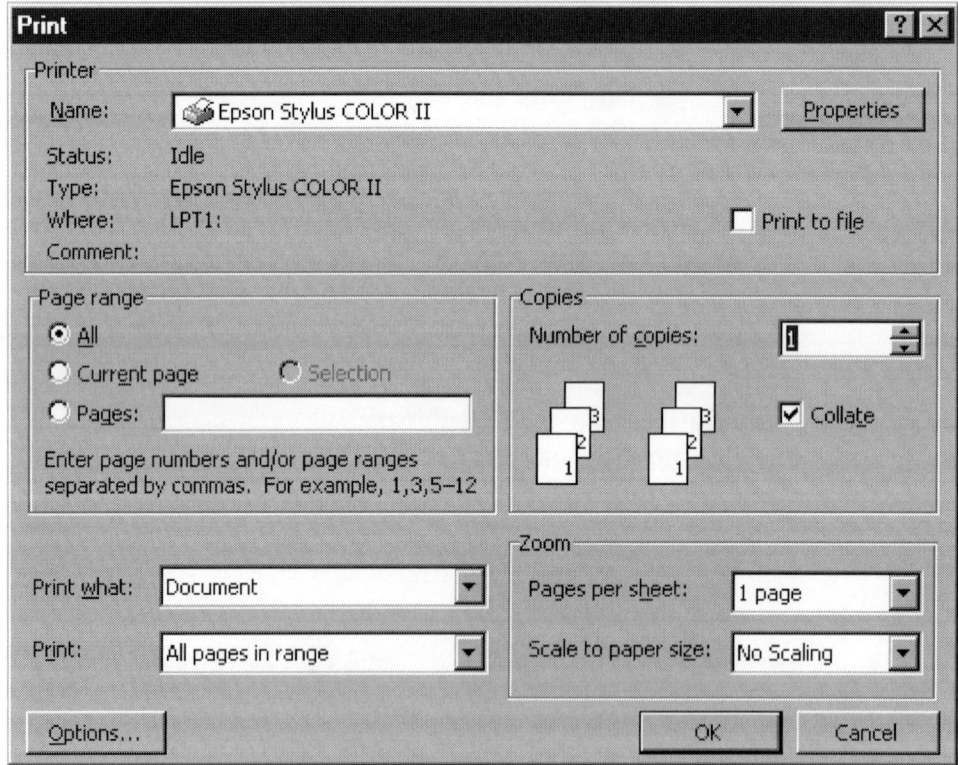

As you can see, the default settings are to print 1 copy and All of the pages. For now just accept the default settings and start the printout.

- ```
  Click OK, or press the Enter key.
  ```
  ```

If everything is connected correctly, you should now be in possession of a fine document!

Using the Print button in the toolbar

If you know that the settings in the Print dialog box are as you want them, you can start a printout by simply clicking the **Print** button in the Standard toolbar. The Print dialog box is not opened, but its settings are used to print the document.

- Click the **Print** button.

The document is printed again.

A few more changes

Before closing the document, try making the following changes on your own. Use the **Delete** or **Backspace** keys to erase the word shown and then type the replacement word.

- In the phrase the phone company, delete the word phone and replace it with the word **power**.

- In the phrase your telephone will be disconnected, delete the word telephone and replace it with the word **electricity**.

> *♪ If you have a little experience of working with Windows you may know that there is a quicker method of deleting a word which involves selecting the word - this is covered later on in the course.*

Saving the document again

When the time comes for you to conclude your session with the program you should always finish off by saving your document. Whenever you have made any changes since the last time the document was saved, Word will warn you if you try to exit without saving.

- Open the **File** menu and choose **Save,** or click the **Save** button in the Standard toolbar, or press **Ctrl+S.**

The document is automatically saved keeping the same filename, i.e., **Computer**. The Save As dialog box is not displayed.

Turning off automatic spelling & grammar checking

If you are happy using automatic spelling & grammar checking, just skip this section. If you want to turn off the automatic spell & grammar checking features, proceed as follows turning off one, or both, of the options as you wish.

- Open the **Tools** menu and choose **Options.**

- Click the **Spelling & Grammar** tab to show these options.

To turn off the automatic spelling checker:

- In the Spelling options, click the **Check spelling as you type** option so that it is no longer ticked.

To turn off the automatic grammar checker:

- In the Grammar options, click the **Check grammar as you type** option so that it is no longer ticked.

- Click **OK**.

The automatic spelling and grammar features are now off.

Ending the session

You have now completed this chapter. You have two choices:

    ➥ Choosing **File**, **Close** will close the current document without exiting Word

    ➥ Choosing **File**, **Exit** will exit Word, closing the current document automatically at the same time

You only need to exit Word if you want to finish working with it altogether. If you want to continue working on another document, it is enough to close the current document without exiting Word.

- Open the **File** menu and choose **Close** to close the current document.

- If you are not continuing directly with the next chapter, open the **File** menu and choose **Exit** to exit Word.

> ♦ *If you have no more than one document open, you can also exit Word by clicking the **Close** button in the top right-hand corner of the Word window.*

Summary ~ Your First Document

Typing text

When typing text, you must always remember that you do not have to press the carriage return, or **Enter** key, at the end of every line. The program adjusts the lines of text for you whenever the text reaches the right-hand margin. This feature is known as *word wrap*.

There are two easy ways to correct mistakes as you type:

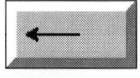

    ✋ Use the **Backspace** key to delete characters to the left of the insertion point

    ✋ Use the **Delete** key to delete characters to the right of the insertion point

Automatic spelling & grammar checker

Word has a spelling & grammar checker that can check your spelling and grammar as you type. If you type a word that Word does not recognise, and the automatic spelling checker is on, a red wavy line will appear underneath the word. Right-click the word to display a shortcut menu. Choose the correct spelling for the word from the list provided. The word is then corrected automatically for you.

Similarly, if you type a phrase which Word thinks is grammatically incorrect, and the automatic grammar checker is on, a green wavy line appears beneath the phrase. Right-click the phrase to display a shortcut menu and, if necessary, choose an alternative from the list provided.

Moving the insertion point

To move the insertion point to a new position in a document, point the mouse pointer to the desired position in the text and click the left-hand mouse button. You can also use the **Arrow** keys on the keyboard.

To move round your document more rapidly, use the **Home**, **End**, **Page Up** and **Page Down** keys.

Saving a document

To save a document, do one of the following:

- Open the **File** menu and choose **Save**
- In the Standard toolbar, click the **Save** button
- Press **Ctrl+S**

If it is the first time the document has been saved, the Save As dialog box is opened and you must choose a filename and location for the document.

Printing a document

To print a document, do one of the following:

- Open the **File** menu and choose **Print**

✎ In the Standard toolbar, click the **Print** button

  ✎ Press **Ctrl+P**

Clicking the **Print** button in the toolbar prints the document using the current settings in the Print dialog box. The other two methods open the Print dialog box where you can change the print settings before printing the document.

Notes

Use this page to make notes of your own.

Page #   Notes

Chapter 4 ~ Your Second Document

In this chapter you will learn about:

- Typing text
- Saving a document on your exercise diskette
- Using Print Preview

In this chapter you will create a second document and save it. You will also use the Print Preview feature to preview the document without printing it.

Getting started

To start, you need to have a new blank document to work with. Follow one of the two instructions given below depending on whether or not Word is already started:

- If Word is already started: close any documents that are currently open (**File, Close**), then open a new document by clicking the **New Blank Document** button in the Standard toolbar, or by pressing **Ctrl+N**.

- If Word is not already started: start your Word program – a new document will be opened automatically.

You should now have a new blank document with the insertion point flashing at the top of the page.

Closing the Office Assistant

If the Office Assistant is displayed, you should hide it before continuing.

- If necessary, right-click the Office Assistant and choose **Hide**.

Microsoft Word 2000 ~ Beginners Course **67**

Typing text

It is not absolutely necessary that you type all the text, but the screen shots assume that you have!

- Type:

    Electronics - General Safety

- Press the **Enter** key twice to conclude the heading and create an empty line after the heading.

You can now continue typing.

- Type:

    Electricity cannot be seen, smelt or heard. However, it can be felt. An electric current passing through the body causes electric shock. It affects the heart, the muscles and the nervous system.

- Press the **Enter** key twice to conclude the paragraph and create an empty line.

- Type:

    The size of the current depends on the voltage involved and the resistance of the body.

- Press the **Enter** key twice to conclude the paragraph and create an empty line.

- Type:

    The most serious injuries and deaths from electric shock occur from contact with the mains electricity supply. The live wire of the mains supply is at a high voltage and touching it, while in contact with the ground, can be fatal.

- Press the **Enter** key to conclude the paragraph.

Your document should now resemble the next picture.

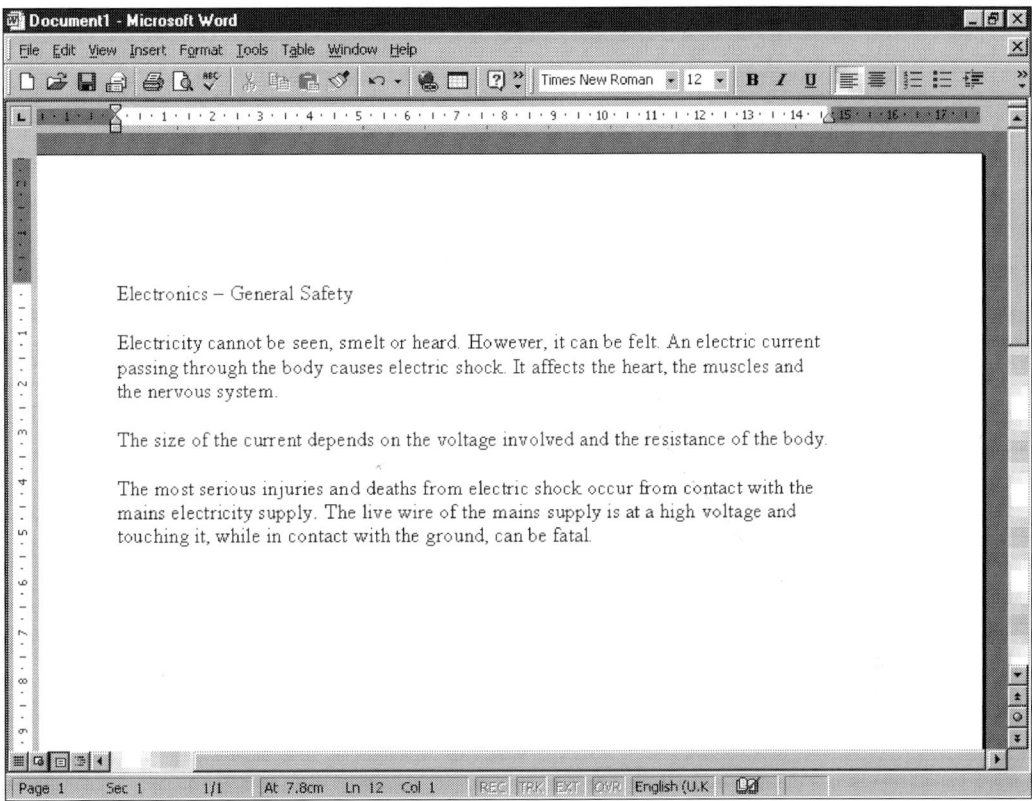

Saving your document

In order to save the text that you have written, you must give your new document a name. Call it **Electronics**.

- Insert your exercise diskette in drive A.
- Open the **File** menu and choose **Save**, or click the **Save** button in the Standard toolbar, or press **Ctrl+S**.

The Save As dialog box is opened.

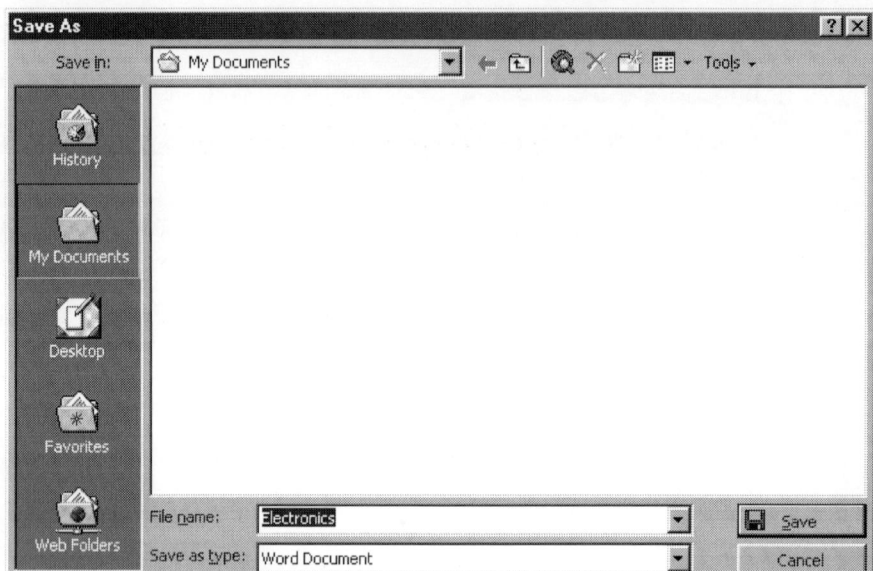

You may see files on your exercise diskette listed

Note how Word suggests the first word from your document for the filename. You are going to call the document Electronics but you also need to tell Word where to save the document. As the entry in the File name box is highlighted it will be replaced by whatever you type.

- In the File name box, type:

  a:Electronics

- Click **Save**, or press the **Enter** key.

> ✍ *Remember, typing **a:** at the beginning of the filename instructs Word to save the document on drive A. Word automatically saves your file as a Word document.*

The name of the document is now shown in the Title bar as Electronics.

Print Preview

Instead of printing the document, you can use Print Preview to view the document on screen. Print Preview will show you exactly what the document will look like when it is printed.

- Open the **File** menu and choose **Print Preview**, or click the **Print Preview** button in the Standard toolbar - it may be in the More Buttons palette.

70 Microsoft Word 2000 ~ Beginners Course

Print Preview is opened showing you a whole page view of your document.

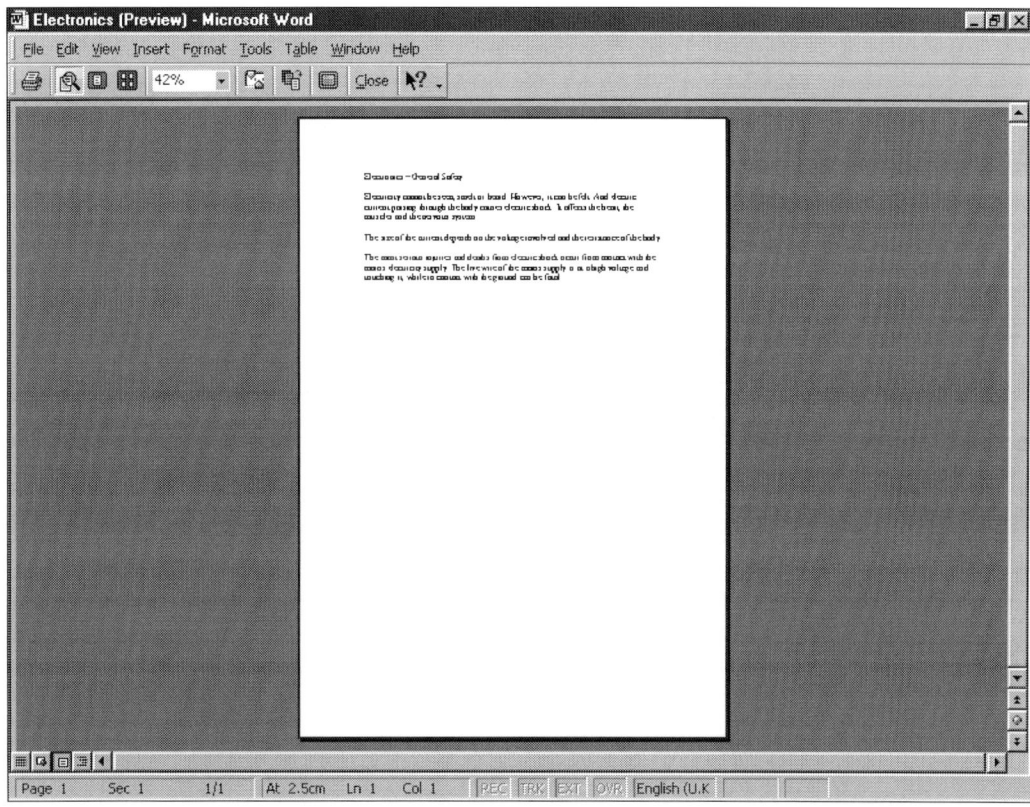

Notice that the mouse pointer now looks like a magnifying glass when it is positioned over the document.

- Move the mouse pointer over the document and click.

The text is magnified.

- Click the document again.

The view is zoomed out and you can see the whole page again. Now close Print Preview.

- Click the **Close Preview** button in the Print Preview toolbar, or press the **Esc** key.

The normal Word window is displayed again.

Adding more text

Now add some more text. Start off by moving the insertion point down to the end of the document.

- Press **Ctrl+End**.

- Press **Enter** to create an empty line.

- Type the following text, adding empty lines where necessary:

   The resistance of the body depends mostly on the resistance of the skin. If the skin is damp, resistance is considerably reduced. Electrical equipment should never be handled with damp or wet hands.

   Electronic engineers run special risks when dealing with equipment that uses high voltages. Colour television receivers, for example, use very high voltages - up to 30kV.

   Equipment designed to be connected to the mains should either have its cover earthed, or should be double-insulated.

- Press the **Enter** key twice to conclude the current paragraph.

- If you wish, type the following:

   An isolation transformer offers a degree of safety when working on equipment that requires the mains voltage, as it separates that piece of equipment from the mains supply. This type of transformer has two separate windings that are insulated from one another. Neither of the two supply wires is live with respect to earth - touching one or the other will not result in shock. An earthed metal screen between the windings offers further protection.

- If you wish, continue with the following:

    ```
    Most domestic equipment is fully insulated.
    All current carrying parts are enclosed in
    an insulated casing so that in normal use
    it is not possible to come into contact
    with the current. Where it is possible to
    come into contact with the metal frame of
    an appliance - such as a metal radiator -
    then the metal frame is earthed.
    ```

Closing the document

You have now finished working with this document so close it!

- Open the **File** menu and choose **Close**, or press **Ctrl+W**.

As you did not save the document before closing it, Word now asks you if you want to save the changes you made.

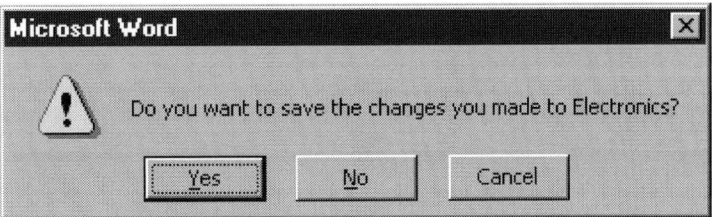

- Click **Yes**.

Ending the session

Three extra exercises follow, but it is not necessary to do them now.

- If you are not continuing directly with the additional exercises or with the next chapter, open the **File** menu and choose **Exit** to exit Word.

Exercise 4a

First you need a new blank document to work on.

- Click the **New Blank Document** button in the Standard toolbar, or press **Ctrl+N**.

- Type the following text:

STROUD

Stroud has a wonderful setting on the edge of the Cotswolds, just where the escarpments are at their most dramatic. Its five valleys, which spread out like the fingers of your hand, provide a perfect backdrop for unlimited exploration.

The resident, let alone the visitor, can never hope to see everything of Stroud. Even those of us who have lived in the district all our lives can still discover isolated countryside and spectacular views quite different from anything we have experienced before. There is a wealth of scenery unlike anywhere else on earth. You can travel the world - across Europe to Asia, even to Australia and the Pacific, but in this spectacular part of the Southern Cotswolds, you will still catch your breath when discovering the hidden valleys and quaint terraced villages.

- When you are ready, save the document on your exercise diskette as **a:Ex04a**.

- Print the document, or use Print Preview to view it.

- Close the document - **File, Close**.

Exercise 4b

First you need a new blank document to work on.

- Click the **New Blank Document** button in the Standard toolbar, or press **Ctrl+N**.

Microsoft Word 2000 ~ Beginners Course

- Type the following text:

> **Classic match finds worthy winner!**
>
> **Minchinhampton 3 Kingswood 2**
>
> **This top of the table clash saw PCP-sponsored Minchinhampton, take both points in the dying minutes of a spectacular match. The Kingswood team will undoubtedly feel disappointed, but none of the large partisan crowd will share their feelings as they tread their way home after a thrilling encounter.**
>
> **Hampton took an early lead when, on their sixth corner within the first 10 minutes, 6ft 4in Mike Kenny climbed higher than the church spire to nod in the opening goal. Kingswood fought back and were awarded a penalty kick after 22 minutes. 1-1. On the stroke of half-time a defensive error let Kingswood in to take the lead.**
>
> **The second half was a tremendous event. Hampton powered forward, wave after wave, hit the post three times and had a goal disallowed. Kingswood defended doggedly, but always looked dangerous on the break. After 67 minutes the match got what it deserved. A seven-man move finished with a superb low cross and a spectacular diving header from John Loveridge. 2-2.**
>
> **It wasn't over yet! With eight minutes to go, player manager Peter Harrison picked up a loose ball on the half-way line, drove forward past two defenders and chipped the advancing goalkeeper from 30 yards. A splendid finish to a splendid match.**

- When you are ready, save the document on your exercise diskette as **a:Ex04b**.

- Print the document, or use Print Preview to view it.

- Close the document – **File, Close**.

Exercise 4c

First you need a new blank document to work on.

- Click the **New Blank Document** button in the Standard toolbar, or press **Ctrl+N**.

When you type the next section of text, you may notice some ScreenTips appear above the text you are writing. When you type <u>Dear Sofia,</u> and press **Enter**, the Office Assistant may spring to life offering to help you write a letter - just click **Cancel** to remove it from your screen.

Microsoft Word 2000 ~ Beginners Course **75**

- Type the text shown in the next picture – ignore any ScreenTips that appear above your text, and click **Cancel** in the Office Assistant bubble if it appears while you are typing the letter.

---

14 Rosewood Terrace
SEAFORD
BN45 4ER

Dear Sofia

It was so nice to see you at the weekend; I really hope you enjoyed your visit. It didn't seem to matter that the weather was so inclement; the thrashing waves were no match for the warmth that a good friend brings.

Thank you so much for the beautiful painting you gave me. I have already hung it in the drawing room where I shall sit and survey it after dinner every evening.

I must tell you that I met your friend Nils from Sweden, lovely lad isn't he! He gave me a message for you in Swedish, so here it is, and goodness knows what it means.

Sofia, jag kan inte forsta hur vacker du ar! Det var sa underbart att vara tillsammans med dig. Jag hoppas att allting blir bra med dig och din familj.

Perhaps I shouldn't know what it means!

I look forward to seeing you in the spring. In the meantime, stay happy and thanks again for the lovely present.

Love and warm hugs

Charlie

- When you are ready, save the document on your exercise diskette as **a:Ex04c**.

- Print the document, or use Print Preview to view it.

- Close the document - **File, Close**.

Summary ~ Your Second Document

Saving a document

To save a document, you must give it a name and choose where to save it. In this course all documents are saved on your exercise diskette, in the A drive of your computer.

To save a document, do one of the following:

- Open the **File** menu and choose **Save**
- In the Standard toolbar, click the **Save** button
- Press **Ctrl+S**

If it is the first time the document has been saved, the Save As dialog box is opened and you must choose a filename and location for the document.

Type the filename, and then choose a location for the document using the Save in list box. Then click the **Save** button, or press **Enter**, to save the document.

Print Preview

You can use Print Preview to see exactly what a document will look like when it is printed. There are two ways to open Print Preview:

- Open the **File** menu and choose **Print Preview**
- In the Standard toolbar, click the **Print Preview** button

Print Preview is opened displaying a whole page of the document. The mouse pointer looks like a magnifying glass when it is positioned over the document. Click the document to magnify it.

Microsoft Word 2000 ~ Beginners Course

To close Print Preview, do one of the following:

- In the Print Preview toolbar, click the **Close Preview** button
- Press the **Esc** key

Notes

Use this page to make notes of your own.

Page #   Notes

Notes

Use this page to make notes of your own.

Page #   Notes

Chapter 5 ~ Open, Close, New & Save As

In this chapter you will learn about:

- Opening an existing document
- Closing a document
- Starting a new document
- Saving a document with a different filename - Save As

It is assumed that:

- You have created the Computer document and the Electronics document in Chapters 3 and 4, and have saved them on your exercise diskette

Getting started

- If necessary, start Word.

- If the Office Assistant is displayed, right-click it and choose **Hide**.

Opening and closing a document

So far in this course you have created and saved two documents on your exercise diskette: Computer and Electronics. As long as these documents are not deleted, they can be opened at any time.

You will now open the Computer document by typing in the drive name and filename, just as you did when you saved it.

- Make sure your exercise diskette is in drive A.

- Open the **File** menu and choose **Open**, or click the **Open** button in the Standard toolbar, or just press **Ctrl+O**.

The Open dialog box is displayed.

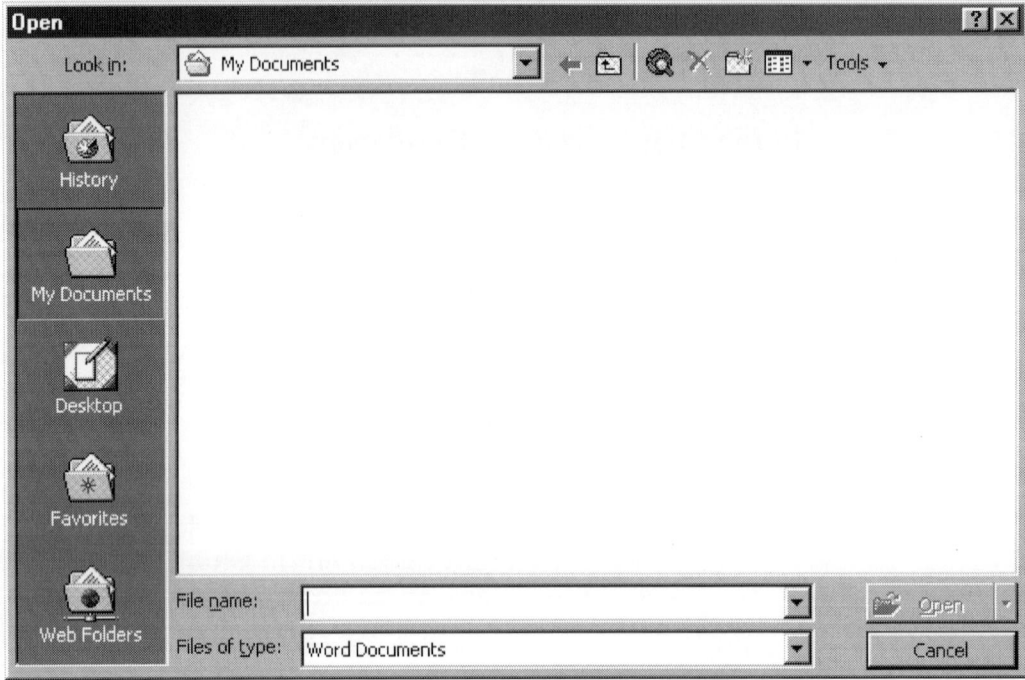

Any documents that are in the current folder are listed. Note that the insertion point is flashing in the File name box. This means that you can simply type the drive and filename of the desired document.

- Type:

    a:Computer

- Click **Open**, or press **Enter**.

The document is opened ready for you to start work on, although just now you will close it again.

- Open the **File** menu and choose **Close**.

The Computer document is closed and you are left with an empty Word window.

Open - using the Look in box

This time, you will open a document using the Look in box, and then look for the document filename in the list of available files. Try opening the Electronics document as follows:

- Make sure your exercise diskette is in drive A.

- Open the **File** menu and choose **Open,** or click the **Open** button in the Standard toolbar, or just press **Ctrl+O**.

The Open dialog box is displayed and any documents that are in the current folder are listed. This may well be the My Documents folder.

- Click anywhere on the Look in box to open the list of available drives.

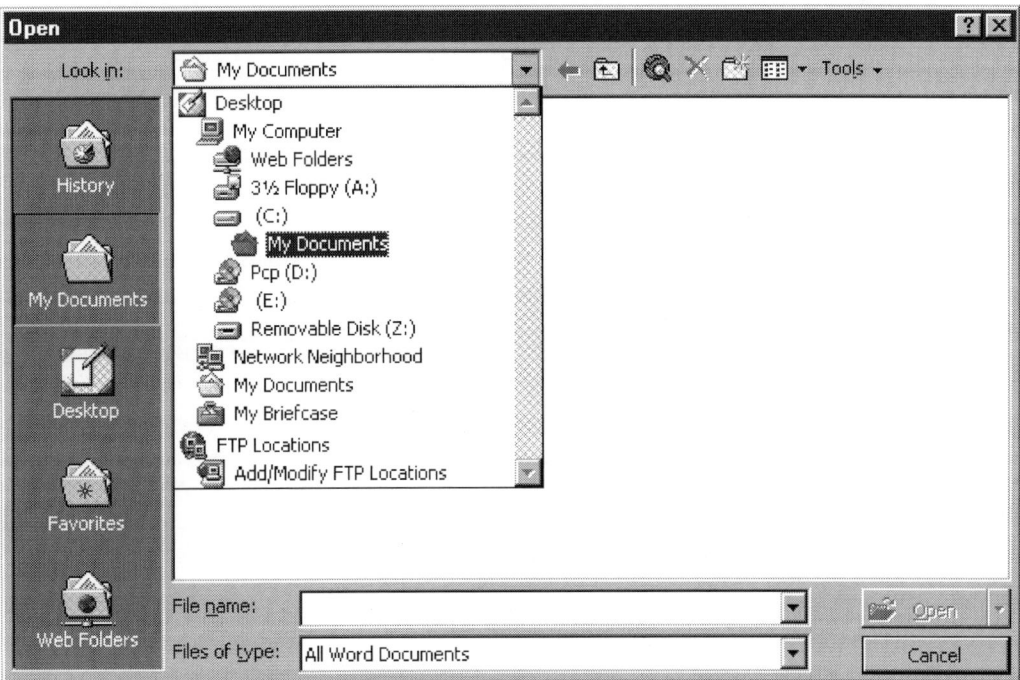

- In the list, click **3½ Floppy (A:)**.

After a short pause, the list of files is updated to show the files available in drive A.

- In the list of files, look for the file **Electronics**.

> ♪ *If the file you are looking for is not visible, you can scroll the list using the horizontal scroll bar. You can also click any filename in the list and use the ↓ key to move down the list of files.*

- Double-click the filename **Electronics,** or click the filename once and then click **Open**.

Your Electronics document is now opened.

Clearing the screen

Assume that you wish to clear the current text from the screen in order to start a new document.

New or Close?

At this stage it is important to clarify the difference between the **New**, **Close** and **Exit** options in the **File** menu.

- If you choose **New**, a new Word document window will be opened *on top of* the current Word window. This is because Word allows you to work with several Word document windows open at any one time.

- If you choose **Close** when there is only one Word window open, the current *document* is closed and removed from the screen. You are left with an empty Word window. You can then choose **New** to open a new document.

- If you choose **Close** and you have several Word document windows open, only the current Word document window is closed.

- If you choose **Exit**, all open Word document windows will be closed (Word will remind you about saving unsaved or changed documents) and the program exited.

If you only work with a single document at a time, to clear the screen you should choose the **Close** option and then open a new document.

> ♪ *A quicker way of closing a Word document window is to click its **Close** button. If you have only one document open, remember that you have to click the **Close Window** button - if you use the **Close** button in the top right-hand corner you will exit the Word program.*

At present you have only one document open.

- Open the `File` menu and choose `Close`.

The Electronics document is closed and you are left with an empty Word window.

Starting a new document

When you open a new document, the **New Blank Document** button and the **File**, **New** menu option have slightly different results.

Using the menu option File, New

- Open the `File` menu and choose `New`.

The New dialog box is displayed.

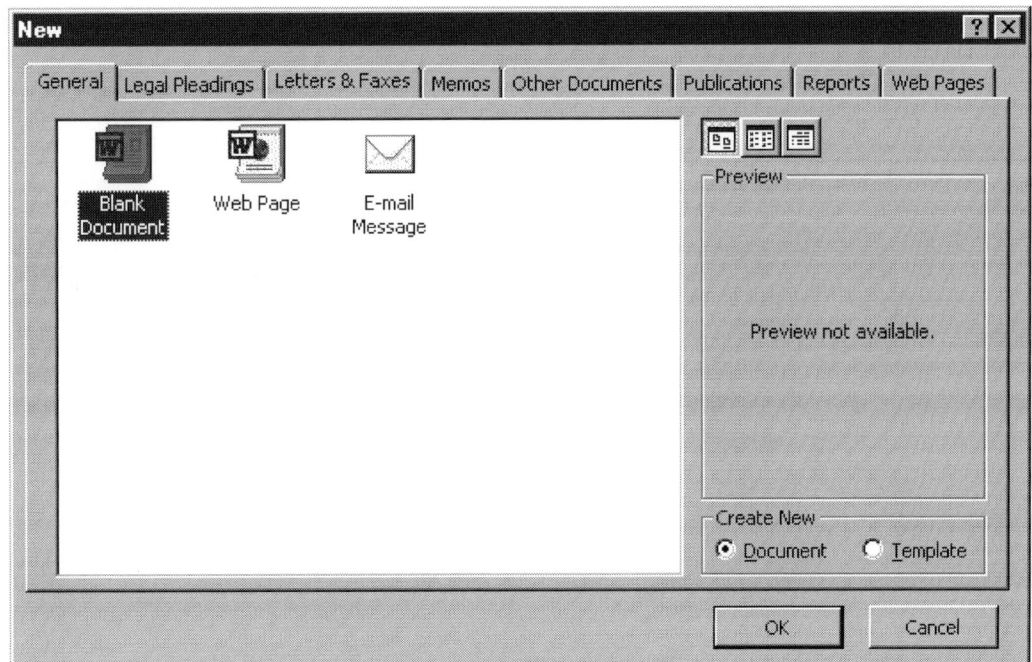

Each time you open a new document in this manner, you will be asked which template you wish to attach to the new document. On the General tab you will have at least three choices:

- **Blank Document** - this is the same as using the **New Blank Document** button or **Ctrl+N** - this provides you with a new document to work on

- **Web Page** - provides you with a blank web page as the starting point for creating your own web page

- **E-mail Message** - gives you a blank message where you can enter the recipient's name, subject and message

You will use the **Blank Document** option, which is currently selected.

- Double-click the `Blank Document` icon, or click **OK**.

A new document is opened for you - it will probably be called Document2. Type something in it.

- Type:

    This is the first document.

- Press **Enter**.

Using the New Blank Document button or Ctrl+N

If you use the **New Blank Document** button in the Standard toolbar, or the shortcut key combination **Ctrl+N**, you do not have to go through the process of choosing a template.

- Click the **New Blank Document** button in the Standard toolbar, or press **Ctrl+N**.

A second Word document window is opened with a blank document ready for you to use - it is probably called Document3.

Working with two Word document windows

Now that you have a second Word document window open, you can see that there is no **Close Window** button just below the **Minimize**, **Restore** and **Close** buttons in the top right-hand corner of the Word document window. These three buttons are for the Document3 window. For example, the **Close** button would close the Document3 window, leaving the Document2 window open.

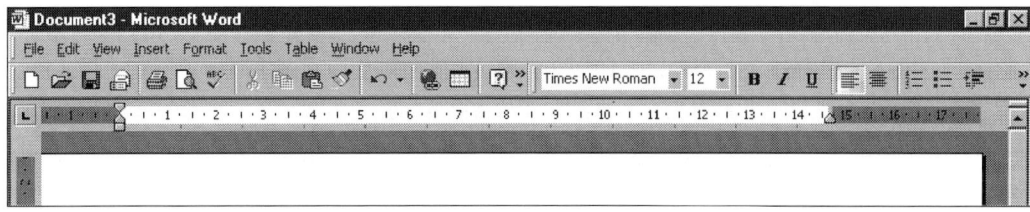

You can switch between the two documents using the Word buttons in the Windows Taskbar.

- In the Windows Taskbar, click the **Document2 Microsoft Word** button.

The first document is displayed. You will notice that this Word document window doesn't have a **Close Window** button either. This is because you still have another Word document window open.

- In the Windows Taskbar, click the **Document3 Microsoft Word** button.

The other Word document window is displayed again. You can close it.

- Click the **Close** button for the Document3 Word window.

The window is closed and you are left with Document2 displayed in the Word window. As this is the only document you have open, you can see that there is a **Close Window** button below the other Window buttons. This would close the document and leave the Word window open.

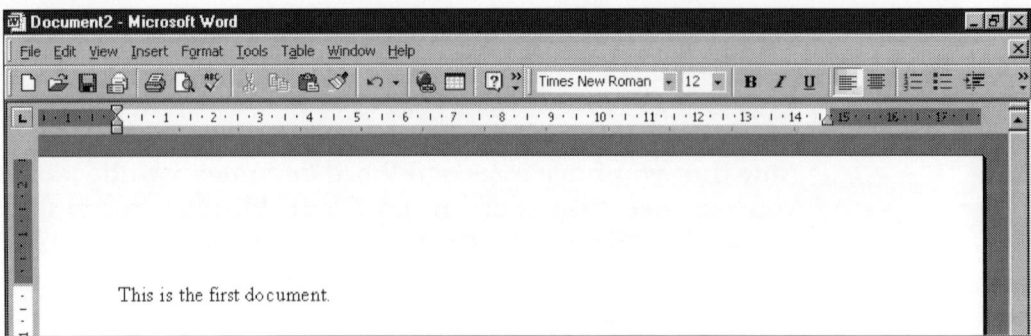

Closing without saving

You will now close a document without saving changes made to it.

- Open the **File** menu and choose **Close,** or press **Ctrl+W.**

A dialog box is opened asking you if you want to save the changes.

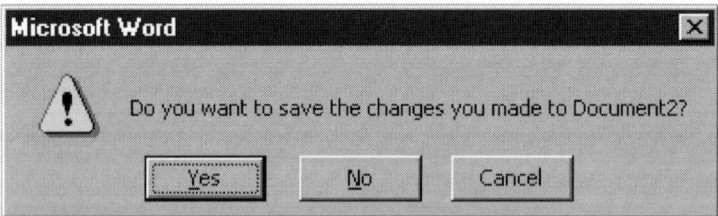

- Choose **No.**

Save As

When you want to save a document, there are two choices in the **File** menu: **Save** and **Save As**. It is worth remembering the following points:

      When you save a document for the first time, because it doesn't already have a filename, the Save As dialog box is opened regardless of whether you choose the **Save** or **Save As** option. You can then give the document a filename.

❧ If your document already has a filename and you wish to save it again with the same name, you should choose **File**, **Save** (or use the **Save** button, or press **Ctrl+S**). No dialog box is opened and your document is saved automatically. You can then close it or carry on working with it.

❧ If your document already has a filename, but you wish to save it with a different filename, then choose **File**, **Save As**. The Save As dialog box is opened and you can give the document the new filename. You can then close it or carry on working.

Try this out now by opening the Computer document and saving it on your exercise diskette with a new name **Computer2**. This means that you will then have two independent copies of the document, one called **Computer** and the other called **Computer2**.

- Make sure your exercise diskette is in drive A.

- Open the `File` menu and choose `Open`, or click the `Open` button in the Standard toolbar, or just press `Ctrl+O`.

The Open dialog box is displayed.

- Locate and double-click the filename `Computer` in the list of files.

The document is opened for you. Now save it with a different name.

- Open the `File` menu and choose `Save As`.

The Save As dialog box is displayed.

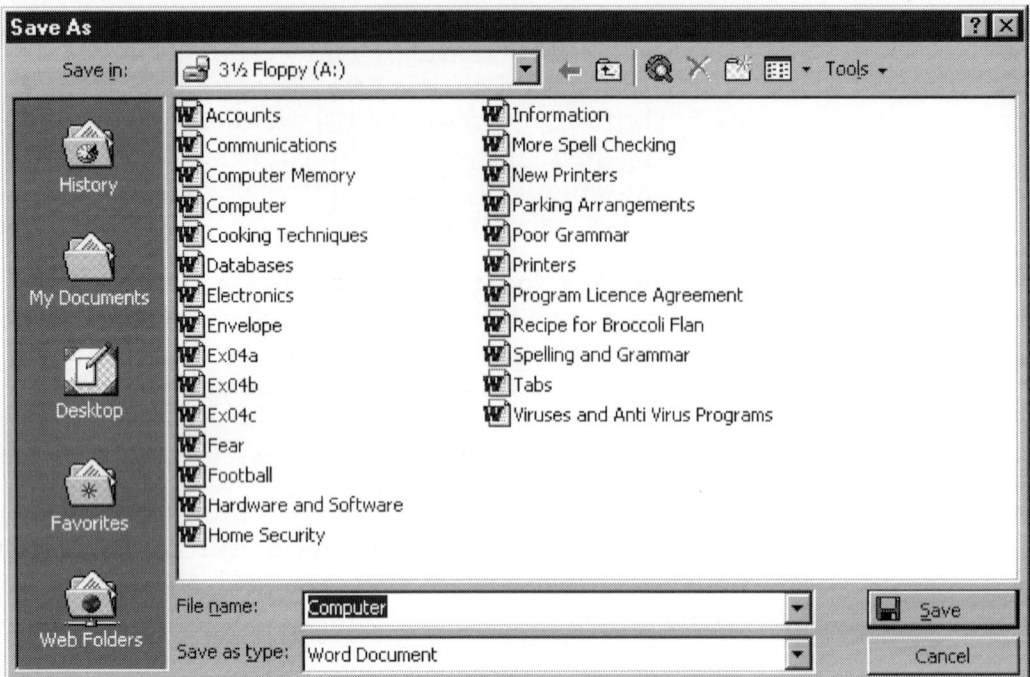

- In the File name box, type:

    `a:Computer2`

- Click **Save**, or press **Enter**.

The old Computer Word window has been renamed, and you are left with the new Computer2 Word window instead. You can continue working with the new document, or close it. The Computer document file will still be on your disk, together with the new Computer2 document file.

- Open the **File** menu and choose **Close**.

Recently opened files

A list of the most recently opened files is shown at the bottom of the **File** menu, allowing you to quickly choose and open them.

- Open the **File** menu and choose one of the files at the bottom of the list.

The file is opened for you.

Word also keeps track of the files and folders that access, and creates a history for you. If you click the **History** button in the Open dialog box this list will be displayed.

Ending the session

You have now completed the tutorial in this chapter. There are two additional exercises that you may wish to do before moving on to the next chapter or exiting Word. First, you should close the current document.

- Open the **File** menu and choose **Close** to close the current document.

- If you are not continuing directly with the extra exercises or the next chapter, open the **File** menu and choose **Exit** to exit Word.

Exercise 5a

In this exercise you will open an existing document, save it with a new name, edit the text, preview the document and then close it.

- Open the **Information** document on your exercise diskette - click the **Open** button to display the Open dialog box.

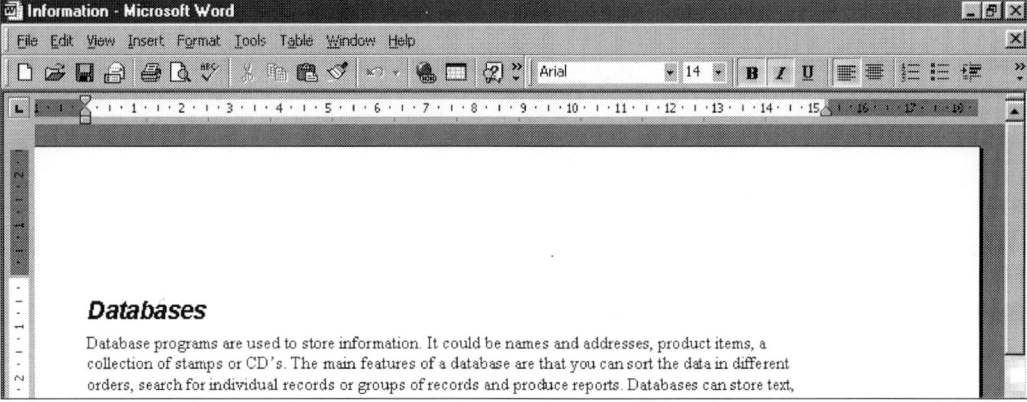

- Before you make any changes, use **File**, **Save As** to save the document on your exercise diskette as **a:Ex05a**.

Microsoft Word 2000 ~ Beginners Course **91**

- Move the insertion point to the end of the document - **Ctrl+End**.

- Replace the word <u>long</u> with the phrase <u>some time</u>.

- Type your name at the end of the document.

- Save the document with the same filename - use either **Ctrl+S**, or the **Save** button in the Standard toolbar.

- Preview the document - open the **File** menu and choose **Print Preview**, or click the **Print Preview** button in the Standard toolbar.

- When you are ready, close Print Preview.

- Move the insertion point to the top of the document - **Ctrl+Home**.

- Press **Enter** to create a blank line before the heading.

- Press **Ctrl+Home** again, and type today's date at the top of the document.

- Save the **Ex05a** document again.

- Close the document - open the **File** menu and choose **Close**.

Exercise 5b

In this exercise you will open an existing document, save it with another name, edit the text, view it in Print Preview and then close it.

- Open the **Viruses and Anti Virus Programs** document on your exercise diskette.

- Before you make any changes, use **File, Save As** to save the document on your exercise diskette as **a:Ex05b**.

- Move the insertion point to the end of the document and press **Enter**.

- Type:

  If you accept a diskette from a friend or work mate, and use that diskette in your computer, then you put yourself at risk, although each time you do so the risk is very very small.

- Use **Ctrl+←** to move the insertion point to the first <u>very</u>.

- Replace the phrase <u>very very</u> with the word <u>extremely</u>.

- Save the changes you have made to the **Ex05b** document.

- Use Print Preview to view the document.

- Close the document.

Summary ~ Open, Close, New & Save As

Opening a document

To open a document, do one of the following:

    ✎   Open the **File** menu and choose **Open**

    ✎   In the Standard toolbar, click the **Open** button

    ✎   Press **Ctrl+O**

The Open dialog box is then displayed. There are several ways of finding your document:

    ✎   If the correct folder is open, your document will be in the list of documents shown - click it to choose it

    ✎   If you are using a diskette and know the name of the document, you can type the drive name and filename

- Use the Look in list box to choose a drive or folder, then double-click the folders listed until your document is displayed

- Use the **History** button to list documents and folders you have used recently

When you have found your document, click **Open** or press **Enter**.

Recently opened documents

A list of the most recently opened documents is shown at the bottom of the **File** menu. To open one of these documents:

- Open the **File** menu

- Choose the document name from the list

Word keeps track of the folders and documents you have used recently - click the **History** button in the Open dialog box to see this list.

Closing a document

To close a document, do one of the following:

- Open the **File** menu and choose **Close**

- Press **Ctrl+W**

- If you have more than one document open, click the **Close** button for the Word document window

- If you have only one document open, click the **Close Window** button

If you have made any changes to the document, you will be given the opportunity of saving it. Click **Yes** if you want to save the changes.

Clearing the screen

You can clear the screen of current text in one of four ways, using the **New**, **Close** and **Exit** options in the **File** menu:

- If you choose **New**, a new Word document window will be opened *on top* of the current Word window.

- If you choose **Close** when there is only one document open, the document is closed and removed from the screen. You are left with an empty Word window. You can then choose **New** to open a new document.

- If you choose **Close** when there are several Word document windows open, only the current Word document window is closed.

- If you choose **Exit**, all the Word document windows that are open will be closed (Word will remind you about saving unsaved or changed documents) and the program exited.

Save As

The Save As dialog box is used the first time a document is saved, or if you want to save a copy of a document in a different folder, give it a different filename or save it as another file type. To open the Save As dialog box:

- Open the **File** menu and choose **Save As**

Notes

Use this page to make notes of your own.

Page #   Notes

Chapter 6 ~ Views, Toolbars & Options

In this chapter you will learn about:

- Normal, Outline, Print Layout, Web Layout and Full Screen views
- The Document Map
- Zooming a document
- Showing and hiding formatting marks
- Showing and hiding different toolbars
- Showing and hiding the rulers
- Options in Word
- Changing the units of measurement

It is assumed that:

- You know how to maximise, minimise, restore, close, re-size and move windows - these basic Windows features were covered in Chapter 2 and are not repeated here

There are a number of options available that will enable you to change the screen display. You can also hide and show different toolbars.

You have already learnt about the Print Preview and it is covered in more detail later on in the course.

Getting started

- If necessary, start Word.
- If the Office Assistant is displayed, right-click it and choose **Hide**.
- Make sure your exercise diskette is in drive A.

- Open the **File** menu and choose **Open,** or click the **Open** button in the Standard toolbar, or just press **Ctrl+O**.

Microsoft Word 2000 ~ Beginners Course

The Open dialog box is displayed.

- In the <u>File name</u> box, type:

    `a:Communications`

- Click **Open,** or press **Enter.**

The Communications document is opened.

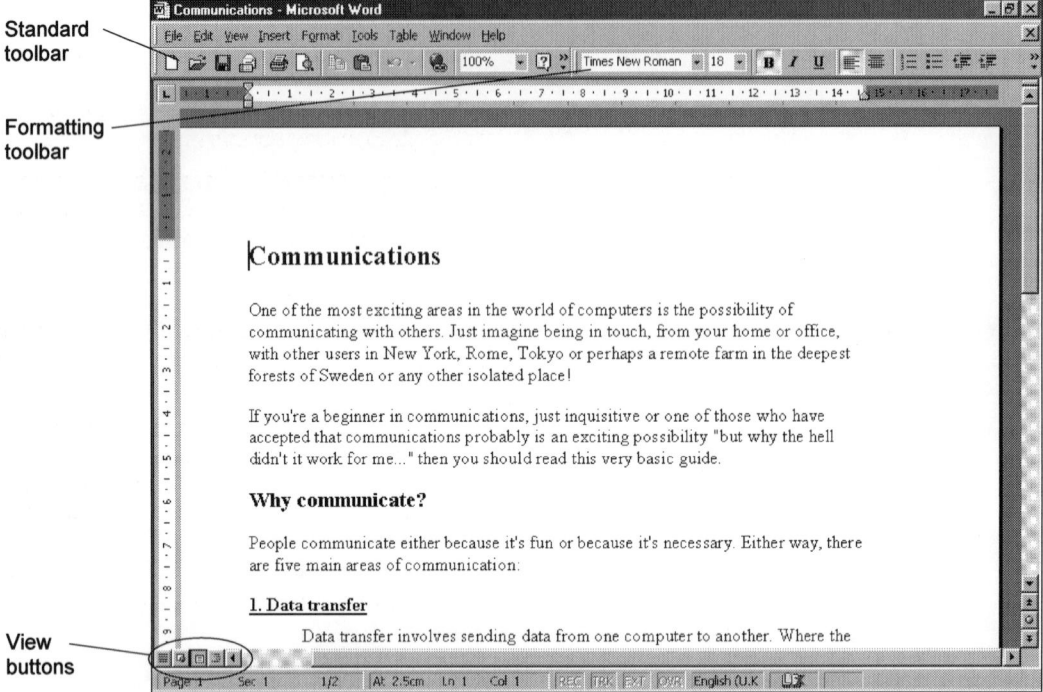

Standard toolbar

Formatting toolbar

View buttons

The different views

Word has different views, each of which can be accessed via the **View** menu. The view determines just how much of the document is visible at one time. The more that is visible, the smaller everything will be. Some of the views also have a button to the left of the horizontal scroll bar in the bottom left-hand corner of the Word window.

Shortcut button	View	Description
▤ (Scroll bar)	Normal	Shows a simplified version of your document and is the best all round view for entering, editing and formatting your document.

Shortcut button	View	Description
▢ (Scroll bar)	Web Layout	Displays your document as if it were a web page so that you can see how it would look if you published it on the Web or your local intranet.
▢ (Scroll bar)	Print Layout	Displays your document as it will be printed, but may slow down your work if you use it for general typing and editing.
▢ (Scroll bar)	Outline	Allows you to collapse a document to see only the main headings and to expand it to see all the document again. This is particularly useful for scrolling through long documents.
	Full Screen	Allows you to clear the screen and show just the document itself.
▢ (Standard toolbar)	Document Map	Displays an outline of your document's paragraph headings in a vertical pane down the left-hand side of the document window. Click the required heading to jump to that section in your main document.
▢ (Standard toolbar)	Print Preview	Shows an entire page at a reduced size. You can also display multiple pages at the same time. This is useful to see the 'balance' of a document spread over several pages.
100% ▾ (Standard toolbar)	Zoom	Allows you to zoom in on, or zoom out of, your document.

To check which view you are currently in, do as follows:

- Open the **View** menu - the current view will have a depressed icon beside the option to show it is chosen.

- Press the **Esc** key to close the menu.

The best way to see the effects of choosing different views is to try them out.

- Open the **View** menu and choose **Normal**, or click the **Normal View** button.

The document is now shown in Normal view.

- Open the **View** menu and choose **Full Screen**.

> **Communications**
>
> One of the most exciting areas in the world of computers is the possibility of communicating with others. Just imagine being in touch, from your home or office, with other users in New York, Rome, Tokyo or perhaps a remote farm in the deepest forests of Sweden or any other isolated place!
>
> If you're a beginner in communications, just inquisitive or one of those who have accepted that communications probably is an exciting possibility "but why the hell didn't it work for me..." then you should read this very basic guide.
>
> **Why communicate?**
>
> People communicate either because it's fun or because it's necessary. Either way, there are five main areas of communication:
>
> **1. Data transfer**
>
> > Data transfer involves sending data from one computer to another. Where the two computers are situated is not very important and the data can really be anything: a document or message, a set of financial reports, a picture, a program. Data transfers can be simple messages or, with the help of a specialised communications program, reports can be sent to hundreds of specified destinations at specified times. Computer programs can also be sent from one place to another.
>
> **2. Information retri**
>
> > Around the w   formation services that provide databases through which you can access information and data on just about anything and everything. You can keep up to date with Wall Street using data provided by Dow Jones, check the times of flights to Seattle, or scan travel news, books,

The screen is cleared of all but the document itself and it is still in Normal view. You can work on the document in this view. If the document window is not maximised it will not cover the entire screen.

There may be a **Close Full Screen** button displayed in a small toolbar of its own.

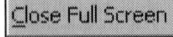

- ```
  Click the Close Full Screen button, or
  press the Esc key to close the Full Screen
  view.
  ```

Now switch to the Print Layout view.

- ```
  Open the View menu and choose Print Layout,
  or click the Print Layout View button.
  ```

The document is now shown in Print Layout view.

The Document Map

The Document Map allows you to split your screen in two. An outline of your document's paragraph headings is shown in the left-hand pane, and the document itself is shown in the right-hand pane.

- Open the **View** menu and choose **Document Map**, or click the **Document Map** button in the Standard toolbar - it may be in the More Buttons palette.

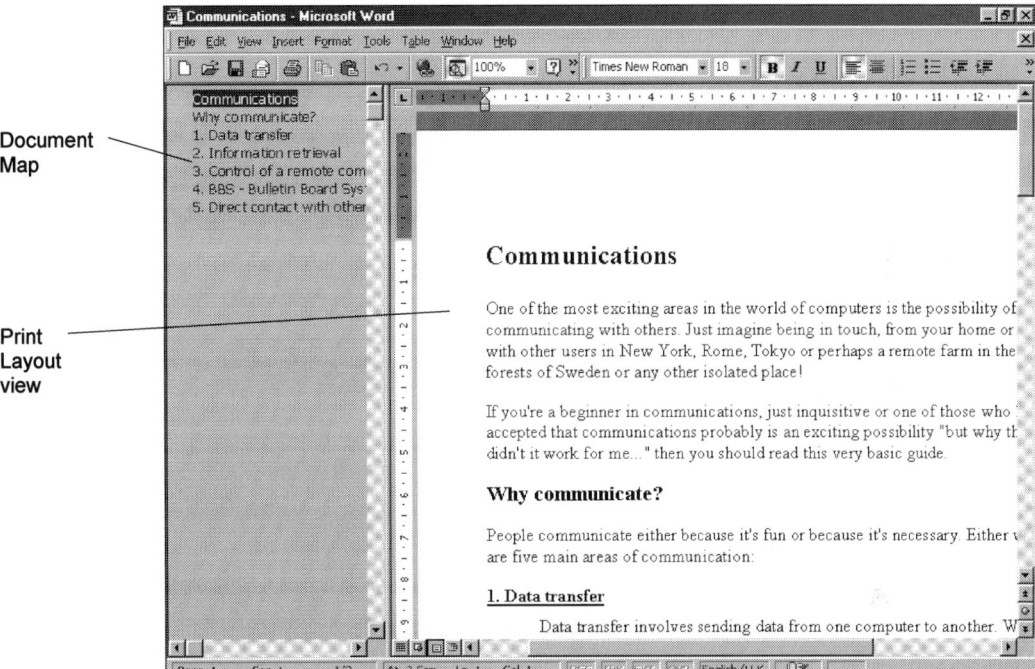

When you click a paragraph heading in the Document Map the insertion point jumps to that position in the main document. Try it now.

- In the Document Map section of the window, click 4. BBS - Bulletin Board….

The insertion point jumps to the 4. BBS - Bulletin Board Systems section in the main document.

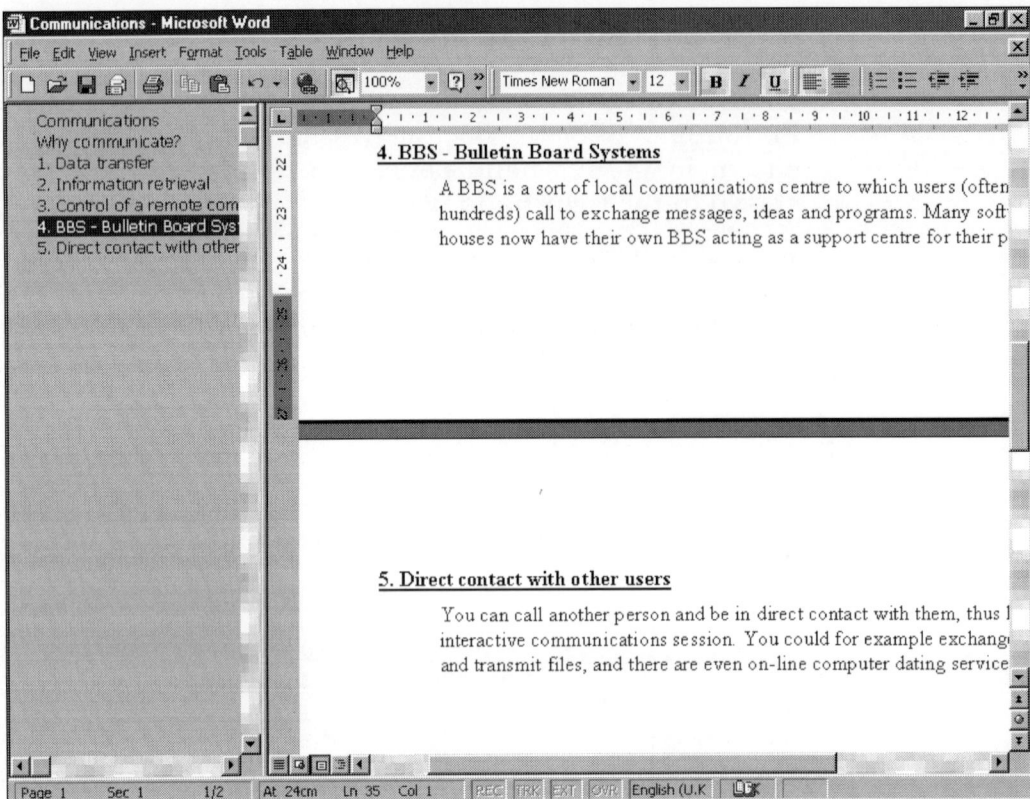

Now return to the start of the document by using the Document Map.

- In the Document Map section of the window, click the main heading: Communications.

The insertion point jumps back to the start of the document. Now close the Document Map.

- Open the **View** menu and choose **Document Map**, or click the **Document Map** button in the Standard toolbar.

Web Layout view

You will now try the Web Layout view. This view displays your document as it would be seen as a web page or if viewed on a screen. The document is displayed at 100% zoom.

- Open the **View** menu and choose **Web Layout**, or click the **Web Layout View** button.

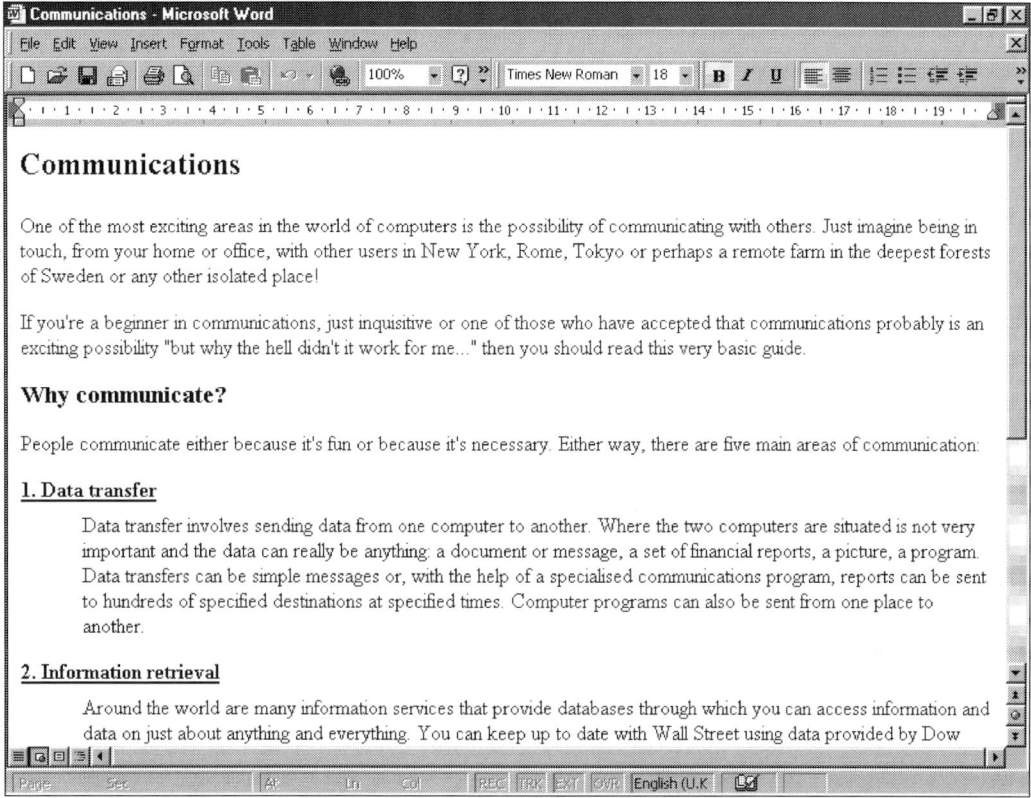

The document now fills the window. Notice that the horizontal scroll box exactly fits the scroll bar - you don't need to scroll the window because the full width of the page is displayed.

- When you are ready, open the **View** menu and choose **Normal,** or click the **Normal View** button.

The document is displayed in Normal view once again.

Zooming a document

The Zoom feature allows you to zoom in on or out of your document.

- If you zoom in, everything looks larger - you can see more detail, but less of the document

- If you zoom out, everything looks smaller - you can see more of the document, but less of the detail

There are two ways to change the zoom:

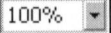

🖐 Use the Zoom dialog box - open the **View** menu and choose **Zoom**

🖐 In the Standard toolbar, use **Zoom** list box

You will try both methods.

- `Open the `**`View`**` menu and choose `**`Zoom`**`.`

The Zoom dialog box is displayed.

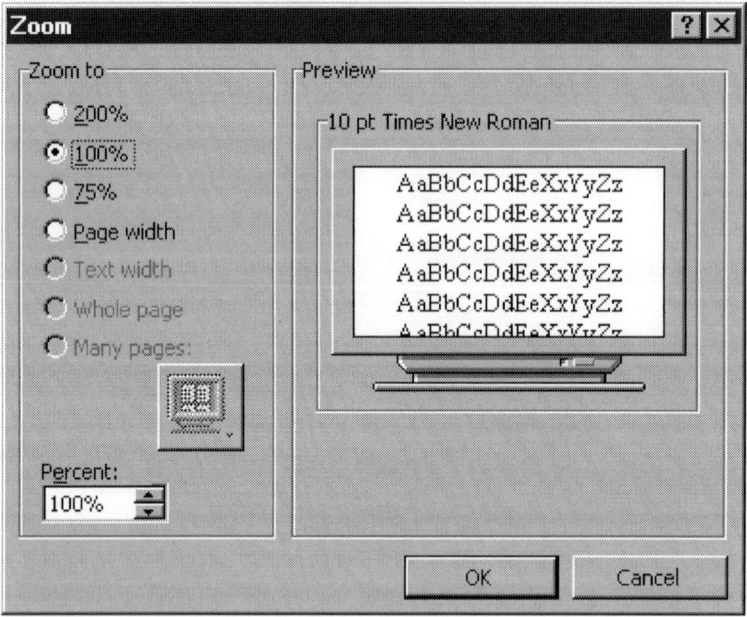

You can either use the pre-defined zoom percentages or set the zoom percentage yourself.

- `Click the `**`200%`**` option so that it is chosen.`

- `Click `**`OK`**`, or press `**`Enter`**`.`

The text in the document is enlarged to twice its original size. Now change it again using the Zoom list box.

- `Find the `**`Zoom`**` list box - it may be in the`
  `More Buttons palette of the Standard`
  `toolbar.`

Click here to open the list box

- `Click the downward-pointing arrow button of`
  `the `**`Zoom`**` list box to display the list of`
  `available zooms.`

- `Choose `**`75%`**`.`

The document is now reduced to show more of it at once.

75%

- Open the **Zoom** list box again and choose **100%**.

The document is now restored to its original display size.

> *♪ If you have a Microsoft IntelliMouse, or equivalent point device, hold down the **Ctrl** key and rotate the wheel button backwards and forwards to zoom out or in on your display.*

Showing formatting marks

When you type in text, only the text itself is displayed. Certain characters - such as paragraph marks, spaces and tab characters - are not shown. These characters are often referred to as *formatting marks* or *non-printing characters*. It is sometimes useful to display these characters in a document. For example, you may want to see where tabs have been inserted, or where two spaces have been typed by mistake.

- In the Standard toolbar, click the **Show/Hide ¶** button.

The formatting marks are displayed.

Microsoft Word 2000 ~ Beginners Course **105**

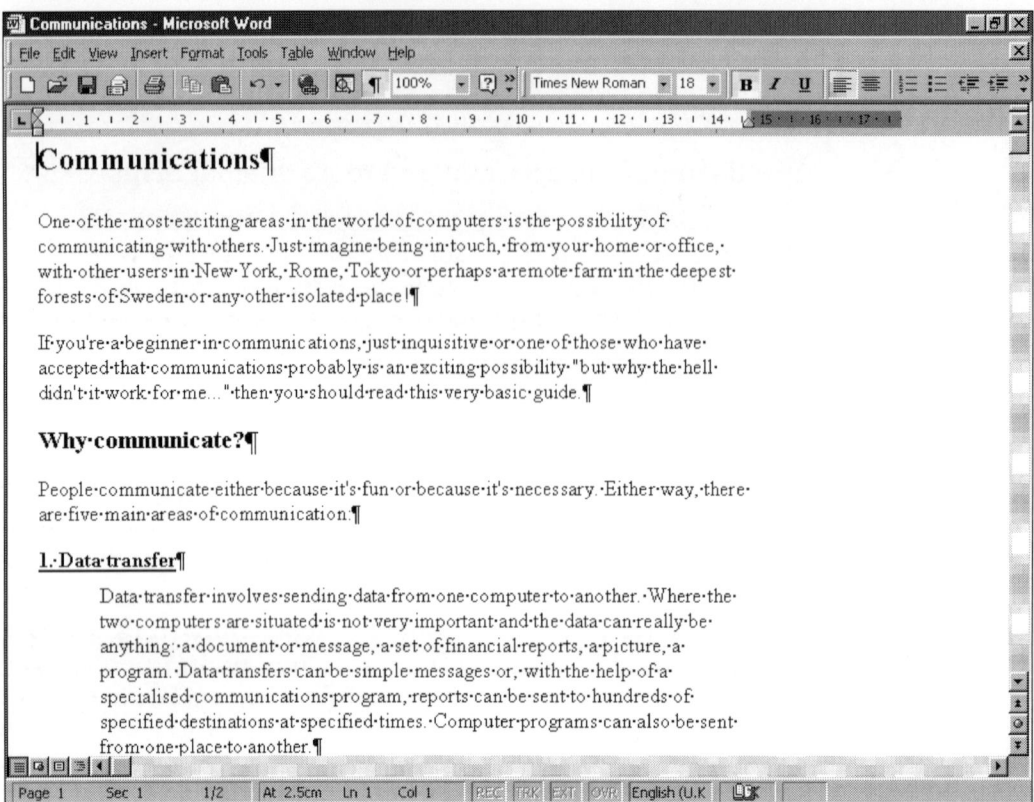

¶ • Click the **Show/Hide ¶** button again to hide the formatting marks.

Toolbars

When Word starts up, the Standard and Formatting toolbars are usually displayed side by side. If you prefer them to be one above the other, you can change the setting in the Customize dialog box:

    ☞   Open the **Tools** menu and choose **Customize**

    ☞   Click the **Options** tab

    ☞   Click Standard and Formatting toolbars share one row so that it is not ticked

You will not make the change for this course but you may like to do it for yourself at some time. One thing to note, if you then decide to make the toolbars share one row again, the Standard toolbar will remain the same length and the Formatting toolbar will be very short.

Resetting a toolbar

As you work with the Standard and Formatting toolbars, buttons that you use frequently will be displayed, while those that you use less often will move to the More Buttons palette of that toolbar.

To reset the toolbars:

- Open the **Tools** menu and choose **Customize**
- Click the **Options** tab
- Click **Reset my usage data**
- Choose **Yes** to confirm that you want to restore the default settings for the menus and toolbars
- Click **Close** to close the Customize dialog box

You may find that the toolbars do not revert back to sharing the space across the top of the document evenly. If this is the case, you can always change the length of the toolbars.

Changing the length of a toolbar

As you use the toolbars, and access the buttons in the More Buttons palettes, you will find that the toolbars change in length. This may mean that the one toolbar grows at the expense of the other.

To change the lengths of the Standard and Formatting toolbars:

- Move the mouse pointer over the boundary between the two toolbars - the mouse pointer will change to double-headed crossed arrows when you are in the right place
- Drag the boundary to the right or to the left, as appropriate - the mouse pointer will change to a double-headed arrow as you drag the boundary

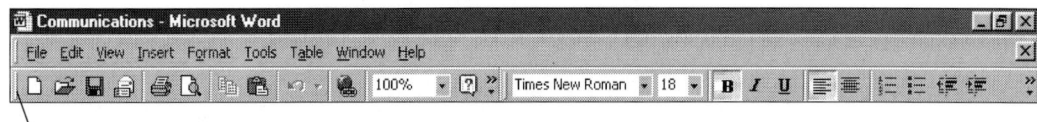

Move handle

> ✋ *If you double-click the Move handle of one of the toolbars, the toolbar will be displayed in full - the other toolbar will then take up the remaining space across the top of the document.*

Other toolbars

Word has several other toolbars. Each toolbar relates to a set of tasks such as drawing, forms and AutoText. Each toolbar can be hidden or displayed. There are three ways of hiding and showing toolbars:

- ✋ Right-click any toolbar to display a list of toolbars
- ✋ Open the **View** menu and choose **Toolbars**
- ✋ Open the **View** menu and choose **Toolbars**, then choose **Customize**

You will try all three methods.

- Right-click any of the current toolbars.

A list of available toolbars is displayed.

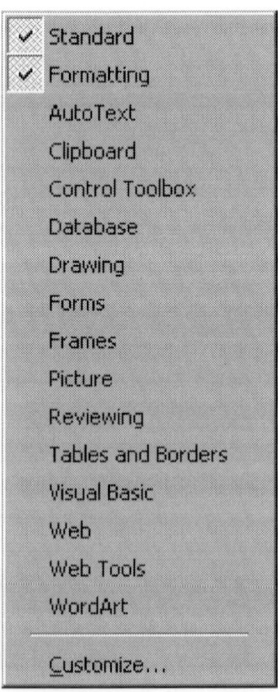

The toolbars that are currently displayed will be ticked.

- In the list, click **Drawing**.

The Drawing toolbar is displayed at the foot of the Word window above the Status bar.

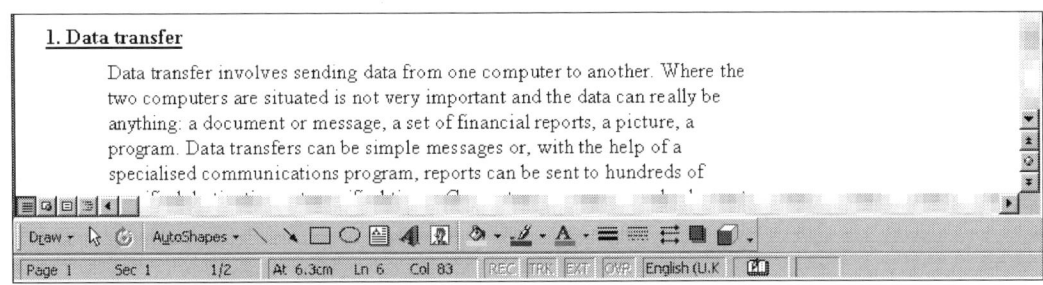

Now open the Forms toolbar using the **View**, **Toolbars** menu option.

- Open the **View** menu and choose **Toolbars**, then choose **Forms**.

The Forms toolbar is displayed. This time, it is shown as a *floating* toolbar.

The following points should be noted about a floating toolbar:

- The small arrow to the left of the toolbar name is the **More Buttons** button - click it to display any buttons that are not currently displayed

- To move the toolbar, drag it by its Title bar

- To dock the toolbar, double-click its Title bar

- To close the toolbar, click the **Close** button in the top right-hand corner

Move, and then dock, the Forms toolbar.

- Position the mouse pointer over the Title bar of the Forms toolbar, and then drag it across to the right to reposition it.

- Double-click the Title bar of the Forms toolbar.

Microsoft Word 2000 ~ Beginners Course

The Forms toolbar is now *docked* - either below the Standard toolbar or at one edge of the screen.

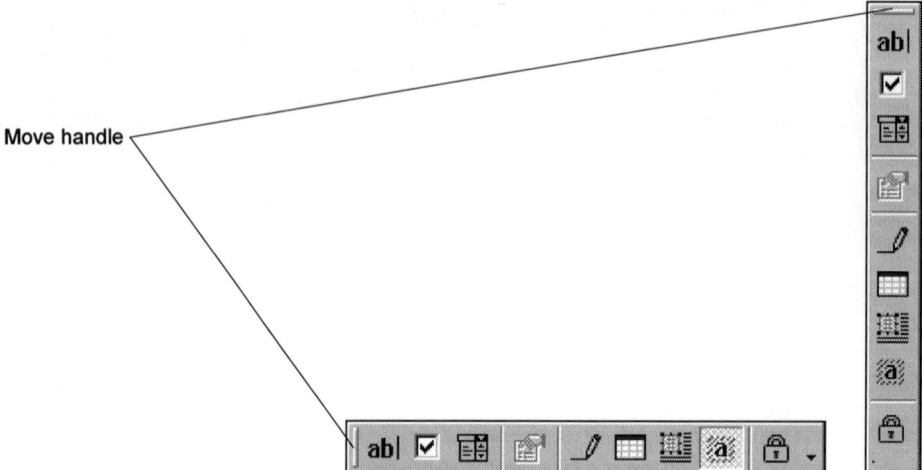

Move handle

Now drag it back again.

- Point very carefully at the Move handle in
  the Forms toolbar, and drag the toolbar
  back onto the document.

You can also display or hide several toolbars at once using the Customize dialog box.

- Open the **View** menu and choose **Toolbars**,
  then choose **Customize**.

The Customize dialog box is displayed.

- Click the **Toolbars** tab.

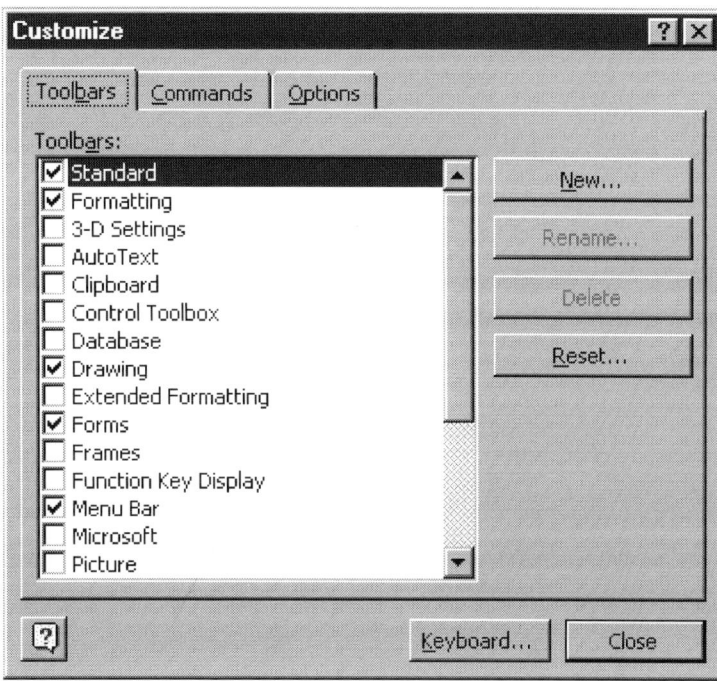

If an option is ticked, the toolbar will be displayed. If it is not ticked, the toolbar will be hidden.

Make sure that only the Standard and Formatting toolbars and the Menu bar will be displayed on your screen.

- In the list of Toolbars, click **Forms** and **Drawing** so that they are not ticked.

- Click **Close**.

The Forms and Drawing toolbars are no longer displayed.

Hiding and showing the ruler

Word has a ruler that can be hidden or shown. It is most useful when working with tab stops. If you are in Print Layout view, a vertical ruler may also be displayed down the left-hand edge of the window. The option for displaying this ruler is chosen in the View tab in the Options dialog box (**Tools**, **Options**). Don't worry if you can't see it - you don't need it for this course.

Ruler —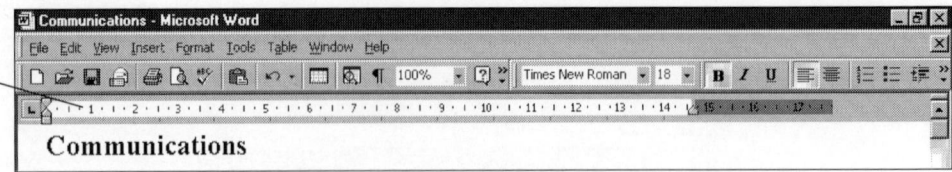

> ☞ *Warning!*
> *Be careful not to click anywhere on the ruler - Word uses this as a quick method of setting tab stops.*

- `Open the` **View** `menu and choose` **Ruler** `- if you can't see the option, click the double-arrow button at the bottom of the menu to display the full menu.`

The ruler is now hidden, but if it was hidden before you started it will now be shown.

- `Open the` **View** `menu and choose` **Ruler** `again.`

The ruler is now displayed again - or hidden.

Options for customising Word

Word has an extensive set of options that will allow you to customise your program. You will not be instructed to change the options in this course, but as you learn more you may want to start making changes. One specific example is given in the section *Changing the units of measurement*.

To view the different options, open the Options dialog box.

- `Open the` **Tools** `menu and choose` **Options.**

There are ten different sets of options each having its own tab. You need to look at the View options.

- `If necessary, click the` **View** `tab to show these options.`

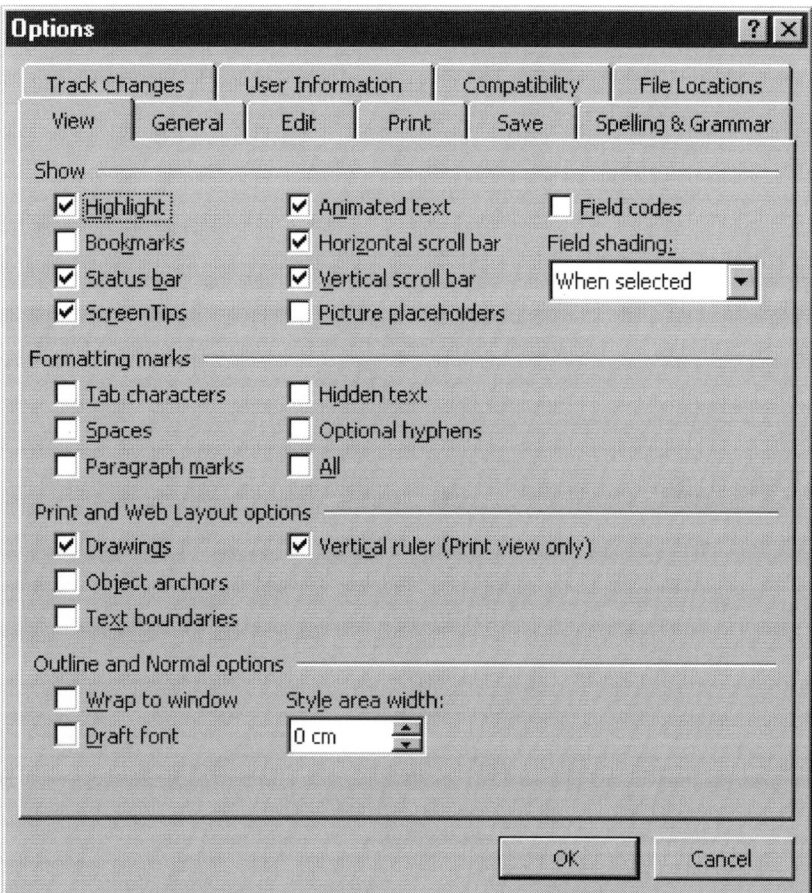

- Look through the options.

- When you are ready, close the Options dialog box without saving any changes - click **Cancel**, or press the **Esc** key.

Changing the units of measurement

One option that you may want to change is the units of measurement. You can choose to display measurements in inches, centimetres, points or picas. (Pica is a printing unit. There are six picas to an inch.)

- Open the **Tools** menu and choose **Options**.

The Options dialog box is displayed again.

- Click the **General** tab to show these options.

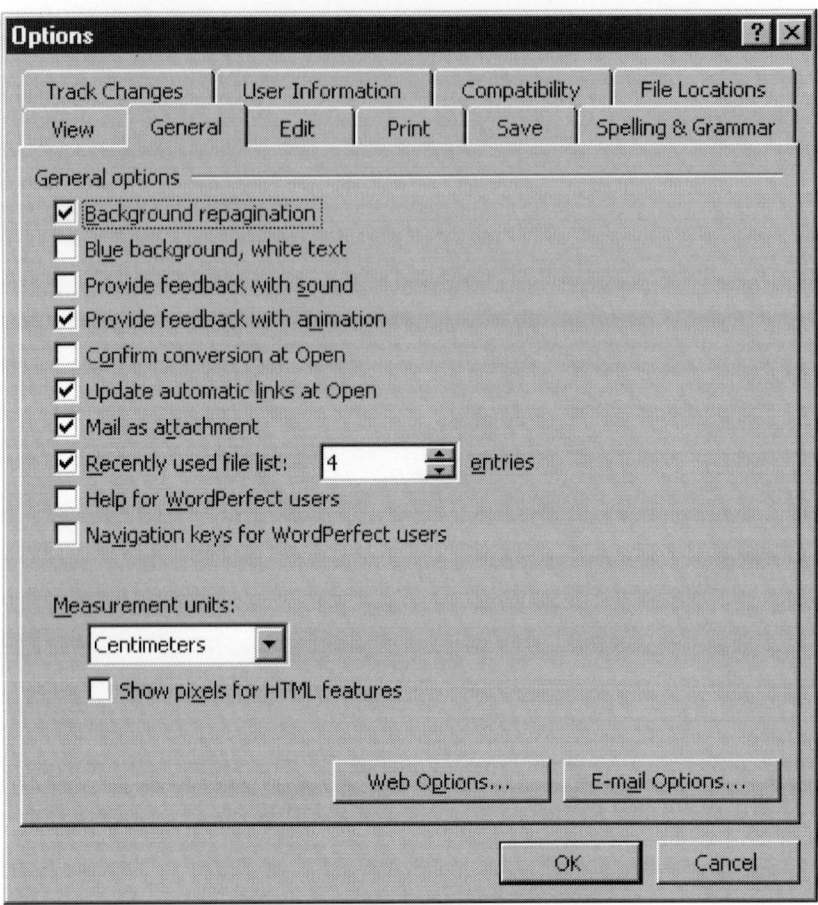

At the foot of the dialog box, there is a Measurement units option.

- Open the Measurement units list box.

- Choose the measurement units you require.

- Click **OK** to confirm the change you have made, or click **Cancel** to close the dialog box without keeping any changes.

Ending the session

You have now completed the tutorial in this chapter. There is an additional exercise that you may wish to do before moving on to the next chapter or exiting Word. First, you should close the current document.

- Open the **File** menu and choose **Close** – there is no need to save any changes.

- If you are not continuing directly with the extra exercise or the next chapter and want to stop now, open the **File** menu and choose **Exit** to exit Word.

Exercise 6a

In this exercise you will open an existing document, display the formatting marks, and also display some additional toolbars.

- Open **Viruses and Anti Virus Programs** document from your exercise diskette.

- Display the formatting marks.

- Hide and show the ruler using the **Ruler** option in the **View** menu.

- Zoom the display to **200%** using the **Zoom** option in the **View** menu.

- In the Standard toolbar, use the **Zoom** list box to zoom the document to **100%**.

- Use **View, Full Screen** to clear all toolbars and show just the document itself.

- Click the **Close Full Screen** button, or press the **Esc** key, to return to the original view.

- Display the **AutoText** and **Picture** toolbars.

- Practise docking and floating the AutoText and Picture toolbars.

- Close the AutoText toolbar - right-click any toolbar and choose **AutoText**.

- Close the Picture toolbar - click its **Close** button.

- Hide the formatting marks.

- Close the document - **File, Close** - don't save the changes.

Microsoft Word 2000 ~ Beginners Course **115**

Summary ~ Views, Toolbars & Options

Different views

Word has different views, each of which can be accessed via the **View** menu. The view determines just how much of the document is visible at one time. The more that is visible, the smaller everything will be. Some of the views also have a button towards the bottom left-hand corner of the Word document window. The main views are summarised on page 98.

The Document Map

The Document Map lists the paragraph headings of a document, in a vertical pane down the left-hand side of the document window. To display the Document Map, do one of the following:

- Open the **View** menu and choose **Document Map**

- In the Standard toolbar, click the **Document Map** button

You can then click a heading to jump to that section of your document.

Zooming a document

The Zoom feature allows you to zoom in on or out of your document.

- If you zoom in, everything looks larger - you can see more detail, but less of the document

- If you zoom out, everything looks smaller - you can see more of the document, but less of the detail

To access the Zoom feature, open the **View** menu and choose **Zoom**, or use the **Zoom** list box in the Standard toolbar.

Showing formatting marks

When you type text, only the text itself is displayed. Certain characters - for example, paragraph marks, spaces and tab characters - are not shown. These characters are often referred to as *formatting marks*. You can display these characters on the screen by clicking the **Show/Hide ¶** button in the Standard toolbar.

Toolbars

The Standard and Formatting toolbars are normally displayed side by side when Word starts up. You can choose to display them one above the other if you wish - use the **Tools**, **Customize** menu option.

Word has several other toolbars each relating to a set of tasks, such as AutoText or drawing. You can choose which toolbars you want to display by choosing the **Toolbars** option in the **View** menu. Then click each toolbar you want to display so that the option is ticked. As a shortcut, you can right-click any toolbar to open up a list of toolbars.

Hiding and showing the ruler

Word has a ruler that can be hidden or shown. It is most useful when working with tab stops. To hide or show the ruler, open the **View** menu. If the **Ruler** option is ticked the ruler is shown. Clicking the **Ruler** option will then hide the ruler on the screen.

In Print Layout view, an additional vertical ruler may be displayed down the left-hand edge of the Word window. The option to display this ruler is chosen in the View tab of the Options dialog box (**Tools**, **Options**).

Options for customising Word

Word has an extensive set of options that will allow you to customise your program. Although you will not make any major changes in this course, to view the options open the **Tools** menu and choose **Options**. The Options dialog box is displayed. It has ten sets of options, each with its own tab - click the tab to show that set of options.

Changing the units of measurement

You can choose to display measurements in inches, centimetres, points or picas. To do this display the General tab in the Options dialog box, then open the Measurement units list box and choose the unit you require.

Notes

Use this page to make notes of your own.

Page #   Notes

Notes

Use this page to make notes of your own.

Page #   Notes

Chapter 7 ~ Selecting Text for Editing

In this chapter you will learn about:

- Scrolling a document
- Using the Microsoft IntelliMouse, or equivalent pointing device, to scroll a document
- Using the mouse to select words, phrases, sentences and paragraphs
- Using the keyboard to select words, phrases and blocks of text in general

Whenever you want to change the style of a particular piece of text - for instance, to put it into italic or bold - you should first select the block of text you want to alter and then select the desired feature. Selecting blocks of text allows you to format letters, words, phrases, sentences or paragraphs at the same time.

> *You will only be able to carry out the section about using the Microsoft IntelliMouse if you have one installed on your computer.*

Getting started

- If necessary, start Word.

- If the Office Assistant is displayed, right-click it and choose **Hide**.

- Make sure your exercise diskette is in drive A.

- Open the **File** menu and choose **Open**, or click the **Open** button in the Standard toolbar, or just press **Ctrl+O**.

The Open dialog box is displayed.

- In the File name box, type:

    a:Fear

Microsoft Word 2000 ~ Beginners Course **121**

- Click **Open**, or press **Enter**.

The Fear document is opened.

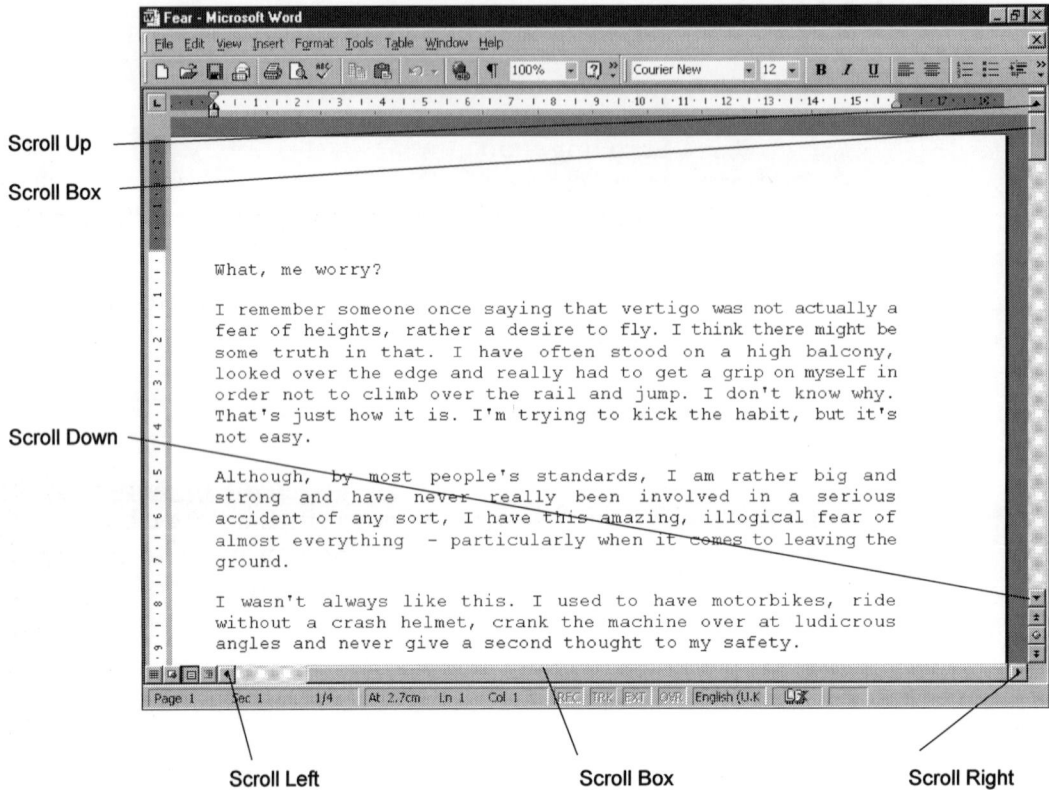

Scrolling a document

The Fear document is too big to fit on the screen so you will have to scroll it to find certain words and phrases. You can use the mouse or the keyboard to scroll a document. The previous picture shows the scroll buttons and scroll boxes for moving up and down and left and right in a document.

If your scroll bars are not displayed - check the previous picture - you will need to follow the next four instructions. If they are displayed, you can skip to the next section - *ScreenTips*.

- If your scroll bars are not visible, open the **Tools** menu and choose **Options**, to display the Options dialog box.

- Click the **View** tab to show these options.

- In the Show options, click **Horizontal scroll bar** and **Vertical scroll bar** so that they are both ticked.

- Click **OK**.

ScreenTips

As you move the scroll box down the scroll bar, a ScreenTip will appear showing the page you are currently scrolling through. Try out the scroll bar ScreenTip now.

- Point at the **Scroll Box** and drag it down the scroll bar.

Note how the ScreenTip changes.

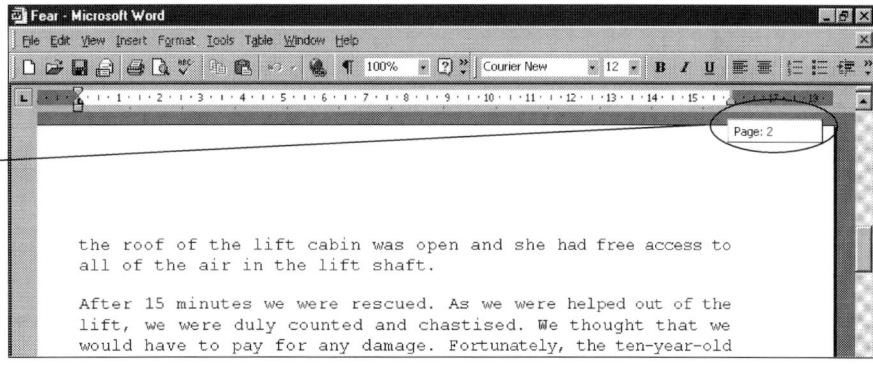

As the Scroll Box is dragged downwards, the ScreenTip shows which page you are scrolling past

- Release the mouse button.

When you release the mouse button, the chosen page will be displayed.

> *It is important to note that scrolling a document using a scroll bar does not move the insertion point.*

Using the mouse and keyboard

The following table lists the different ways of scrolling through a document using the mouse and the keyboard.

Movement	Mouse	Keyboard
Up/down one line at a time	Click ▲ or ▼ on the scroll bar	↑/↓
Left/right	Click ◄ or ► on the scroll bar	←/→
Up/down one screen at a time	Click above or below the Scroll Box	**Page Up/Page Down**
To approx. position in text	Drag the Scroll Box	N/a
Beginning of next/previous paragraph	N/a	**Ctrl+↓/Ctrl+↑**
Beginning/end of document	N/a	**Ctrl+Home/Ctrl+End**

Try out a few of the movements.

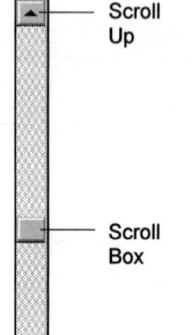

- On the vertical scroll bar, click the **Scroll Down** button a few times.

- On the vertical scroll bar, click the **Scroll Up** button a few times.

- Drag the **Scroll Box** to the middle of the scroll bar.

- Click anywhere on the scroll bar above the Scroll Box to scroll one screen upwards.

- Click anywhere on the scroll bar below the Scroll Box to scroll one screen downwards.

- Press **Ctrl+Home** to move to the beginning of the document again.

- Press **Ctrl+↓** a few times to move down one paragraph at a time.

- Press **Page Down** a few times to move down the document.

- Finish off by pressing **Ctrl+Home** to move to the beginning of the document again.

Scrolling with the Microsoft IntelliMouse

The Microsoft IntelliMouse is like an ordinary mouse pointing device, except for a small wheel button between the left-hand and right-hand mouse buttons.

If you have a Microsoft IntelliMouse or equivalent pointing device, you can scroll your document by using the wheel button on the device.

- If you do NOT have a Microsoft IntelliMouse or equivalent pointing device, skip to the next section in this chapter - *About selecting text*.

Movement	IntelliMouse
Up/down one line at a time	Rotate wheel forwards or backwards.
Pan up/down	Hold down the wheel button and drag the mouse up or down.
Continuous scroll up/down	Click the wheel button, then drag the mouse above/below the origin mark in the vertical scroll bar.

Try out a few movements now.

- Rotate the wheel backwards a little to move down by a few paragraphs.
- Hold down the wheel button, and keep it held down, while you drag the mouse down slightly.
- Hold down the wheel button, and keep it held down, while you drag the mouse up slightly.
- Click the wheel button.

An origin mark appears on the vertical scroll bar and your document starts to scroll down slowly.

- Drag the mouse down slightly and notice how the scrolling speeds up.

- Click, or press **Esc**, to stop scrolling.

- Finish off by pressing **Ctrl+Home** to move the insertion point to the beginning of the document again.

About selecting text

You can select any continuous section of text. There are shortcuts for selecting words, sentences and paragraphs, and the whole document. Any section of text will remain selected until you click the mouse anywhere in the document window, or press one of the **Arrow** keys.

It is possible to use the mouse or the keyboard to select blocks of text - both methods are covered in this chapter. The method you use will be a matter of personal preference, but being able to use and combine both methods has its advantages.

Selecting text using the mouse

First of all, concentrate on using the mouse to select text. The area to the left of the text is called the selection bar. It is used for selecting text.

> *When you move the mouse pointer over the selection bar, the mouse pointer changes, pointing up to the right.*

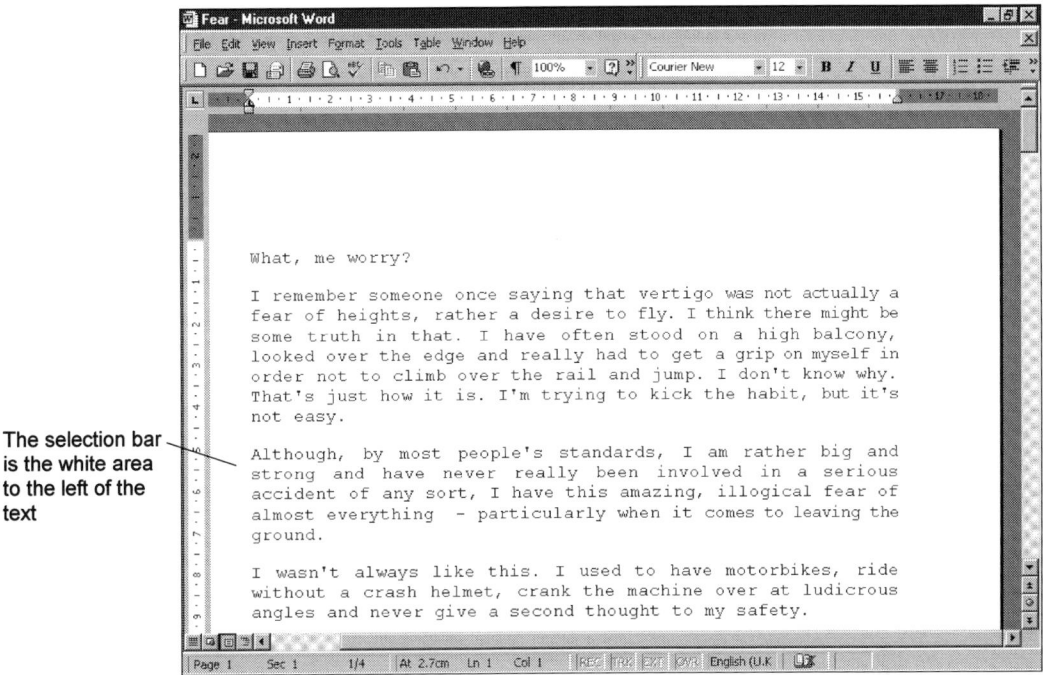

The selection bar is the white area to the left of the text

- Position the mouse pointer over the selection bar - it changes to an arrow that points to the right.

Selecting a phrase

To use the mouse to select a phrase, simply drag the mouse over the text you want to select. Try selecting the phrase desire to fly.

- Position the mouse pointer just before the letter d in desire.

- Hold down the left-hand mouse button and drag the mouse to the right until the phrase desire to fly is selected, then release the mouse button - if you extend your selection too far, you can reverse the end of the selection by pressing **Shift+←**.

Microsoft Word 2000 ~ Beginners Course **127**

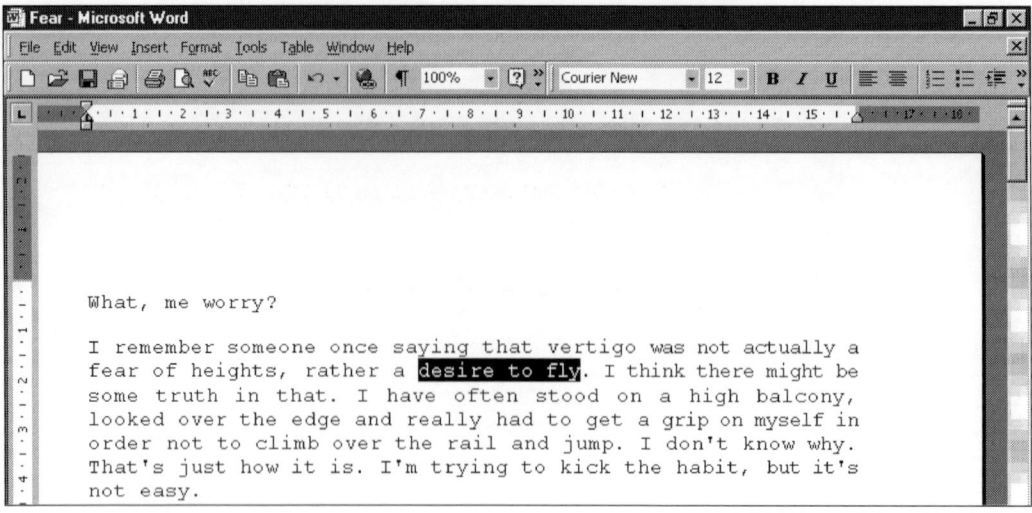

- Click anywhere in the document to cancel the selection.

Selecting a single word

You can also select individual words by double-clicking them.

- Point to the word vertigo.
- Double-click the word.

The whole word is selected.

- Click anywhere in the document to cancel the selection.

Selecting a sentence

A sentence can be selected by using the **Ctrl** key together with the mouse. Try selecting any sentence as follows:

- Hold down the **Ctrl** key and click anywhere in the desired sentence.

The sentence is selected.

- Click anywhere in the document to cancel the selection.

Selecting a line of text

To select a complete line of text using the mouse, click the selection bar to the left of the line.

- ```
  In the selection bar, click to the left of
  any line of text.
  ```

The chosen line of text is selected.

- ```
  Click anywhere in the document to cancel
  the selection.
  ```

Selecting a paragraph

There are two ways of selecting a paragraph with the mouse:

- ✎ Triple-click anywhere in the paragraph
- ✎ In the selection bar, double-click to the left of the paragraph

Try the first method.

- ```
  Triple-click anywhere in the third
  paragraph.
  ```

The paragraph is selected.

- ```
  Click anywhere in the document to cancel
  the selection.
  ```

Selecting a whole document

To select the whole document, triple-click the selection bar.

- ```
  Point to the selection bar and then triple-
  click the mouse.
  ```

The whole text is selected.

- ```
  Click anywhere in the document to cancel
  the selection.
  ```

Shift & click - selecting large sections of text

The easiest method to select large sections of text is to use *Shift & click*. Click at the start point, then hold down the **Shift** key and click at the end point - you can scroll the document with the mouse between the two clicks.

- Click at the beginning of the first paragraph - the insertion point is moved there.

- Hold down the **Shift** key and click at the end of the sixth paragraph - ending considerably more.

- Click anywhere in the document to cancel the selection.

Selecting text using the keyboard

Now try using the keyboard to select some text.

Selecting a phrase

To select a phrase, first position the insertion point at one end of the text you want to select, then extend the selection. Try selecting the phrase not actually a fear.

- In the first paragraph, position the insertion point just before the n in not actually a fear.

- Press **Shift+→**.

Note how the n is selected.

Each time you press **Shift+→** or **Shift+↓**, the selection is extended one character or line in the direction of the arrow.

- Press **Shift+→** again.

Note how the selection is extended.

- Press **Shift+→** a further 17 times.

You should now have selected the phrase not actually a fear.

> ☞ *If you extend your selection too far, you can reverse the end of the selection by using **Shift+←**.*

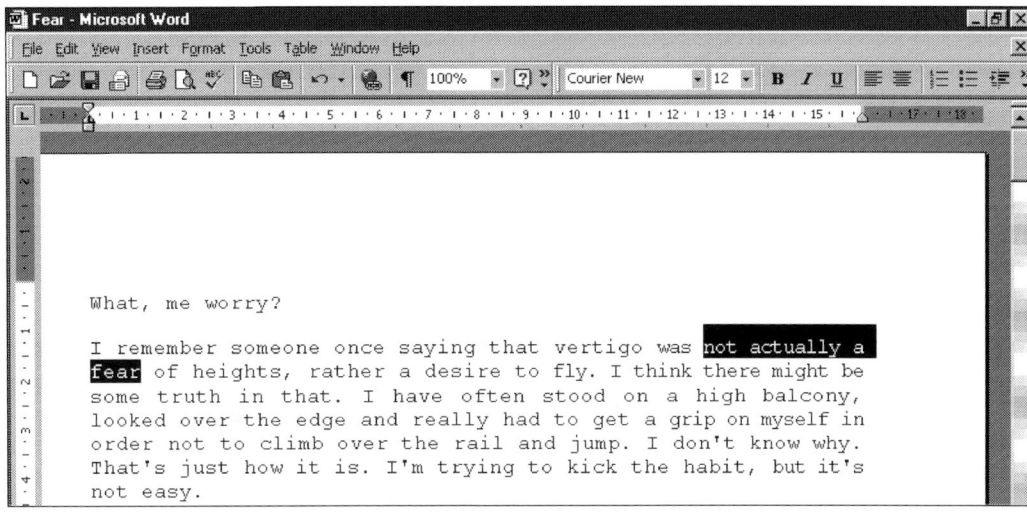

- Press one of the **Arrow** keys (←→↑ or ↓) to cancel the selection.

Selecting a single word

To select a word at a time press **Shift+Ctrl+→**.

- Position the insertion point just before the word vertigo.

- Press **Shift+Ctrl+→**.

> ☞ *You can skip forward selecting the next words by pressing **Shift+Ctrl+→** again, or skip backwards using **Shift+Ctrl+←**.*

- Press one of the **Arrow** keys to cancel the selection.

Selecting a sentence

To select a sentence, you can use the same method as selecting a word. If the sentence is longer than a line of text, you can quickly select the line using **Shift+End**. Try selecting the very first sentence.

- Position the insertion point at the beginning of the first sentence (not the title).

- Press **Shift+End** to select the line.

- Press **Shift+↓** to extend the selection downwards.

- Press **Shift+←** until the selection coincides with the end of the sentence.

- Press one of the **Arrow** keys to cancel the selection.

Selecting a paragraph

To select a paragraph, you need to position the insertion point at the beginning of the paragraph, and then press **Shift+Ctrl+↓**. Try selecting the second paragraph now.

- Position the insertion point at the beginning of the second paragraph.

- Press **Shift+Ctrl+↓**.

The whole paragraph is selected.

- Press one of the **Arrow** keys to cancel the selection.

Selecting a whole document

To select the whole document, use **Ctrl+A**.

- Press **Ctrl+A**.

The whole text is selected.

- Press one of the **Arrow** keys to cancel the selection.

Extending selected text

Any selected text can be extended, or shortened, a character or line at a time using **Shift+ArrowKey**.

- ```
  Try selecting some blocks of text, and then
  extend and shorten them.
  ```

Ending the session

You have now completed this chapter. Close the current document and then exit Word, or continue working with the next chapter.

- ```
  Open the File menu and choose Close -
  choose No to avoid saving the changes.
  ```

- ```
  If you are not continuing directly with the
  next chapter, open the File menu and choose
  Exit to exit Word.
  ```

Summary ~ Selecting Text for Editing

Scrolling a document

When a document is too big to fit onto one screen you may need to scroll it to find certain words and phrases. You can use the mouse or the ↑ and ↓ keys on the keyboard to do this. To move in small increments, click one of the scroll arrows, at either end of the vertical or horizontal scroll bar. To move in big increments, click above or below, to the right or to the left, of the scroll box in the appropriate scroll bar.

You can also drag the scroll box up and down the scroll bar. As you do this, a ScreenTip will appear showing the page you are currently scrolling through.
  ```

Scrolling with the Microsoft IntelliMouse

If you have a Microsoft IntelliMouse or equivalent pointing device, you can scroll your document by using its wheel button.

- To scroll up/down one line at a time, rotate the wheel backwards or forwards

- To pan up/down, hold down the wheel button and keep it held down while you drag the mouse up or down

- To automatically scroll up/down, click the wheel button, then drag the mouse above/below the origin mark in the vertical scroll bar

Selecting text

You can use the mouse or the keyboard to select any continuous section of text. There are also a few shortcuts for selecting complete words, sentences, paragraphs or the whole document.

The following table summarises the selection procedures.

To select...	Mouse	Keyboard
Any text block	Left-hand button and drag	**Shift+Arrow keys**
One character left/right		**Shift+←/Shift+→**
One line up/down		**Shift+↑/Shift+↓**
Word	Double-click word	**Shift+Ctrl+→/ Shift+Ctrl+←**
Sentence	Hold down **Ctrl** and click sentence	
Line of text	Point on selection bar and click	**Shift+End**
Paragraph	Triple-click paragraph, or double-click selection bar beside paragraph	**Ctrl+Shift+↓/ Ctrl+Shift+↑**
Whole document	Triple-click selection bar	**Ctrl+A**

Any section of text will remain selected until you click the mouse anywhere in the document or press one of the **Arrow** keys (←→↑↓).

Notes

Use this page to make notes of your own.

Page #   Notes

_____   _____

_____   _____

_____   _____

_____   _____

_____   _____

_____   _____

_____   _____

_____   _____

_____   _____

_____   _____

_____   _____

_____   _____

_____   _____

_____   _____

Chapter 8 ~ Simple Text Formatting

In this chapter you will learn about:

- Applying **bold**, *italic* and underlining to selected text
- Applying **bold**, *italic* and underlining as you type
- Changing the font and font size

It is assumed that:

- You know how to select text using the keyboard or mouse

In order to emphasise headings and other important sections of your text, you can apply **bold**, *italic* and underlining. You can also choose different character styles, known as fonts, and different font sizes.

Getting started

- If necessary, start Word.
- If the Office Assistant is displayed, right-click it and choose **Hide**.
- Make sure your exercise diskette is in drive A.

- Open the **File** menu and choose **Open**, or click the **Open** button in the Standard toolbar, or just press **Ctrl+O**.

The Open dialog box is displayed.

- In the File name box, type:

  `a:Computer Memory`

- Click **Open**, or press **Enter**.

The Computer Memory document is opened.

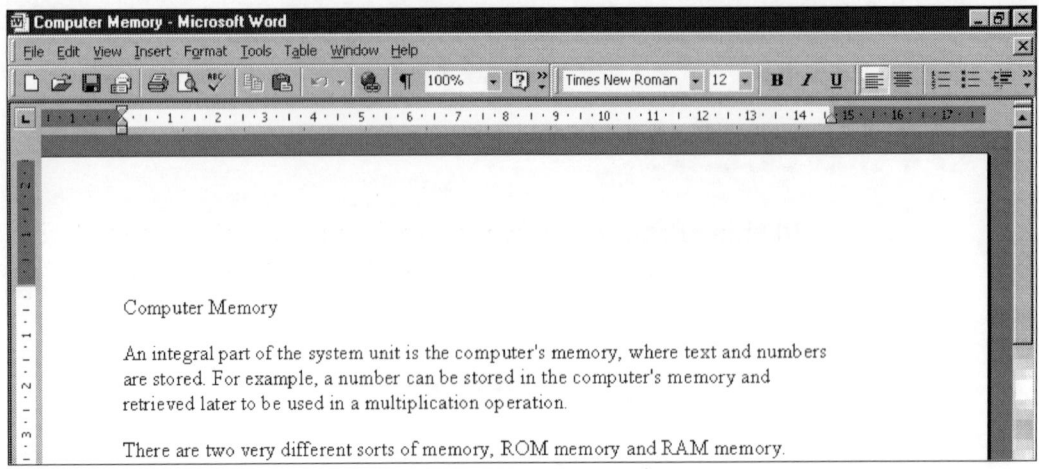

Applying bold, italic and underlining to selected text

Bold, *italic* and underlining formatting can be applied to existing text by first selecting the desired text and then choosing the required feature. There are two easy ways of applying each formatting feature:

- In the Formatting toolbar, click the **Bold**, **Italic** and **Underline** buttons

- Use the shortcut key combinations **Ctrl+B**, **Ctrl+I** and **Ctrl+U**

You can also apply text formatting using the Font dialog box. This method is covered in the *Microsoft Word 2000 Intermediate Course*.

Undoing changes

If you apply formatting and decide that you preferred the text the way it was before, you can use Undo to remove it. There are three ways to undo your last action:

- Open the **Edit** menu and choose **Undo**

Click here

- In the Standard toolbar, click the **Undo** button - the blue circular arrow, not the black downward-pointing arrow that opens the Undo list

- Press **Ctrl+Z**

138 Microsoft Word 2000 ~ Beginners Course

To undo a series of changes use any of these methods repeatedly.

Bold

You can make any existing text in your document bold by first selecting the text and then applying the bold font style.

- Select the first heading, Computer Memory - triple-click it.

- Click the **Bold** button, or press **Ctrl+B**, to apply the bold font style.

The first heading is now displayed as bold text. Note that the **Bold** button is depressed, showing that this formatting is applied.

- Click anywhere in the document to cancel the selection.

- Select the second heading, ROM Memory - triple-click anywhere in it.

- Click the **Bold** button, or press **Ctrl+B**, to apply the bold font style.

- Click anywhere in the document to cancel the selection.

Both headings now have bold font style.

Computer Memory

An integral part of the system unit is the computer's memory, where text and numbers are stored. For example, a number can be stored in the computer's memory and retrieved later to be used in a multiplication operation.

There are two very different sorts of memory, ROM memory and RAM memory. These are described below.

ROM Memory

ROM stands for Read Only Memory. It is a pre-programmed memory chip containing vital information for the computer to function. Read Only means that the data stored can only be read and not changed.

- Finally, make the other three headings bold.

Microsoft Word 2000 ~ Beginners Course **139**

Underlining text

You can underline any existing text in your document by first selecting the text and then clicking the **Underline** button in the Formatting toolbar, or pressing **Ctrl+U**.

- In the third paragraph, select the phrase Read Only Memory.

- Click the **Underline** button, or press **Ctrl+U**, to apply underlining.

The phrase is underlined. Note that the **Underline** button is depressed showing that this formatting is applied.

- Click anywhere in the document to cancel the selection.

- In the next paragraph, select the phrase Random Access Memory.

- Click the **Underline** button, or press **Ctrl+U**, to apply underlining.

The phrase is underlined.

- Click anywhere in the document to cancel the selection.

Now try undoing the underline.

Click here

- Open the **Edit** menu and choose **Undo Underline,** or click the **Undo** button, or press **Ctrl+Z**.

The phrase Random Access Memory is no longer underlined.

- Open the **Edit** menu again and choose **Undo Underline** again.

The phrase Read Only Memory in the third paragraph is no longer underlined.

If you continued to use **Edit, Undo,** or click the **Undo** button, or press **Ctrl+Z**, you would gradually remove all the text formatting that you had applied in this exercise.

Italic

You can make any existing text italic by first selecting the text and then clicking the **Italic** button in the Formatting toolbar, or pressing **Ctrl+I**.

- In the section headed Bits and Bytes, select the phrase 1 kilobyte.

- Click the **Italic** button, or press **Ctrl+I**, to apply italic font style.

- Click anywhere in the document to cancel the selection.

Combining features

You can combine the different formats so that text can be bold, italic and underlined - or any combination of the three. You can also remove formatting from selected text - just click the button, or press the shortcut keys, for the format you want to remove.

Change the first heading to be bold, italic and underlined - it already is bold.

- Select the first heading, Computer Memory.

- Click the **Italic** button, or press **Ctrl+I**, to apply italic font style.

Without removing the selection highlight, you can continue to apply different features.

- Click the **Underline** button, or press **Ctrl+U**, to apply underlining.

- Click anywhere in the document to cancel the selection.

Removing a feature

You can remove the bold font style from selected text by clicking the **Bold** button, or pressing **Ctrl+B**, as this in effect turns the feature on or off. The same applies for italic and underlining.

Remove the italic font style from the main heading.

Microsoft Word 2000 ~ Beginners Course **141**

- Select the first heading, Computer Memory.

- Click the **Italic** button, or press **Ctrl+I**, to remove the italic font style.

- Click anywhere in the document to cancel the selection.

The title is now bold and underlined only.

> ✎ *If a section of text is part bold, part not bold, applying the feature may first remove the bold font style from all the selected text. Applying it again will then apply the bold font style to all the selected text.*

Applying the features as you type

All these features can be applied as you type - just click the appropriate button, or press the shortcut keys, and then start typing.

- Press **Ctrl+End** to move the insertion point to the end of the document.

- Press **Enter** to create an empty line.

- Click the **Bold** button, or press **Ctrl+B**, to turn on the bold feature.

Notice how the **Bold** button is depressed, indicating that the bold feature is active.

- Type:

  Good Advice

- Click the **Bold** button again, or press **Ctrl+B**, to turn off the bold feature.

- Press **Enter** to conclude the paragraph.

- Click the **Underline** button, or press **Ctrl+U**, to turn on the underline feature.

Notice how the **Underline** button is depressed, indicating that the underline feature is active.

- Type:

  If you use Windows

- Click the **Underline** button again, or press **Ctrl+U**, to turn off the underline feature.

- Click the **Italic** button, or press **Ctrl+I**, to turn on the italic feature.

- Type, starting with a space:

  make sure you have plenty of memory!

- Click the **Italic** button again, or press **Ctrl+I**, to turn off the italic feature.

- Press **Enter** to move down one line.

Changing the font and font size

Fonts and font sizes can be set quickly using the **Font** and **Font Size** list boxes in the Formatting toolbar.

- In the second paragraph, select the phrase ROM memory and RAM memory.

- In the Formatting toolbar, open the **Font** list box - click its arrow button.

You will be presented with a list of available fonts - Word shows you what each font looks like.

> ♪ *The contents of the list of available fonts will depend on which fonts are installed on your computer and which have been used recently. It will be different from the picture above.*

- Click one of the available fonts.

The font for the selected phrase has been changed. Keep the phrase selected for now.

- In the Formatting toolbar, open the **Font Size** list box - click its arrow button.

A list of available font sizes is displayed.

- Click one of the available font sizes - **14** if it is there.

- Click anywhere in the document to cancel the selection.

The new font and font size have been applied to the selected text.

If you decide you preferred the original font and font size, you can easily undo these changes:

      ✎ Open the **Edit** menu and choose **Undo** - the name of the option will change according to what is being undone e.g., **Undo Font Size Select**, **Undo Font**

      ✎ Click the **Undo** button

✏ Press **Ctrl+Z**

Use Undo now to undo the changes you have made to the font.

- ```
  Open the Edit menu and choose Undo Font
  Size Select.
  ```
- ```
  Open the Edit menu again and choose Undo
  Font.
  ```

The font is now back to Times New Roman with a font size of 12 pt.

Printing the document

Now print the document to see the changes you have made.

- ```
  Make sure your printer is ready to print.
  ```

- ```
  In the Standard toolbar, click the Print
  button.
  ```

Experiment

- ```
  Spend a little time selecting phrases and
  applying different fonts, font sizes, and
  bold, italic and underlining.
  ```

Ending the session

You have now completed the tutorial in this chapter. There are three additional exercises that you may wish to do before moving on to the next chapter or exiting Word. First, you should close the current document.

- ```
  Open the File menu and choose Close -
  choose No to avoid saving the changes.
  ```
- ```
  If you are not continuing directly with the
  extra exercises or the next chapter, open
  the File menu and choose Exit to exit Word.
  ```

Microsoft Word 2000 ~ Beginners Course
  ```

Exercise 8a

In this exercise you will practise applying bold, italic and underlining.

- Open the **Hardware and Software** document from your exercise diskette.

- Before you make any changes, use **File, Save As** to save the document on your exercise diskette as **a:Ex08a**.

- Apply bold, italic and underlining as indicated in the next picture.

Hardware and Software

A **personal computer** is a complete system that can be placed on your desk. It can perform a <u>whole range</u> of tasks at very high speeds, but it needs two specific parts to make it work, hardware and software.

Hardware is the <u>physical components</u> of a computer that you can see and touch, for example, the screen, the keyboard, the **printer** and the system unit.

Software refers to the <u>programs</u> that are run on your computer to turn it into something useful, for example, word processing, spreadsheet, database and games programs.

What can a computer do?

The tasks that a computer performs can be broken down into four main categories as follows:

Receive information
Process information
Send out information
Store information

By <u>information</u> we mean text, numbers, pictures and even electrical voltages. It is the combination of these four processes, controlled with the help of programs, which allows computers to be so versatile.

Word processing, for example, is only a matter of <u>receiving data</u> via the keyboard, <u>processing the data</u> and sending it out to the screen and probably <u>sending it out</u> to a printer too. Finally, the document will probably be stored on a diskette or hard disk.

- Save your changes to the **Ex08a** document.

- If you wish, print the document.

- When you are ready, close the document.

Exercise 8b

The exercise text that is shown in the next picture has various formatting features applied. Your aim is to make your document look the same.

- Open the **Program Licence Agreement** document from your exercise diskette.

- Before you make any changes, use **File, Save As** to save the document on your exercise diskette as **a:Ex08b**.

- Format the document as indicated - the fonts and font sizes are given; the bold, italic and underlining are clear from the text. All occurrences of PC Press Limited should be **Times New Roman, 10 pt, bold** and *italic*.

Times New Roman 18 pt bold

Program Licence Agreement

Times New Roman 10 pt

PC Press Limited aims to provide high-quality computer books and programs at an affordab order to achieve this goal we need to keep sales volumes high and thus respectfully request t observe the following:

Courier New 11 pt underlined

1 You may:

Courier New 10 pt

Use this program on a single computer. Make copies of this pro for your own use. Transfer this product to a third party who these conditions. If you transfer this product to a third par must also transfer all copies you have made or destroy all cop that are not transferred.

Courier New 11 pt underlined

2 You must not:

Courier New 10 pt

Use this product on more than one computer. Disassemble, decon change the program in any way. Export the program commercially without the prior written consent of *PC Press Limited*.

Times New Roman 14 pt bold and underlined

Warranty

Times New Roman 10 pt

PC Press Limited hereby guarantees that, on delivery, your diskette is free from material fau processing errors. Beyond this, *PC Press Limited* does not provide any form of guarantee re characteristics of the program, nor does it guarantee that the program will be suitable for you applications. *PC Press Limited* does not accept any responsibility whatsoever for any damag occur in connection with the use of the program/product.

- Save your changes to the **Ex08b** document.
- If you wish, print the document.
- When you are ready, close the document.

Exercise 8c

This exercise uses various formatting features.

- Open the **Parking Arrangements** document from your exercise diskette.

A copy of the document is shown on the next page.

- Before you make any changes, use **File, Save As** to save the document on your exercise diskette as **a:Ex08c**.

- Format the document as indicated in the next picture - the fonts and font sizes are given; the bold, italic and underlining are clear from the text.

Times New Roman 16 pt

Parking Arrangements

Times New Roman 12 pt

GLP Parking Limited give notice to all car park users of the following:

Times New Roman 12 pt

1 Responsibility

Times New Roman 11 pt

GLP Parking Limited accept no responsibility for loss or damage to individuals o property whilst using their premises. Children (under age 16) should not enter the without an accompanying adult.

Times New Roman 12 pt

2 Hours of Opening

Times New Roman 11 pt

This car park is open during the following hours:

Times New Roman 14 pt

Mon-Fri 07:00 to 20:00
Saturday 07:00 to 18:00
Sunday 09:00 to 18:00

Times New Roman 10 pt

Concessions may be made by prior arrangement for 24 hour parking.

Courier New 10 pt

```
The car park will operate Sunday hours on all Bank Holidays,
exception of Christmas Day when it will be closed all day.
```

Times New Roman 12 pt

3 Tariff

Times New Roman 14 pt

0 to 2 hours £0.50
2 to 4 hours £1.50
4 to 6 hours £2.50
Over 6 hours £3.00

Times New Roman 12 pt

4 Loss of Tickets

Times New Roman 11 pt

Loss of car park entry/exit ticket will result in a minimum payment of £5.00. In a security reasons, evidence will have to be given for proof of ownership of the veh proof of address. A form will have to be completed on departure, declaring your responsibility for the vehicle being removed from the premises. *GLP Parking Li* the right to transfer information given to the Police.

Times New Roman 10 pt

Note. This procedure has been instigated to protect the property of persons using this faci

- Save your changes to the **Ex08c** document.
- Print the document, or use Print Preview to view it.
- When you are ready, close the document.

Summary ~ Simple Text Formatting

Applying bold, italic and underlining to selected text

To apply bold, italic and underlining to existing text, first select the text and then choose the required formatting feature:

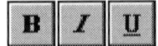

- In the Formatting toolbar, click the **Bold**, **Italic** or **Underline** button

- Use the shortcut key combinations **Ctrl+B**, **Ctrl+I** or **Ctrl+U**

Combining bold, italic and underlining

All these features can be used in combination. For example, a heading can be bold, italic and underlined. Just select the text and then apply each feature in turn.

You can add formatting features to, and remove formatting features from, any selected text.

Applying bold, italic and underlining as you type

All these features can be applied as you type. Click the button(s) to apply the feature(s) you want before you start to type. When you have finished with the feature(s), click the appropriate button(s), or use the shortcut key combination(s), to turn off the feature(s) and return to regular text.

Changing the font and font size

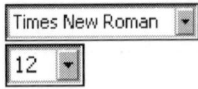

Fonts and font sizes can be set quickly using the **Font** and **Font Size** list boxes in the Formatting toolbar. As with the other formatting features you can either apply different fonts and font sizes to selected text, or set up the character style you require before you type the text.

Notes

Use this page to make notes of your own.

Page #   Notes

Notes

Use this page to make notes of your own.

Page #   Notes

Chapter 9 ~ Simple Paragraph Formatting

In this chapter you will learn about:

- Paragraph alignment
- Indents
- Typing anywhere on the page - Click and Type
- Bullets and numbering
- Aligning text using the default tab stops

You have already selected text and applied different formatting features. There are also a number of styles that you can apply directly to paragraphs.

Getting started

- If necessary, start Word.
- If the Office Assistant is displayed, right-click it and choose **Hide**.
- Make sure your exercise diskette is in drive A.

- Open the **File** menu and choose **Open**, or click the **Open** button in the Standard toolbar, or just press **Ctrl+O**.

The Open dialog box is displayed.

- In the File name box, type:

    a:Fear

- Click **Open**, or press **Enter**.

The Fear document is opened.

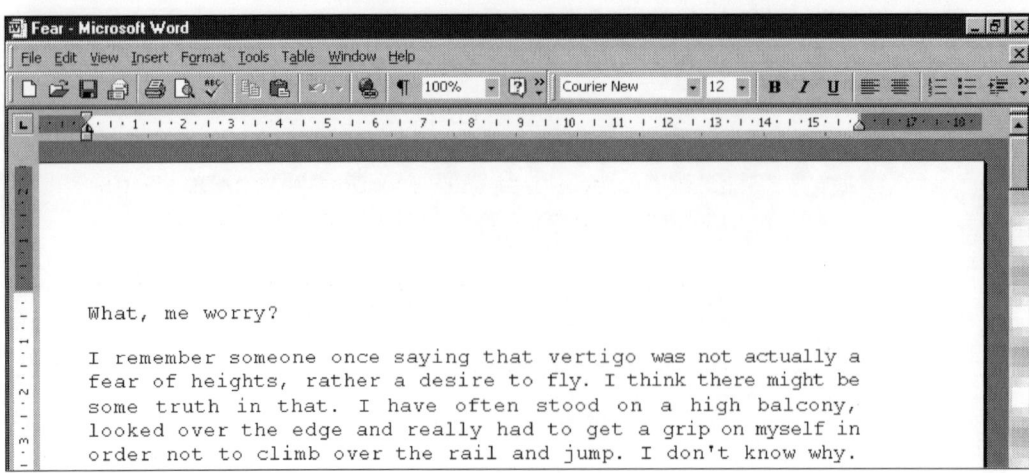

Paragraph alignment

The four alignment options are summarised in the following table.

Alignment	Toolbar buttons	Shortcut keys	Description/Example
Left	Align Left	Ctrl+L	The paragraph has a straight left-hand edge and ragged right-hand edge - default setting.
Centre	Center	Ctrl+E	All text centred on each line.
Right	Align Right	Ctrl+R	The paragraph has a ragged left-hand edge, straight right-hand edge.
Justify	Justify	Ctrl+J	Both left-hand and right-hand edges, apart from the very last line if it is short, have straight edges. Spacing between words is adjusted to achieve this.

Notice that the paragraphs in the Fear document are justified.

Try out the different alignments now. When formatting a single paragraph it is not necessary to select the whole paragraph, but the insertion point must be positioned somewhere within the paragraph you want to format.

- Click anywhere in the second paragraph, starting Although, by most people.

- Click the **Align Right** button, to see the effect of right-aligning the paragraph - the button may be in the More Buttons palette of the Formatting toolbar.

- Click anywhere in the third paragraph, starting I wasn't always.

- Click the **Center** button, to see the effect of centring the paragraph.

- Click anywhere in the fifth paragraph, starting When I was a kid.

- Click the **Align Left** button, to left-align the paragraph.

The document should now resemble the following picture.

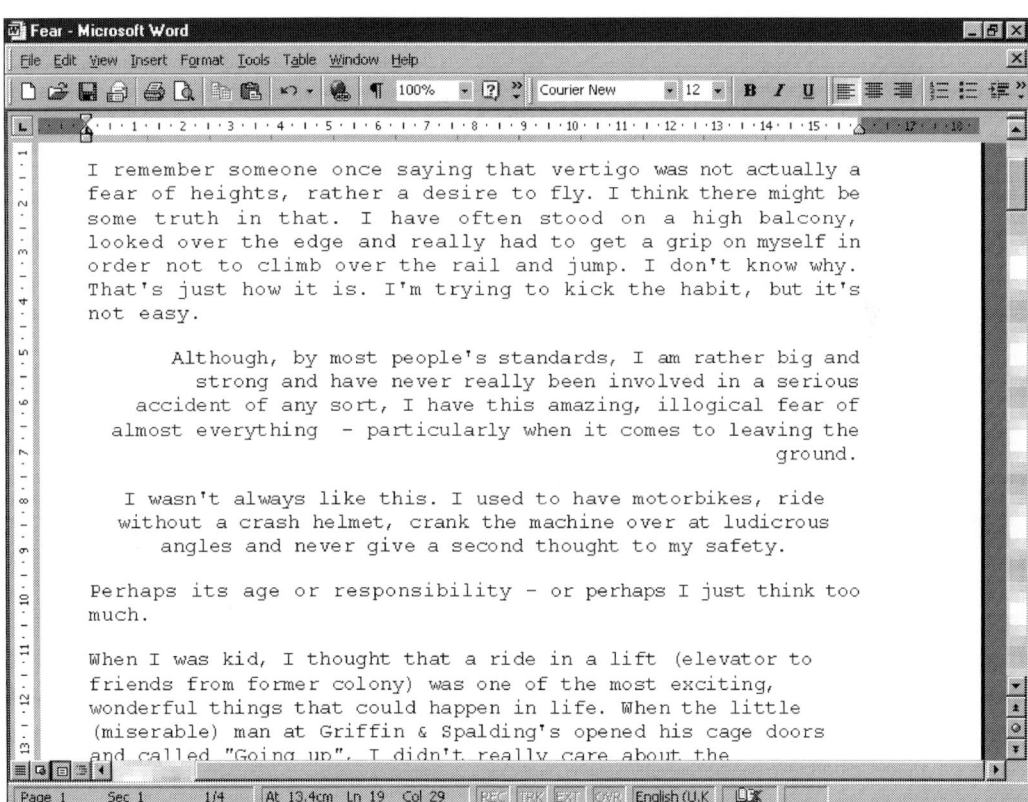

Now try undoing the paragraph alignment using the Undo feature.

- Open the **Edit** menu and choose **Undo Paragraph Alignment,** or click the **Undo** button in the Standard toolbar, or just press **Ctrl+Z**.

The change to the fifth paragraph is undone and it will now be justified as before. Repeating the Undo process would undo the changes made to the other paragraphs in turn.

Now use the **Justify** button to justify the second and third paragraphs.

- Select the second and third paragraphs all at once.

- Click the **Justify** button - it may be in the More Buttons palette of the Formatting toolbar.

Indents

You can indent a paragraph from the left-hand margin.

- Position the insertion point anywhere in the first paragraph.

- Click the **Increase Indent** button - it's probably in the More Buttons palette of the Formatting toolbar.

The whole paragraph is shifted in from the left-hand margin - just how far is controlled by the *tab stops* - more about that later in this chapter.

- Click the **Increase Indent** button again - it should now be in the toolbar.

The whole paragraph is shifted inwards one more step.

- Click the **Decrease Indent** button.
- Click the **Decrease Indent** button again.

The paragraph is moved back. Now close the Fear document.

- Open the **File** menu and choose **Close** - do not save the changes.

Click and Type

Word 2000 allows you to type anywhere in the blank areas of a page - to the left, right or below existing text. To take advantage of this, you must have the current document displayed in Print Layout view or Web Layout view. The mouse pointer changes shape according to where it is positioned on the page - the shape indicating the formatting that will be applied to any text that you type.

To use Click and Type:

> ↳ Display your document in Print Layout view or Web Layout view

> ↳ Click in any blank area of the page to activate the Click and Type pointer - if the mouse pointer is below the end of the document, the Click and Type pointer will automatically be displayed

> ↳ Double-click where you want to start typing

The Click and Type pointer can take on the following shapes:

Mouse pointer	Formatting
I≡	The text will be left-aligned with the first line indented from the margin.
I≡	The text will be left-aligned and start from where you double-click.
I	The text will be centre-aligned about the centre of the page.
≡I	The text will be right-aligned and start at the right-hand margin.

To try this out, open a new blank document and display it in Print Layout view.

- Click the **New Blank Document** button, or press **Ctrl+N**.

- If necessary, open the **View** menu and choose **Print Layout**, or click the **Print Layout View** button next to the Status bar.

Microsoft Word 2000 ~ Beginners Course **157**

The insertion point is flashing in the top left-hand corner of the page.

- Change the font size to **16 pt**.

- Move the mouse pointer over the page and note the different shapes of the Click and Type pointer.

The Click and Type pointer will be displayed over most of the page because no text has been entered yet. Note that it is not displayed where you cannot enter text - in the margins of the page.

- Move the Click and Type pointer to the middle of the page and double-click anywhere it displays the Center icon.

Note that the insertion point is now centred on the page and the **Center** button appears depressed. Whatever you type now will be centre-aligned about the centre of the page.

- Type:

This is in the middle of the page.

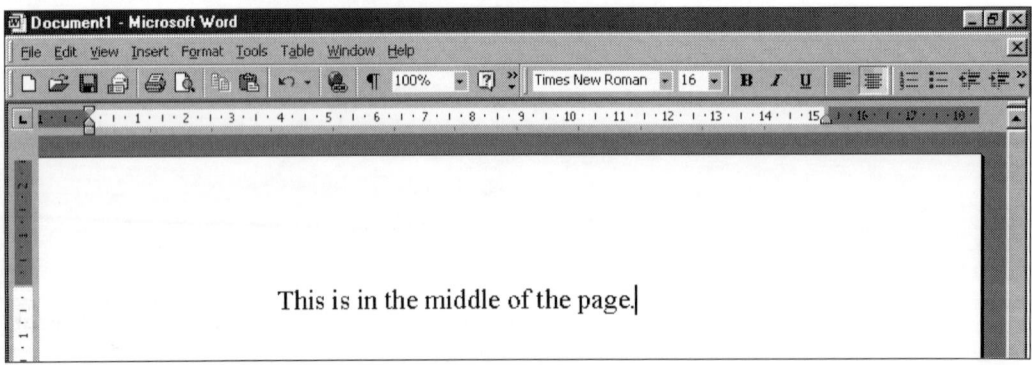

Now try the right-alignment.

- Move the Click and Type pointer to the right-hand side of the page and double-click anywhere it displays the Align Right icon.

- Type:

This is on the right.

Note how the words spread out across the page from the right-hand margin as you typed.

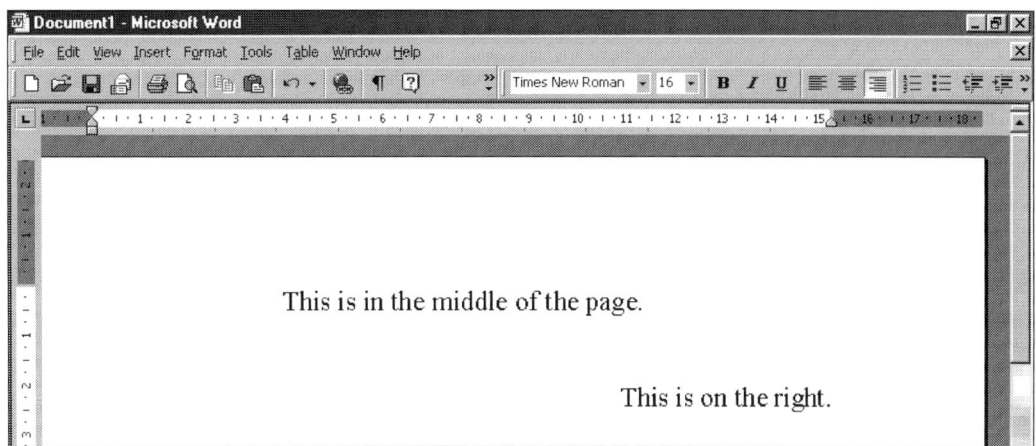

Now try using Click and Type to type to the right or left of existing text.

- Click anywhere to the left of the line of text you have just entered, This is on the right.

The mouse pointer changed from a simple I-beam to the Click and Type pointer.

- Move the Click and Type pointer to the left-hand side of the page and double-click anywhere it displays the Align Left icon.

The insertion point is now on the left-hand side of the page and the **Align Left** button appears depressed.

- Type:

This is on the left.

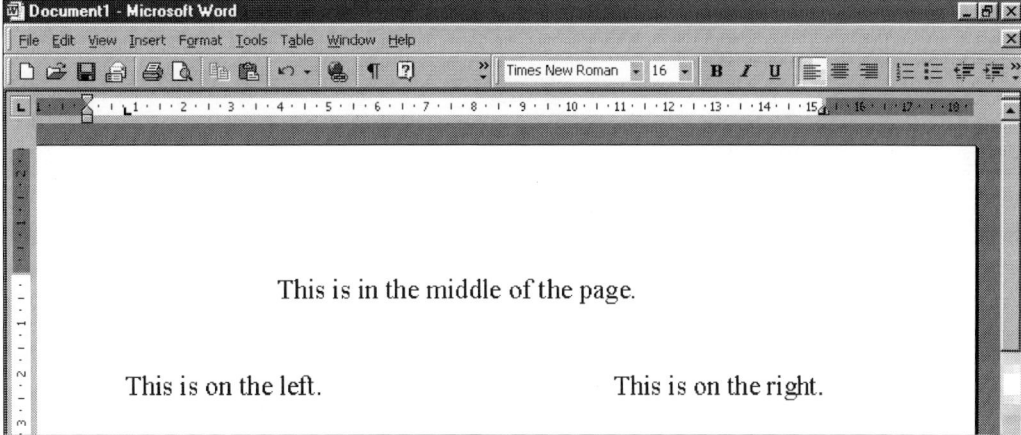

Microsoft Word 2000 ~ Beginners Course

You have succeeded in using three different alignments just using Click and Type. This is clearly a very versatile feature.

- On your own, experiment with Click and Type.

- When you are ready, close the document without saving your changes.

Bullets

You can assign a bulleted indent to a paragraph. For example, all the instructions in this training course are bulleted with a dot. The **Bullets** button will automatically create a bulleted indent using the current settings.

To continue, open the Printers document.

- Open the **Printers** document from your exercise diskette.

Now create a bullet.

- In the list of printer types, click anywhere in the text Dot matrix.

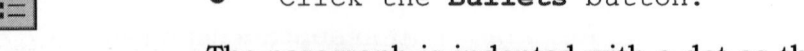

- Click the **Bullets** button.

The paragraph is indented with a dot as the bullet. Repeat this for the other printer types.

- Select the three other printer types in the list.

- Click the **Bullets** button again.

All four printer types are now indented with a dot as the bullet. The document should resemble the following picture.

160 Microsoft Word 2000 ~ Beginners Course

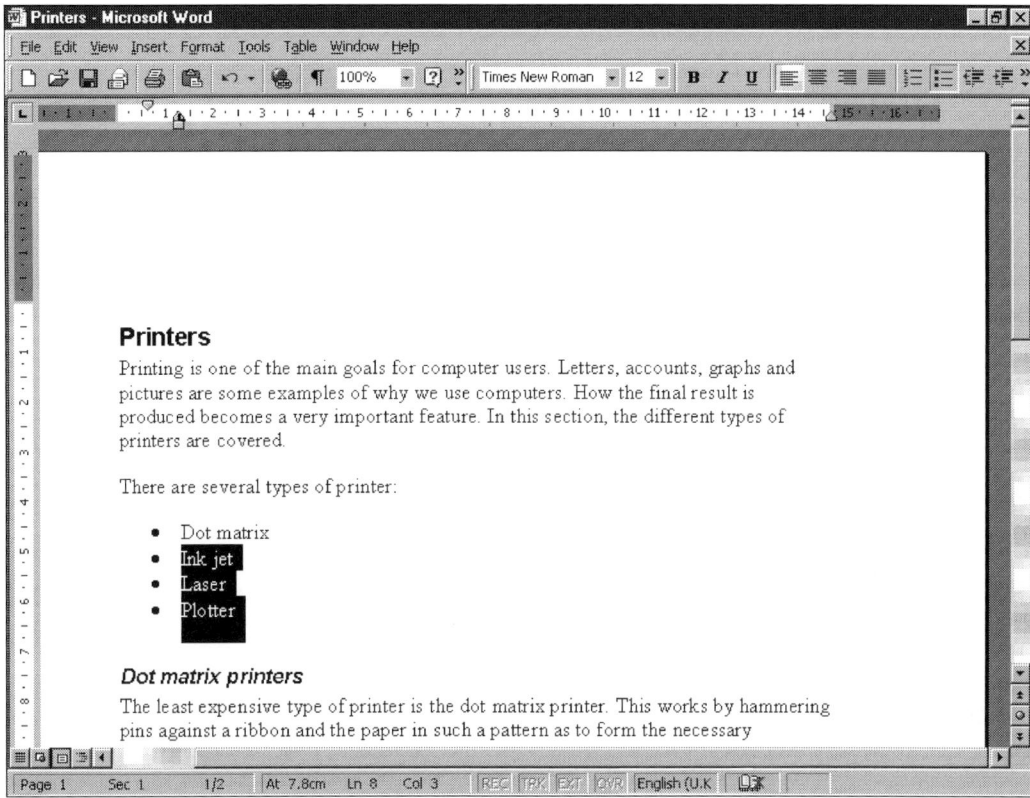

Automatic bullets as you type

Word provides the capability to produce bullets automatically as you type.

- ```
  Press Ctrl+End to move the insertion point
  to the end of the document.
  ```

- ```
  If necessary, create a couple of empty
  lines.
  ```

- ```
  Type:
  ```

  ```
  * Times Roman
  ```

- ```
  Press Enter.
  ```

You will notice that Word has started a bulleted list for you. You can continue to add items to this list.

- ```
  Type:
  ```

  ```
  Courier
  ```

- ```
  Press Enter.
  ```

Microsoft Word 2000 ~ Beginners Course **161**

Algerian

- Press **Enter**.

The bulleted list is continued until you press **Enter** twice.

- Type:

  Arial

- Press **Enter** twice.

The bulleted list is now complete.

Removing bullets

To remove a bullet, select the paragraph(s) with a bullet to be removed, and then click the **Bullets** button.

- Use **Ctrl+Home** to move the insertion point to the top of the document.

- In the list of printer types, click anywhere in the text Dot matrix.

- Click the **Bullets** button.

The bullet is removed.

- Select the three other printer types in the list.

- Click the **Bullets** button again.

The bullets are removed.

- Click anywhere in the document to cancel the selection.

Lists of numbered points

In much the same way as creating bulleted indents, you can easily create paragraphs as a list of numbered points. Once again there is a shortcut button in the Formatting toolbar.

- Select the four printer types.

- In the Formatting toolbar, click the **Numbering** button.

- Click anywhere in the document to cancel the selection.

The paragraphs are numbered 1 to 4.

Printers

Printing is one of the main goals for computer users. Letters, accounts, graphs and pictures are some examples of why we use computers. How the final result is produced becomes a very important feature. In this section, the different types of printers are covered.

There are several types of printer:

1. Dot matrix
2. Ink jet
3. Laser
4. Plotter

Dot matrix printers

Automatic numbering as you type

Word also provides an automatic numbering facility that enables you to number a list as you type. You can use Arabic numbers (1, 2, 3, etc.), Roman numerals (I, II, III, etc.) or letters.

The steps to take are as follows:

- Type a number or letter
- Type a full stop or a bracket
- Type a space
- Type the first item
- Press **Enter**

When you press **Enter**, the first item is formatted automatically and the next item is numbered automatically.

- Press **Ctrl+End** to move the insertion point to the end of the document.
- If necessary, create a couple of empty lines.

Microsoft Word 2000 ~ Beginners Course

- Type:

    1. HP LaserJet 4

- Press **Enter**.

- Type:

    Canon BJ10e

- Press **Enter**.

You will see that Word has created a numbered list for you. This will continue until you press **Enter** twice.

- Type:

    IBM Proprinter

- Press **Enter** twice.

The list is now concluded.

- Close the document without saving the changes.

Aligning text as type

This section will give you a little practice at formatting paragraphs as you type. Start off by opening a new document.

- Click the **New Blank Document** button.

You should now have a new document.

- Click the **Center** button, or press **Ctrl+E**.

The insertion point will now be flashing in the middle of the current line. Any text that you type will spread out on either side.

- Type:

    Mr & Mrs Ponsonby-Smythe

- Press **Enter** twice.

Notice how the centred format continues to be applied to new paragraphs.

164 Microsoft Word 2000 ~ Beginners Course

> ✦ *Important principle:*
> *Whenever you press **Enter** to conclude a paragraph, the format of the paragraph you are concluding is carried forward and will apply to the new paragraph. You can of course alter the format of the new paragraph if you want to.*

- Type:

  Request the pleasure of your company

- Press **Enter** twice.

- Type:

  At the saddling of their foal

- Press **Enter** three times.

- Set the alignment to right by clicking the **Align Right** button, or by pressing **Ctrl+R**.

- Type:

  Please reply promptly to:
  Kendrick Hall
  Kendrick Park
  CIRENCESTER
  Glos.

- Press **Enter** three times.

- Set the alignment to left by clicking the **Align Left** button, or by pressing **Ctrl+L**.

- Type:

  Remember our rules!

- Press **Enter** twice.

- Click the **Numbering** button.

- Type – the numbers will automatically appear:

  No animals
  No smoking
  Don't be late

Save the document and print it if you wish. Then close it.

- Save the document on your exercise diskette as **a:Saddling**.

Microsoft Word 2000 ~ Beginners Course **165**

- Print the document.

- When you are ready, close the document - **File, Close**.

Using default tab stops

So far in this chapter you have learnt how to align paragraphs. Another important way to line up information is by using tab stops. These can be used to line up information to create simple tables. To see a table aligned in this way open the Football document.

- Open the **Football** document from your exercise diskette.

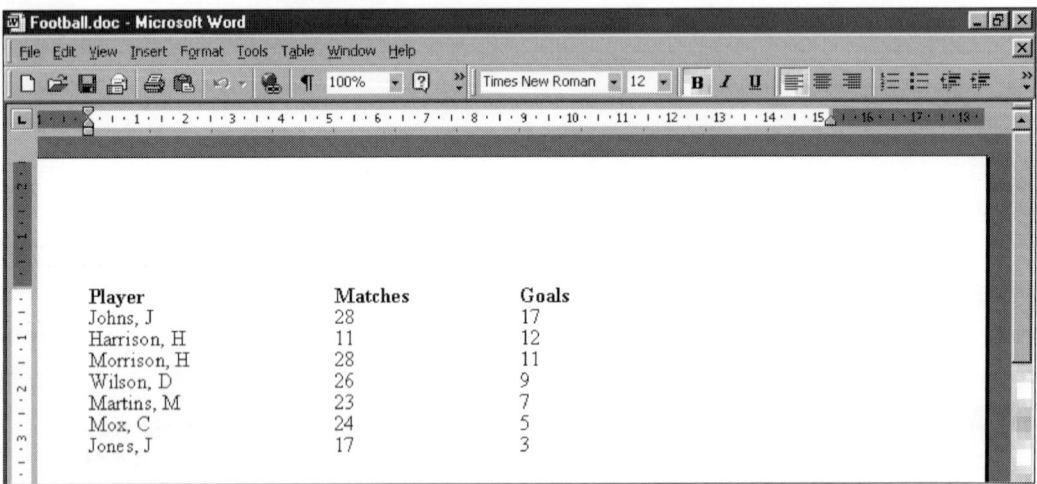

Showing tab characters in text

When dealing with tabs, it is useful to display the formatting marks.

- In the Standard toolbar, click the **Show/Hide ¶** button.

As you can now see, this simple table has been created by typing the information and using a number of tabs (shown as →) to line up the columns.

Adding some more entries

Now add three more entries, pressing the **Tab** key where necessary to line up the columns.

- Move the insertion point to the end of the document - **Ctrl+End**.

- Type the following entries:

  ```
  Wise, K          14        3
  Loveshore, J     21        2
  Pates, P         19        1
  ```

You can use this simple method to set out data in table form. An additional exercise is included at the end of this chapter.

Now hide the formatting marks.

- In the Standard toolbar, click the **Show/Hide ¶** button.

Ending the session

You have now completed the tutorial in this chapter. There are two additional exercises that you may wish to do before moving on to the next chapter or exiting Word. First, you should close the current document.

- Open the **File** menu and choose **Close** - choose **No** to avoid saving the changes.

- If you are not continuing directly with the extra exercises or the next chapter, open the **File** menu and choose **Exit** to exit Word.

Exercise 9a

- Open the **Recipe for Broccoli Flan** document from your exercise diskette.

- Before you make any changes, use **File, Save As** to save the document on your exercise diskette as **a:Ex09a**.

The picture on page 168 shows you what you are aiming for.

Microsoft Word 2000 ~ Beginners Course

- Centre the main heading.
- Apply bullets to the <u>Pastry</u> and <u>Filling</u> headings.
- Indent the ingredients so that they are aligned with their headings.

- Number the three instructions under the heading <u>For the pastry:</u>.
- Number both the instructions under the heading <u>For the filling:</u>.

Recipe for Broccoli Flan

- **Pastry**

    175g wholemeal flour
    100g butter
    50g porridge oats

- **Filling**

    350g broccoli
    3 eggs
    300ml milk

<u>For the pastry:</u>

1. Rub flour, oats and a pinch of salt with the butter until the mixture resembles breadcrumbs.

2. Add water to form a firm pastry.

3. Line a 25cm flan dish, baking blind at 200 deg.C for 10-12 minutes.

<u>For the filling:</u>

1. Whisk eggs and milk together and pour over broccoli, which has been cooked and laid onto the flan base.

2. Bake at 190 deg.C for about 35 to 40 minutes.

- Print the document or use Print Preview to view it.

- Save the changes you have made to the **Ex09a** document.

- As an additional exercise you may wish to practise putting the alignments back to how they were originally.

- When you are ready, close the document without saving your changes.

Exercise 9b

- Open the **Tabs** document from your exercise diskette.

- Before you make any changes, use **File**, **Save As** to save the document on your exercise diskette as **a:Ex09b**.

- Add the additional titles, subjects, authors and number of copies sold - as shown in the next picture.

Book Title	Subject	Author	Number of Copies Sold
Birdie	Golf	Mr G Tee	564
The Stage	Acting	A Actor	225
Going West	Travel	Ms G Far	234
PC's R Us	Computing	S Chip	153
Motormania	Cars	A Mobile	245
Aerobike	Keep Fit	E Nergetic	789

- Save the changes you have made to the **Ex09b** document.

- Print the document or use Print Preview to view it.

- When you are ready, close the document.

Summary ~ Simple Paragraph Formatting

To make a document clearer:

- Use different paragraph alignments
- Indent the text
- Use bullets or numbering

These features can be easily applied using buttons in the Formatting toolbar.

Paragraph alignment

There are four options for paragraph alignment:

- Left-aligned - like this list

- Centred - with all text centred on each line

- Right-aligned - with each line of text lined up with the right margin

- Justified - like the main text of this document

To change the alignment of a paragraph, click anywhere in the paragraph and then click the appropriate button.

To choose a paragraph alignment before you type any text, just click the appropriate button and then start typing.

To type in a blank area of a page, click once to activate the Click and Type pointer. Then double-click where you want to type. The text will be formatted according to the shape of the Click and Type pointer when you double-clicked.

Indents

You can indent a paragraph from the left-hand margin. Position the insertion point anywhere in the paragraph you wish to indent and click the **Increase Indent** button. The text will move in, in accordance with the pre-set tab stops. To indent the text further, click the button again.

To decrease the indent, use the **Decrease Indent** button. Click once for every step you want to move the paragraph back to the left-hand margin. The text will move back to the margin in accordance with the pre-set tab stops.

Bullets

To format paragraphs as a list of bulleted points, select the paragraph(s) and click the **Bullets** button. This creates bullets using the current default settings.

Automatic bullets as you type

To create automatic bullets as you type, first type an asterisk followed by a space, and then type your paragraph or list item. When you press **Enter** the paragraph will be indented and preceded with a bullet. Subsequent paragraphs will be indented and bulleted until you press **Enter** twice.

Lists of numbered points

To format paragraphs as a list of numbered points, select the paragraphs and click the **Numbering** button. Each paragraph is indented and numbered using the current default settings.

Automatic numbering as you type

To create a list of numbered points as you type, first type a number, or letter, followed by a full stop, or bracket, and then a space. Then type your first list item. When you press **Enter** the item will be automatically indented and numbered. Subsequent items will be indented and numbered until you press **Enter** twice.

Aligning columns using default tab stops

Tabs can be used to line up information to create simple tables.

 Type the first item in the first column, and then use the **Tab** key to move the insertion point across the page to where you want to position the second column. Type the item for this column then press **Enter**. Type subsequent items in each column using the **Tab** key to line them up.

Notes

Use this page to make notes of your own.

Page #   Notes

Notes

Use this page to make notes of your own.

Page #   Notes

Chapter 10 ~ Undo & Redo

In this chapter you will learn about:

- Immediate 'undos'
- Using Undo
- Using Redo

Whenever you make changes to a document, there is always a possibility that you will change your mind and want to undo some or all of the changes. You can also undo your undos - this is known as *redo*.

Getting started

- If necessary, start Word.

- If the Office Assistant is displayed, right-click it and choose **Hide**.

- Make sure your exercise diskette is in drive A.

- Open the **File** menu and choose **Open**, or click the **Open** button in the Standard toolbar, or press **Ctrl+O**.

The Open dialog box is displayed.

- In the File name box, type:

    `a:Home Security`

- Click **Open**, or press **Enter**.

The Home Security document is opened.

Microsoft Word 2000 ~ Beginners Course   **175**

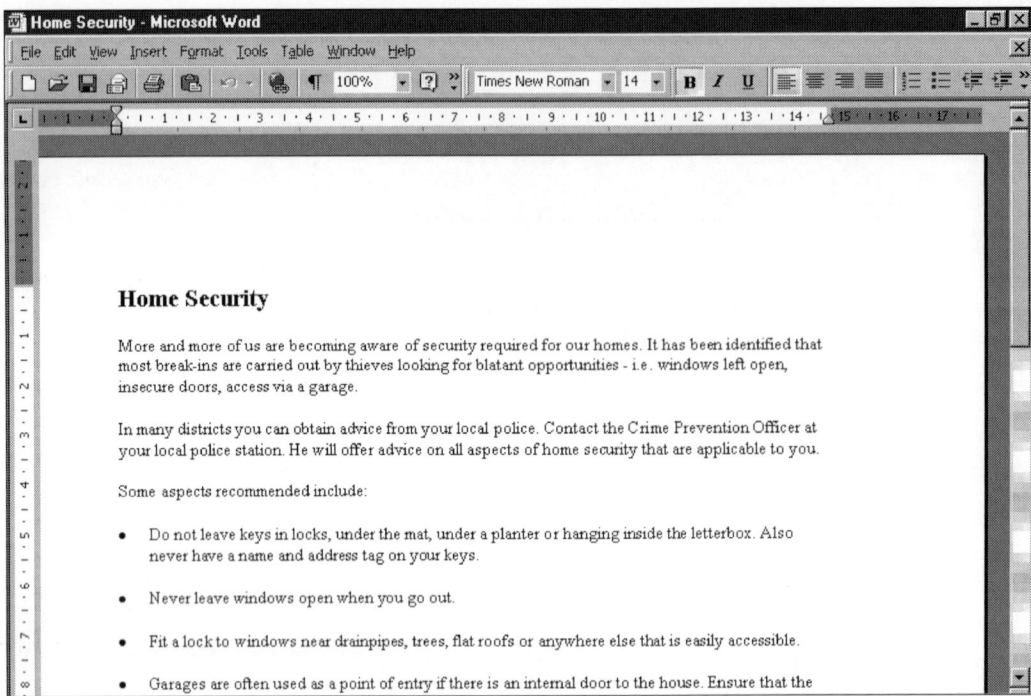

Immediate undos

There are three ways of immediately undoing the most recent operation you have done:

  ✤ Open the **Edit** menu and choose **Undo** - the actual wording of the **Undo** option will change according to the operation you last performed, e.g., **Undo Italic**, **Undo Clear**.

  ✤ In the Standard toolbar, click the **Undo** button - the blue circular arrow not the black downward-pointing arrow that opens the Undo list. The actual wording of the ScreenTip for the **Undo** button will change according to the operation you last performed, e.g., **Undo Italic**, **Clear**.

  ✤ Press **Ctrl+Z**.

Try this out now - first apply some formatting that you can then undo.

- `Select the title `<u>`Home Security`</u>`.`
- `Click the `**`Italic`**` button.`

The italic font style is applied to the selected text.

- ```
  Click anywhere in the document to cancel
  the selection.
  ```

- ```
  Open the Edit menu and choose Undo Italic,
  or press Ctrl+Z.
  ```

The italic font style you applied is automatically removed and the text is re-selected.

- ```
  Click anywhere in the document to cancel
  the selection.
  ```

Repeated undos

All three ways of undoing the last operation can also be used to undo a number of operations. The next section describes in detail the use of the **Undo** button. For now just try undoing two operations using **Edit**, **Undo** or **Ctrl+Z**.

- ```
  In the title, select the word Security.
  ```

- ```
  Press Delete to delete the word.
  ```

The word Security is deleted.

- ```
  Click anywhere in the second paragraph,
  starting In many districts.
  ```

- ```
  Centre the current paragraph.
  ```

Now undo this paragraph alignment.

- ```
  Open the Edit menu and choose Undo
  Paragraph Alignment, or press Ctrl+Z.
  ```

The most recent change is undone - the paragraph is no longer centred. As the change has been undone, the deletion of the word Security becomes the most recent change.

- ```
  Open the Edit menu and choose Undo Clear,
  or press Ctrl+Z.
  ```

The word Security is restored.

- ```
  Click anywhere in the document to cancel
  the selection.
  ```

Using the Undo and Redo lists

The Undo and Redo features allow you to undo and redo multiple changes, so you could make 15 changes and go back and undo all of them, or just some of them.

You cannot pick out individual changes and redo them. If you choose the sixth most recent change and undo it, all of the six most recent changes are undone.

> *There are a few changes that you cannot undo, such as printing and saving documents.*

Using Undo

To try the feature out, you will need to make a few more changes first.

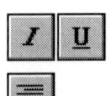

- Select the title Home Security.
- Open the **Font Size** list box and choose **16**.
- Click the **Italic** and **Underline** buttons.
- Click anywhere in the first paragraph and click the **Align Right** button.
- At the start of the third paragraph, select the whole of the line Some aspects recommended include: and then press **Delete**.

Now try undoing some of the changes.

Click here

- In the Standard toolbar, click the downward-pointing arrow of the **Undo** button to open the list of changes.

A list of the changes you made is displayed.

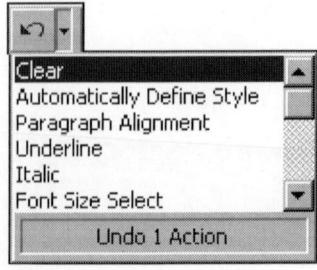

178   Microsoft Word 2000 ~ Beginners Course

The changes that you have just made are shown in the list with the last change at the top. Clear refers to the deletion of the line in the third paragraph, Paragraph Alignment refers to aligning the first paragraph, etc. If you did things in a different order the list would be different.

> ♪ *It is important to note that you cannot choose individual changes from within the list and undo just that operation.*

If you choose the third change in the list you will undo all of the three most recent operations. Choose the fifth change in the list and all of the five most recent changes are undone.

- In the list of changes, choose **Italic**.

All the changes down to Italic are now undone. The first line of the third paragraph is re-instated, the first paragraph is re-aligned and the heading has its underline and italic features removed. The title still has a font size of 16 pt as you did not undo this change.

- In the Standard toolbar, click the downward-pointing arrow of the **Undo** button to open the list of changes again.

The Font Size Select change is still available to undo.

- In the list of changes, choose **Font Size Select**.

The change to the font size is undone - it will be 14 pt again.

Using Redo

As mentioned, Word allows you to redo undos! So if you make some changes and change your mind and undo them, you can change your mind again and redo the changes. Try it.

- Locate the **Redo** button - it may be in the More Buttons palette of the Standard toolbar.

Click here

- Click the downward-pointing arrow of the **Redo** button to open the list of undone changes.

A list of undone changes that can be redone is displayed.

This time the list is in the order you originally made the changes, so you can repeat your steps up to and including any item in the list. Again you cannot choose individual items from the list and apply only that change.

Assume now that you want to redo the three changes to the title - the font size, italic and underline features.

- In the **Redo** list, choose **Underline**.

The **Redo** button is now displayed in the Standard toolbar.

All the changes down to Underline are redone. The heading should be larger, italic and underlined again. Needless to say, you could open the Undo list again and undo one or more of these changes!

- Open the **Undo** list again to see for yourself!

- Press **Esc** to close the list.

> *You can also redo changes using **Edit**, **Redo** or the shortcut key combination **Ctrl+Y**. Use either of these methods repeatedly to work your way through the list of Redos, redoing each one in turn.*

Ending the session

You have now completed the tutorial in this chapter. There is an additional exercise that you may wish to do before moving on to the next chapter or exiting Word. First, you should close the current document.

- Open the **File** menu and choose **Close** - choose **No** to avoid saving the changes.

- If you are not continuing directly with the extra exercise or the next chapter, open the **File** menu and choose **Exit** to exit Word.

Exercise 10a

In this exercise you will create a notice, and apply and remove some text formatting as you type. First of all you need a new blank document to work on.

- Click the **New Blank Document** button, or press **Ctrl+N**.

- Type the following text and format it as required:

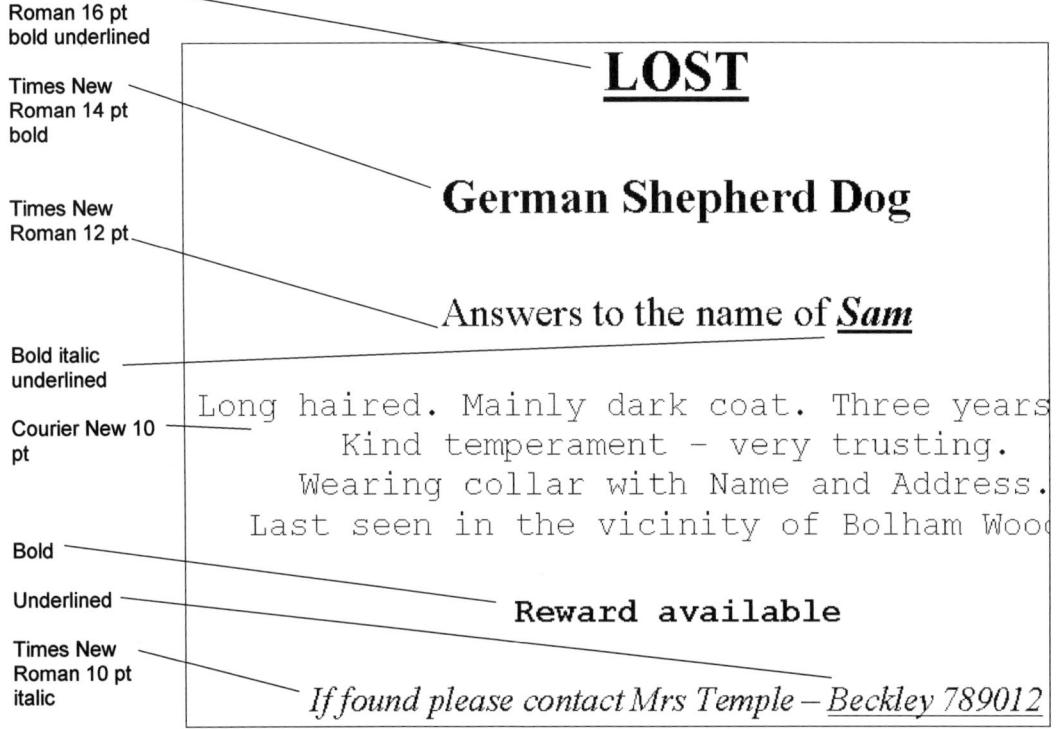

- Save the document on your exercise diskette as **a:Ex10a**.

You will now make some changes that you can then undo.

- Select the title LOST and make it italic.

- Select the line Last seen in the vicinity of Bolham Woods and delete it.

- Select the entire document - **Ctrl+A**.

Microsoft Word 2000 ~ Beginners Course **181**

- Left-align the text.
- Select the line If found please call Mrs Temple - Beckley 789012 and change the font to Courier New.

Now undo the font change in the last line and make the document centre-aligned again.

- In the **Undo** list, choose Paragraph Alignment - the second from the top of the list.

Now restore the deleted line and remove the italic formatting of the title.

- In the **Undo** list, choose **Italic**.

In fact, the italic title looked quite effective. Redo it.

- In the **Redo** list, choose **Italic**.
- Save the changes you have made to the **Ex10a** document.
- When you are ready, close the document.

Summary ~ Undo & Redo

Immediate undos

In Word there are three ways of undoing the last operation:

- Open the **Edit** menu and choose **Undo**

Click here

- In the Standard toolbar, click the **Undo** button - the blue circular arrow
- Press **Ctrl+Z**

If you repeatedly use Undo, each of the latest operations is undone, one at a time.

Undo

Click here

The Undo feature allows you to undo multiple changes. By clicking the downward-pointing arrow of the **Undo** button you can see a list of the last changes you made. You can choose to undo any number of these changes starting with the most recent. For example, click the third item to change your last three actions. Note that you cannot choose just one change from within the list.

Redo

The Redo feature allows you to redo Undos. Click the downward-pointing arrow of the **Redo** button to see the list of undone changes that you can redo. The list is in the order in which you originally made the changes. This means that you can repeat your steps up to and including any item on the list. Like Undo, you cannot choose one redo from the middle of the list.

Undone changes can also be redone in succession using **Edit**, **Redo** or **Ctrl+Y** repeatedly.

Notes

Use this page to make notes of your own.

Page #   Notes

_____   _____

_____   _____

_____   _____

_____   _____

_____   _____

_____   _____

_____   _____

_____   _____

_____   _____

_____   _____

_____   _____

_____   _____

_____   _____

_____   _____

Chapter 11 ~ The Spelling and Grammar Checker

In this chapter you will learn about:

- Automatic spelling and grammar checking
- Spell and grammar checking on demand
- Changing mistakes found
- Ignoring mistakes found
- Using the **Spelling and Grammar Status** icon
- Spell checking options
- Grammar checking options
- Custom dictionaries
- Word Count

The Spelling and Grammar Checker is a very useful tool when you need to check your document for spelling mistakes, and for mistakes in grammar and punctuation. It can be set to check spelling and grammar automatically as you type, or on demand. The Word Count feature will quickly tell you how many characters and words your document contains.

Getting started

- If the Office Assistant is displayed, right-click it and choose **Hide**.
- Make sure your exercise diskette is in drive A.

- Open the **File** menu and choose **Open**, or click the **Open** button in the Standard toolbar, or just press **Ctrl+O**.

The Open dialog box is displayed.

- In the File name box, type:

    a:Spelling and Grammar

- Click **Open**, or press **Enter**.

The Spelling and Grammar document is opened.

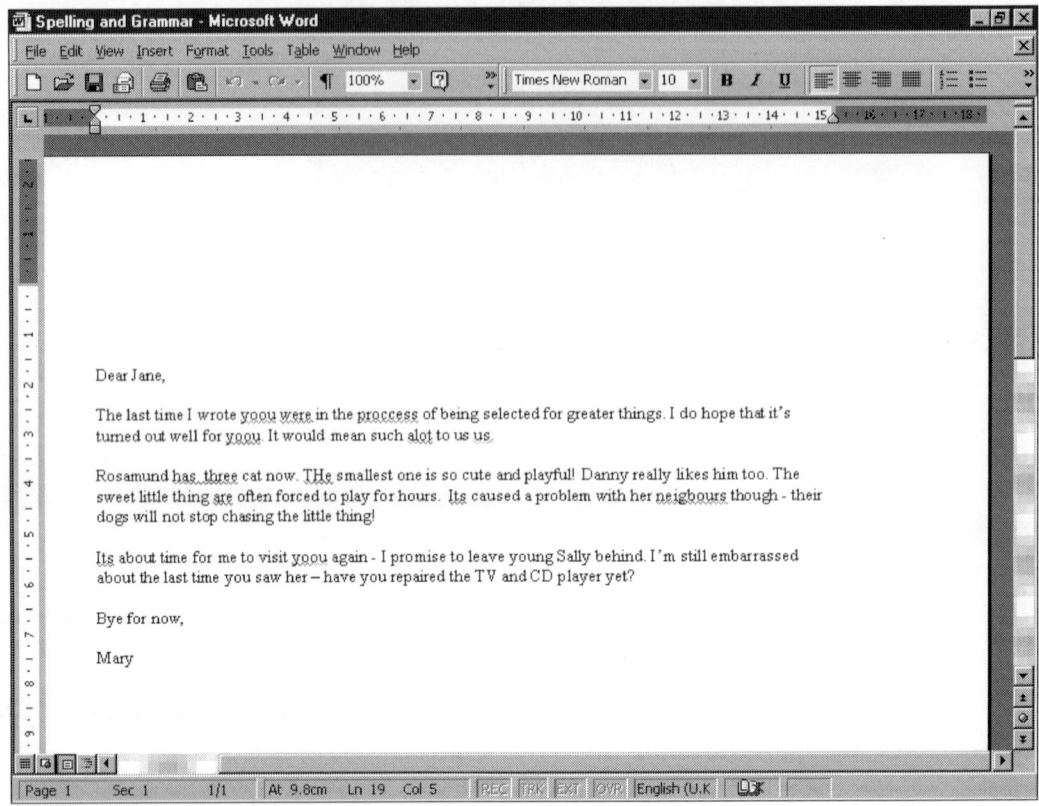

Using the Spelling and Grammar Checker

The Spelling and Grammar Checker is simple to use. It rapidly scans your documents to find spelling, typing, punctuation and grammar errors, and also checks for duplicates, i.e., the same word used twice in a row. Any word that it does not recognise is immediately underlined with a red wavy line. Any grammar or punctuation problems are immediately underlined with a green wavy line. If you right-click the errors, Word will suggest possible alternatives in the shortcut menu.

However, you should bear in mind that no spelling and grammar checker is infallible; neither is it the answer to all your problems. It will pick up things that you are quite happy with and will also miss things that are glaringly wrong. Don't run the Spelling and Grammar Checker and then assume that everything is perfect!

The Spelling and Grammar Checker will sometimes question a word even though it is spelt correctly. This may simply be due to the fact that the word has not been included in the standard dictionary. However, you can add words to the dictionary as you work with Word.

The Spelling and Grammar Checker always carries out its check on the current document, i.e., the document that is displayed in the active Word document window.

In Microsoft Word 2000, the Spelling and Grammar Checker can also be set up to check different languages in the same document. This is not covered in this course. However, if you want to know more about this, ask the Office Assistant.

The Spelling and Grammar Checker can be set up to work in two ways. It can:

- Check your spelling as you type and also check your grammar as you type
- Check spell checking and grammar on demand

Checking spelling and grammar as you type

The Spelling and Grammar Checker can automatically check your spelling and grammar as you type. If you type a word that Word does not recognise, and automatic Spell Checking is on, a red wavy line will appear underneath the word. You can then right-click the offending word and Word will suggest some alternatives.

Likewise, if you type a phrase, or use punctuation that Word considers to be grammatically incorrect, a green wavy line appears beneath the phrase or punctuation. Right-click the phrase or punctuation mark and, if necessary, choose an alternative from the list provided.

Automatic spelling and grammar checking was covered in the chapter *Your First Document* and is not practised again here. However, you are reminded how to turn this feature on and off:

- Open the **Tools** menu and choose **Options**, then click the **Spelling & Grammar** tab
- Turn the **Check spelling as you type** option on or off, as required
- Turn the **Check grammar as you type** option on or off, as required
- Click **OK** to close the dialog box

If you want to run through a document correcting errors, you can:

- Right-click any word underlined with a red wavy line

- Double-click the **Spelling and Grammar Status** icon to automatically find the next error

Spelling & grammar checking on demand

The Spelling and Grammar document, currently displayed on your screen, has several mistakes and is ready to be checked. There are several different ways to start spell and grammar checking on demand:

- Open the **Tools** menu and choose **Spelling and Grammar**

- In the Standard toolbar, click the **Spelling and Grammar** button - remember, it may be in the More Buttons palette
- Press **F7**

Try this now.

- Open the `Tools` menu and choose `Spelling and Grammar`, or click the `Spelling and Grammar` button, or just press `F7`.

The Spelling and Grammar dialog box is displayed.

188 Microsoft Word 2000 ~ Beginners Course

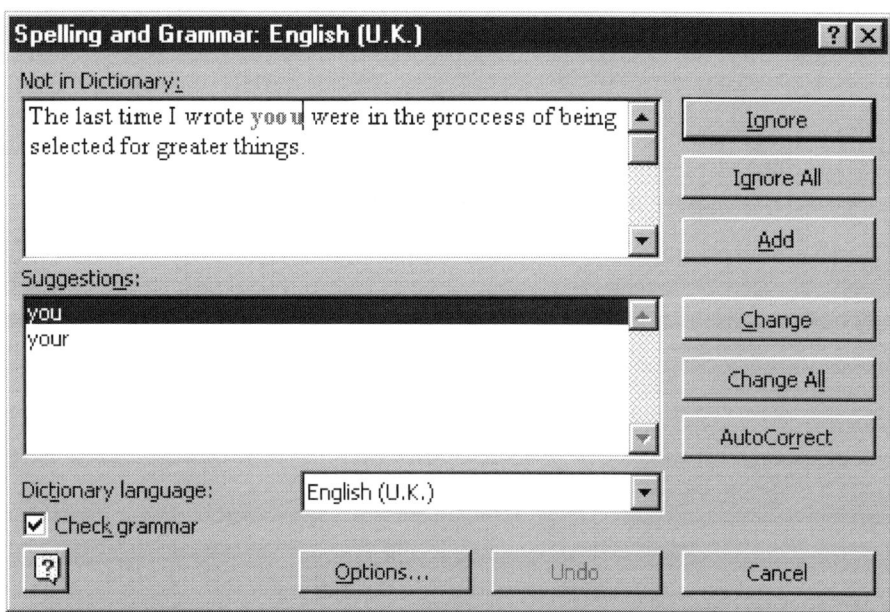

The first mistake that is found is the word youu in the first paragraph. It is shown in the document with a selection highlight and also in the Not in Dictionary box in the Spelling and Grammar dialog box.

> You can move the Spelling and Grammar dialog box, if necessary, by dragging it by its Title bar

The Suggestions box contains a list of suggestions for the correct spelling - in this case, the correct spelling you is shown at the top of the list.

The next table describes the main options that are available in the Spelling and Grammar dialog box. The options you see will depend on whether a spelling or a grammar problem has been found.

Option	Description
Ignore/Ignore All	Skips any changes to the incorrect word or phrase and carries on with the next check - Ignore All skips all further occurrences of the item.
Change/Change All	Changes the incorrect word or phrase to the chosen suggestion in the Suggestions box. Change All corrects all further occurrences of the item.
Add	Adds a word to the chosen custom dictionary.
Delete	Only appears when a duplicate word is found, i.e., the same word found twice in succession, and allows you to delete the

Option	Description
	duplicate.
AutoCorrect	This allows you to add the word to the Replace text as you type list in AutoCorrect. Word will then automatically correct the word the next time you mis-spell it this way. AutoCorrect is covered in detail in the *Microsoft Word 2000 Intermediate Course*.
Options	Allows you to change some default settings.
Undo	Undoes the last change you made.
Check grammar	When ticked will check the grammar in the document at the same time as checking the spelling.
Next Sentence	Only appears for a grammar problem - ignores the current grammar problem and any others found in the same sentence, and moves on to check the next sentence.
Cancel	Closes the Spelling and Grammar Checker.

You can also obtain help by clicking the **Help** button in the top right-hand corner of the dialog box. The mouse pointer then has a question mark attached. Click any button you want to know about and a small text box will appear describing its function.

Changing and ignoring suggestions

The first mistake, yoou, should be changed to the correct spelling. It would make sense to change all occurrences of this mistake throughout the document. The correct spelling, you, is shown in the Suggestions box so you don't need to look for an alternative suggestion.

- In the Suggestions box, make sure **you** is chosen.

- Click **Change All** to replace all occurrences of the word in the document with the chosen word in the Suggestions box.

The next problem is the word proccess, which should be process. Word has correctly analysed this and suggests you change it to process.

- In the Suggestions box, click **process**.

190 Microsoft Word 2000 ~ Beginners Course

- Click **Change**.

The next problem is the missing space in alot. Word provides the correct answer in its list of suggestions.

- In the Suggestions box, choose **a lot**.
- Click **Change** to confirm the correction.

The next error is the repetition of the word us.

- Click **Delete** to delete the repetition.

The Spell Checker next picks up on the name Rosamund, which is correct but Word doesn't recognise it. You can ignore this problem.

- Click the **Ignore All** button.

Correcting grammar problems

Next Word finds a grammar problem. It has found an extra space between two words - has and three in Rosamund has three cat now.

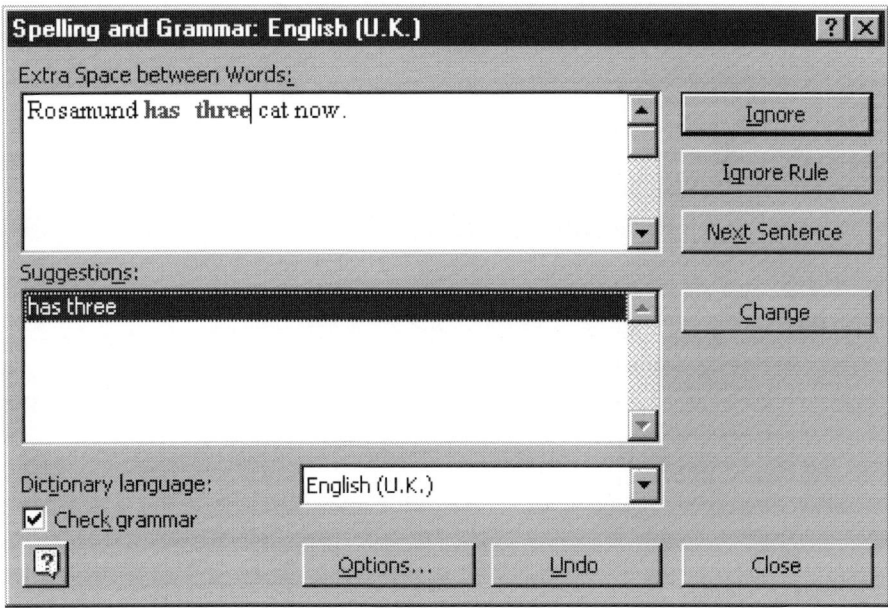

For an explanation of a grammar problem, you can open the Office Assistant.

- In the Spelling and Grammar dialog box, click the **Microsoft Word Help** button.

Microsoft Word 2000 ~ Beginners Course **191**

The Office Assistant springs to life, with an explanation of the problem that has been found.

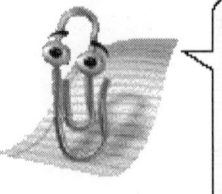

Extra Space between Words

Generally, words in a sentence should have only one space between them.

- Instead of: The line was extra long.
- Consider: The line was extra long.

- Instead of: She laughed all the way to the bank.
- Consider: She laughed all the way to the bank.

- Read what the Office Assistant has to say, and then right-click it and choose **Hide**.

- In the Spelling and Grammar dialog box, click **Change** to accept the suggestion.

The next error the Spelling and Grammar Checker finds is Rosamund has three cat now. It is obvious that it should be cats instead of cat.

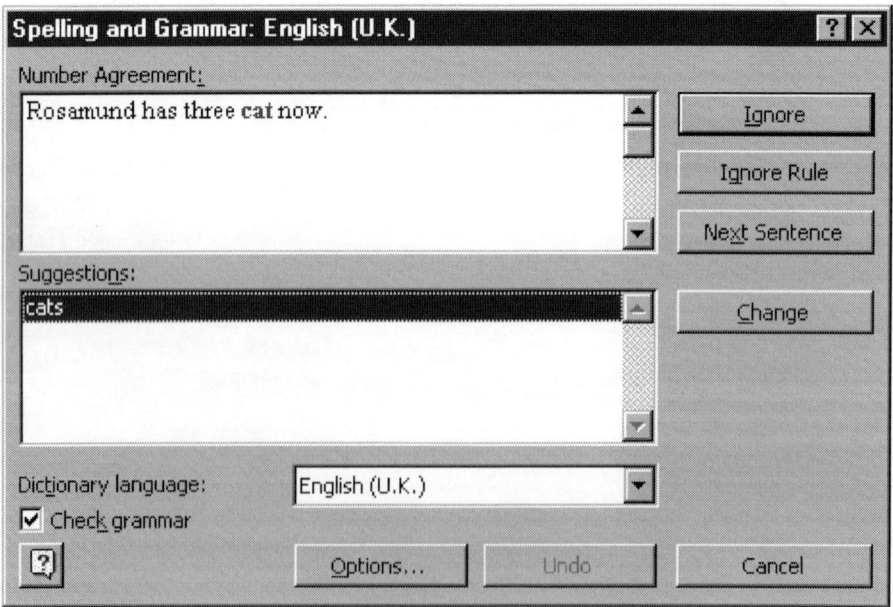

- Click **Change**, to replace cat with **cats**.

The next problem is the word THe, which has two capital letters at the start. Again, Word picks this problem out and suggests the correct alternative.

- Click **Change All**.

192 Microsoft Word 2000 ~ Beginners Course

Word now recognises the incorrect use of are, in the phrase The sweet little thing are often forced to play for hours.

- Click **Change**, to replace are with is.

Adding words to AutoCorrect

Word now questions the spelling of neigbours.

> If this was a mistake you made frequently you could click the **AutoCorrect** button and add the word to the list of words for Replace text as you type. The next time you spelt the word incorrectly, Word would correct it for you as you typed.

> *AutoCorrect is covered fully in the Microsoft Word 2000 Intermediate Course.*

For now, just change the word to the correct spelling.

- Click **Change** to confirm the correction.

Next Word picks out the use of Its instead of It's. Note that although this error came before the spelling error in the sentence, Word chose to correct the spelling before the grammar. It will always do this - sometimes correcting a spelling error may also correct a grammatical error.

- Click **Change**.

Word may question the use of TV if the Spelling and Grammar Checker is not set up to ignore words in upper case. However, this word is correct.

- If necessary, click **Ignore All**.

The spelling check is now complete and you are finally asked to click **OK**.

- Click **OK**, or press **Enter**.

Spelling and grammar checking options

The Spelling and Grammar Checker has a few options that you may find convenient to change. You won't be instructed to make any changes now, but you can decide yourself when and if you make changes. Indeed, different types of document may benefit from different settings.

There are two ways to open the Spelling & Grammar tab and view the options:

> Open the **Tools** menu and choose **Options**

> Click the **Options** button in the Spelling & Grammar dialog box

If you tried to run the Spelling and Grammar Checker now, the dialog box would not be opened because there are no errors in your current document.

- Open the **Tools** menu and choose **Options**.

The Options dialog box is displayed.

- Click the **Spelling & Grammar** tab to show these options.

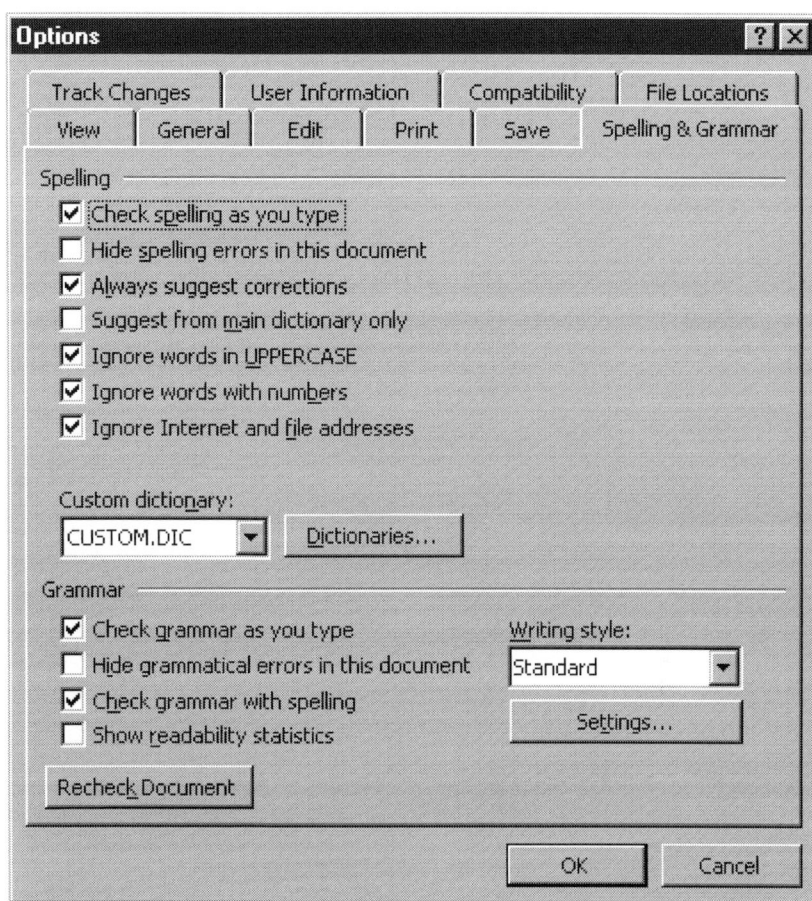

The following table describes the various Spelling options.

Option	Description
Check spelling as you type	Checks your spelling as you type and underlines words it does not recognise with a red wavy line.
Hide spelling errors in this document	Allows you to turn off the red wavy lines.
Always suggest corrections	Will always try to suggest alternative spellings.
Suggest from main dictionary only	Will only look for words in the main dictionary and will not refer to any custom dictionaries.
Ignore words in UPPERCASE	Will ignore uppercase words, e.g., NATO, BBC.
Ignore words with numbers	Will ignore words with numbers, e.g., postcodes.
Ignore Internet and file addresses	Will ignore internet and filenames, e.g., Filename.doc, Train@xxx.u-net.com.

The following table describes the various Grammar options.

Option	Description
Check grammar as you type	Checks your grammar as you type and underlines problems with a green wavy line.
Hide grammatical errors in this document	Allows you to turn off the green wavy lines.
Check grammar with spelling	Will check the grammar at the same time as checking the spelling.
Show readability statistics	When ticked, will automatically show a statistics box at the end of the check.
Writing style	Choose from a list of writing styles: Casual, Standard, Formal, Technical, or customise your own. Rules of grammar are interpreted more strictly for formal writing.
Settings button	Opens the Grammar Settings dialog box where you can set various options for the Writing style you have chosen.
Check Document/ Recheck Document button	Checks the document after you have made changes to the settings in the Spelling and Grammar dialog box, or rechecks the whole document, including any errors you have told Word to ignore on previous spelling and grammar checks.

Custom dictionaries

You will also notice a Custom dictionary list box in the Spelling options. You can build up your own dictionary to contain words you know are correct but the standard Word dictionary doesn't like. You could set up different dictionaries for different types of document, e.g., accounting, computing, medical, or just create one personal dictionary for everything.

> ✤ To create your own personal dictionary, click the **Dictionaries** button in the Options dialog box. Then click the **New** button and give your dictionary a name.

✥ You can choose to edit a dictionary using the **Edit** button, or remove one using the **Remove** button - this doesn't delete the dictionary file, it just removes it from the list. The **Add** button lets you add an existing dictionary to the list of available dictionaries.

✥ When you run the spelling checker, choose the dictionary you want to use. Then, when you click **Add** for a word that Word thinks is incorrect, the word will be added to the dictionary you have chosen to use. The default dictionary for this purpose is **CUSTOM.DIC**.

You are not advised to make changes now.

- `Click **Cancel**, or press **Esc**, to close the Options dialog box.`

Word count

As an added bonus, Word can do a word count for you.

- `Open the **Tools** menu and choose **Word Count**.`

The Word Count dialog box is displayed.

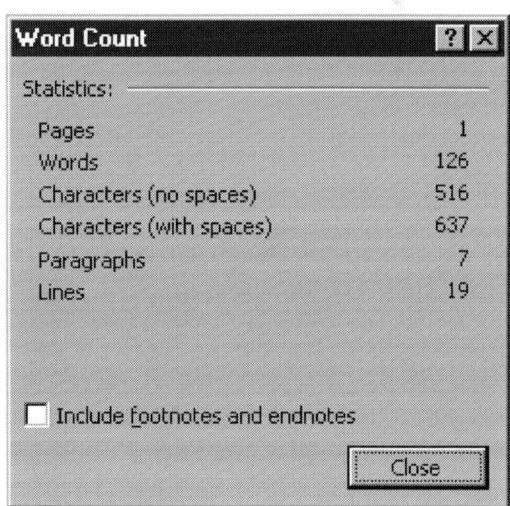

After a short pause, Word displays a message box telling you how many words there are in the document, along with various other statistics.

- `Read what Word has counted for you.`

- When you are ready, click **Close**.

Ending the session

You have now completed the tutorial in this chapter. There are two additional exercises that you may wish to do before moving on to the next chapter or exiting Word. First, you should close the current document.

- Open the **File** menu and choose **Close** – choose **No** to avoid saving the changes.

- If you are not continuing directly with the extra exercises or the next chapter, open the **File** menu and choose **Exit** to exit Word.

Exercise 11a

This exercise provides a document for spell checking.

- Open the **More Spell Checking** document from your exercise diskette.

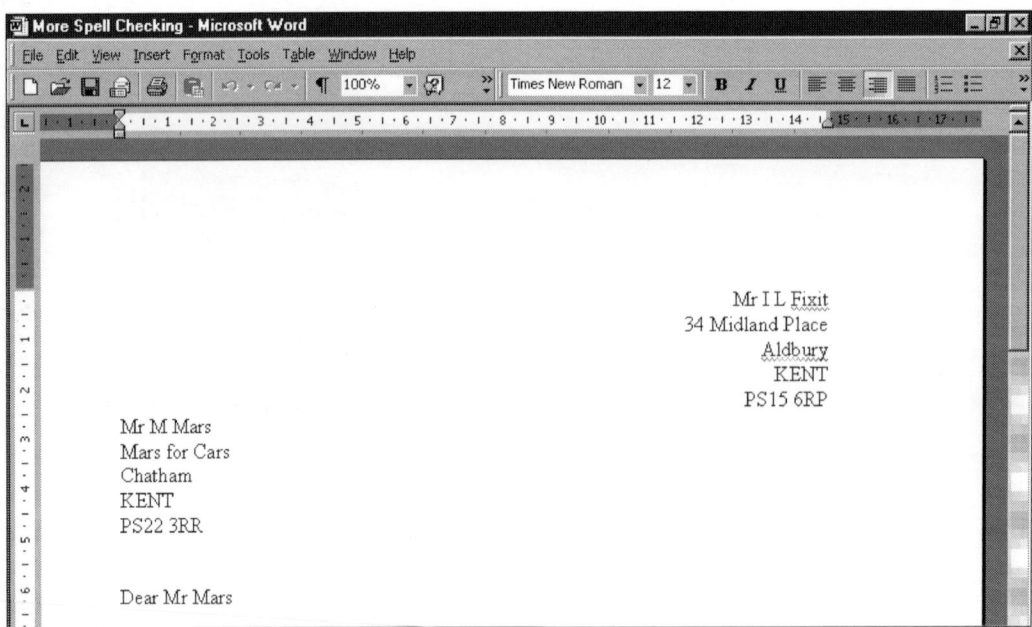

- Run the Spelling and Grammar Checker.
- Use your own judgement to tackle the problems that arise.

- When you have finished, close the document without saving the changes.

Exercise 11b

This exercise provides a document for spelling and grammar checking.

- Open the **Poor Grammar** document from your exercise diskette.

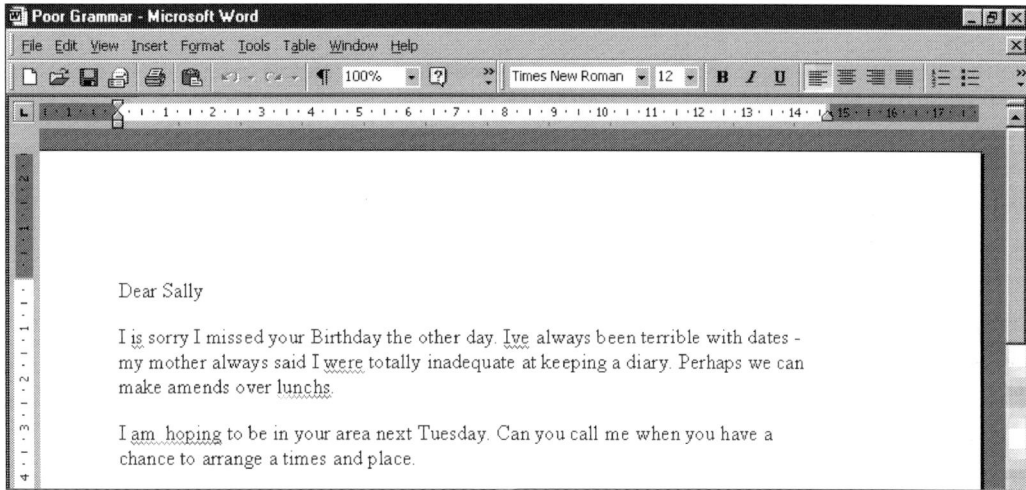

- Use the Spelling and Grammar Checker to help you correct this letter.

- Read through the letter to check the corrections.

Note that the Spelling and Grammar Checker does not find several mistakes - it is not infallible!

- When you are ready, close the document without saving the changes.

Microsoft Word 2000 ~ Beginners Course   **199**

Summary ~ The Spelling & Grammar Checker

Word has a spelling and grammar checker that rapidly scans the current document to find spelling, typing, punctuation and grammar errors. You can set up the Spelling and Grammar Checker to check spelling and grammar as you type, or to check spelling and grammar on demand.

Check spelling as you type

The **Check spelling as you type** option is set using **Tools**, **Options**, **Spelling & Grammar**. When activated, if you type a word that Word does not recognise:

- A red wavy line appears underneath the word
- Right-click the offending word
- A shortcut menu is displayed with some alternative words
- Options are available to ignore all occurrences of the word, add the word to the Custom dictionary, add the error and its correction to the AutoCorrect list, open the Spelling dialog box or set the language

Check grammar as you type

The **Check grammar as you type** option is set using **Tools**, **Options**, **Spelling & Grammar**. When activated, if you type a phrase that Word finds grammatically incorrect:

- A green wavy line appears underneath the phrase
- Right-click the offending phrase
- A shortcut menu is displayed offering alternatives
- Options are available to ignore the sentence, or open the Grammar dialog box

Using the Spelling and Grammar Status icon

When the **Check spelling as you type** and **Check grammar as you type** options are active, the **Spelling and Grammar Status** icon is displayed in the Status bar. A red tick means there are no errors in the current document; a red cross means errors are still present. Double-click this icon to find the next red or green wavy line.

Spell checking on demand

To start the Spelling and Grammar Checker on demand:

- Open the **Tools** menu and choose **Spelling and Grammar**, or click the **Spelling and Grammar** button, or press **F7**

You can choose to do any of the following as appropriate:

- **Ignore** the incorrect word or grammar problem
- **Ignore All** occurrences of the incorrect word or problem
- **Change** the word/phrase to that in the Suggestions box
- **Change All** occurrences of the word/phrase to that in the Suggestions box
- **Add** the word to the dictionary or the **AutoCorrect** list
- Move on to the **Next Sentence** ignoring the current problem and any others found in the same sentence
- **Delete** duplicates
- **Undo** the last change

Spelling and grammar checking options

To see the spelling and grammar checking options, choose **Tools**, **Options**, **Spelling & Grammar**, or click the **Options** button in the Spelling and Grammar dialog box.

Microsoft Word 2000 ~ Beginners Course **201**

- **Check spelling as you type** - as described on page 200
- **Hide spelling errors in this document** allows you to turn off the red wavy lines
- **Always suggest corrections** - Word will try to find suggestions and list them in the Suggestions box
- **Suggest from main dictionary only** - Word will only look for words in the main dictionary
- **Ignore words in UPPERCASE**, e.g., NATO, BBC
- **Ignore words with numbers**, e.g., postcodes
- **Ignore Internet and file addresses**, e.g., Filename.doc, Train@xxx.u-net.com
- **Check grammar as you type** - as described on page 200
- **Hide grammatical errors in this document** allows you to turn off the green wavy lines
- **Check grammar with spelling**
- **Show readability statistics** to display the readability statistics at the end of the grammar check

Also, during a spell check, Word keeps a list of all the words where you clicked **Ignore All**. Click the **Recheck Document** button to clear the list.

Word count

Use the **Tools**, **Word Count** option to see how many pages, words, characters, paragraphs and lines there are in your document.

Notes

Use this page to make notes of your own.

Page #   Notes

Notes

Use this page to make notes of your own.

Page #   Notes

Chapter 12 ~ Printing & Print Preview

In this chapter you will learn about:

- Choosing a printer
- Printing using the **Print** button
- Choosing what to print - pages, number of copies, etc., using the Print dialog box
- Print Preview
- Editing in Print Preview

It is assumed that:

- You have a printer installed and ready to print

You have already created and printed a few documents in earlier chapters, but this chapter concentrates on printing.

Getting started

- If necessary, start Word.

- If the Office Assistant is displayed, right-click it and choose **Hide**.

- Make sure your exercise diskette is in drive A.

- Open the **File** menu and choose **Open**, or click the **Open** button in the Standard toolbar, or just press **Ctrl+O**.

The Open dialog box is displayed.

- In the File name box, type:

    a:Food

- Click **Open**, or press **Enter**.

The Food document is opened.

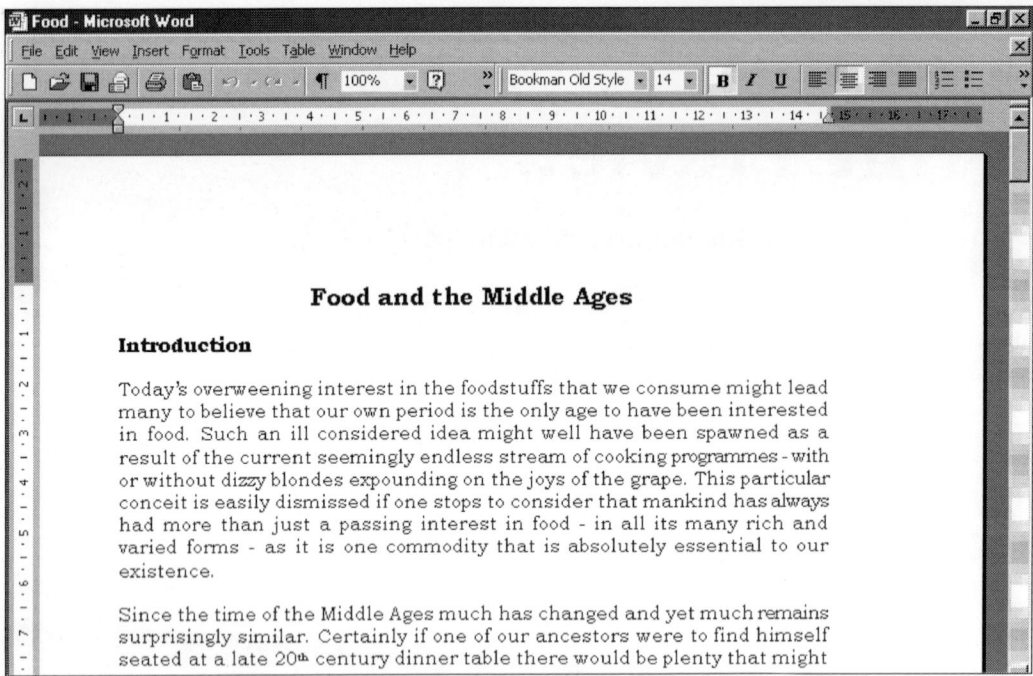

Choosing a printer

If you have more than one printer installed on your system - you may be connected to several via a network - you can choose which printer you want to use. Note that if you click the **Print** button in the Standard toolbar the Print dialog box is not displayed.

- Open the `File` menu and choose `Print`, or press `Ctrl+P`.

The Print dialog box is displayed.

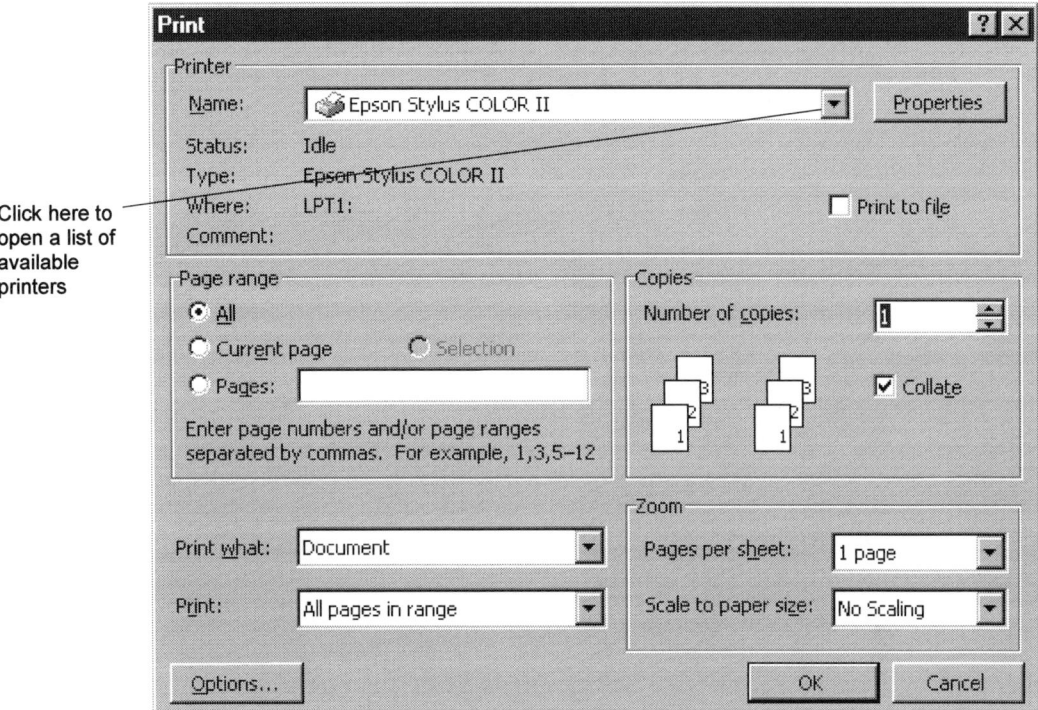

Click here to open a list of available printers

- Click the downward-pointing arrow of the Name list box to open the list of available printers.

A list of available printers is displayed - it will almost definitely be different from the list shown in the next picture.

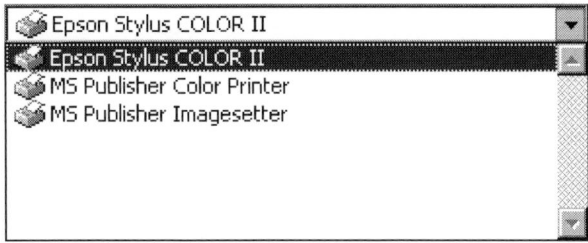

- For now, press **Esc** to close the list of printers.

- Click **Cancel,** or press **Esc** again, to close the Print dialog box without making any changes.

Microsoft Word 2000 ~ Beginners Course **207**

Using the Print button in the toolbar

The quickest way to print the current document is to click the **Print** button in the Standard toolbar. Using this method, the printout is started automatically. You don't get a chance to change any of the settings.

- ```
  In the Standard toolbar, click the Print
  button.
  ```

> ♪ *If somebody else has changed any of the settings, what is printed may not be what you expect!*

The document is printed according to the current settings.

Choosing what to print

You can choose to print the whole document, the current page, selected pages, odd or even pages only, or both, and more. All this is done via the Print dialog box.

- ```
  Open the File menu and choose Print, or
  press Ctrl+P - don't use the Print button
  in the Standard toolbar this time.
  ```

The Print dialog box is displayed.

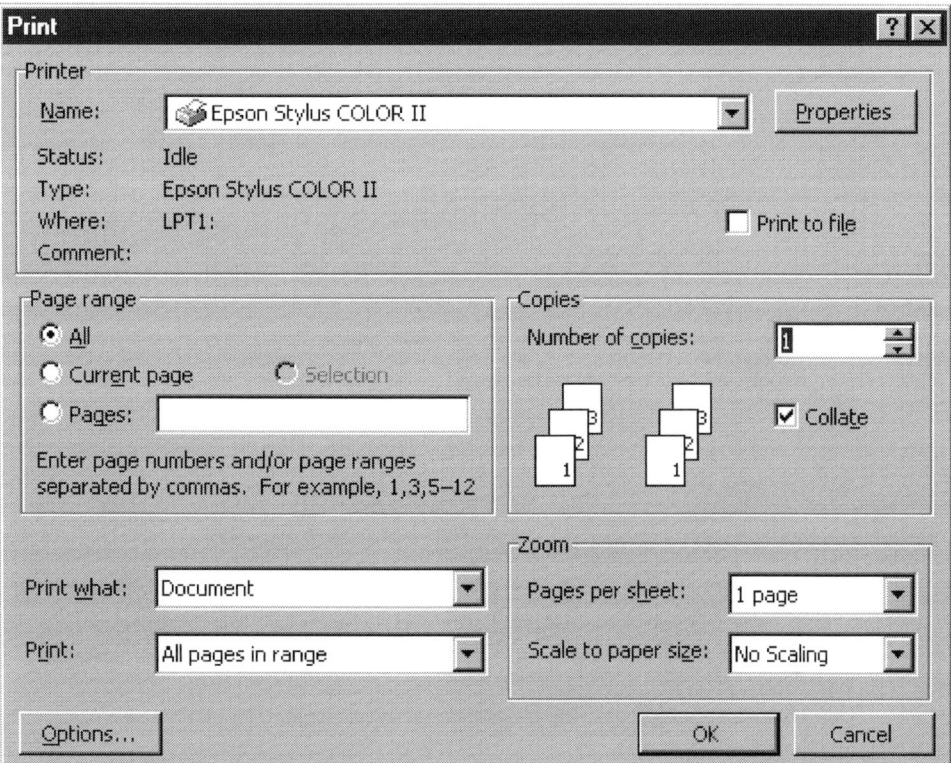

The options are as follows:

Option	Description
All	Prints all the pages in the document.
Current page	Prints the current page only.
Pages	Prints a specified range of pages.
Selection	Prints text currently selected in the document.
Print what	Allows you to print the document itself, or other components of the document.
Print	Allows you to print all pages in the chosen range, or odd or even pages only.
Pages per sheet	Allows you to choose the number of pages that are printed on a single sheet.
Scale to paper size	Allows you to fit the document to a different paper size - either by enlarging or by reducing the font size and any graphics.

Printing the current page only

During the course of your work, you may create a longer document, edit it and print it, then make alterations to a single page. It is not always necessary to re-print the whole document - you can choose to print just the current page, or a specific page.

- Click the **Current page** option.

- Click **OK**.

Only the current page will be printed.

Printing specific pages

You can also print specific pages. Page ranges can be separated by commas, for individual pages, or by a hyphen for a continuous range, e.g., 2,5,8 or 2-3.

Try printing pages 2-3.

- Open the **File** menu and choose **Print**, or press **Ctrl+P** - <u>don't</u> use the **Print** button in the Standard toolbar.

- In the <u>Pages</u> box, type:

    2-3

- Click **OK**.

Pages 2 and 3 are printed.

Printing selected text

In certain instances, you may wish to print a selection of text, a few paragraphs for example. To do this, use the mouse or keyboard to select the text, then open the Print dialog box.

- Select the first two paragraphs.

- Open the **File** menu and choose **Print**, or press **Ctrl+P**.

- In the <u>Page range</u> group of options, click the **Selection** option.

- Click **OK**.

Only the selected text is printed.

How many copies?

The <u>Number of copies</u> box allows you to print multiple copies of a document.

- Open the **File** menu and choose **Print,** or press **Ctrl+P** – <u>don't</u> use the **Print** button in the Standard toolbar.

- Click the **Current page** option.

- In the <u>Number of copies</u> box, type:

    3

- Click **OK.**

The current page will be printed three times.

Previewing a document

To see what your document will look like, without having to print it out, you can use Print Preview. There are two ways to open this view:

    ✤   Open the **File** menu and choose **Print Preview**

    ✤   In the Standard toolbar, click the **Print Preview** button

Try this now.

- Open the **File** menu and choose **Print Preview,** or click the **Print Preview** button in the Standard toolbar – remember it may be in the More Buttons palette.

Print Preview is displayed.

- If necessary, click the **One Page** button.

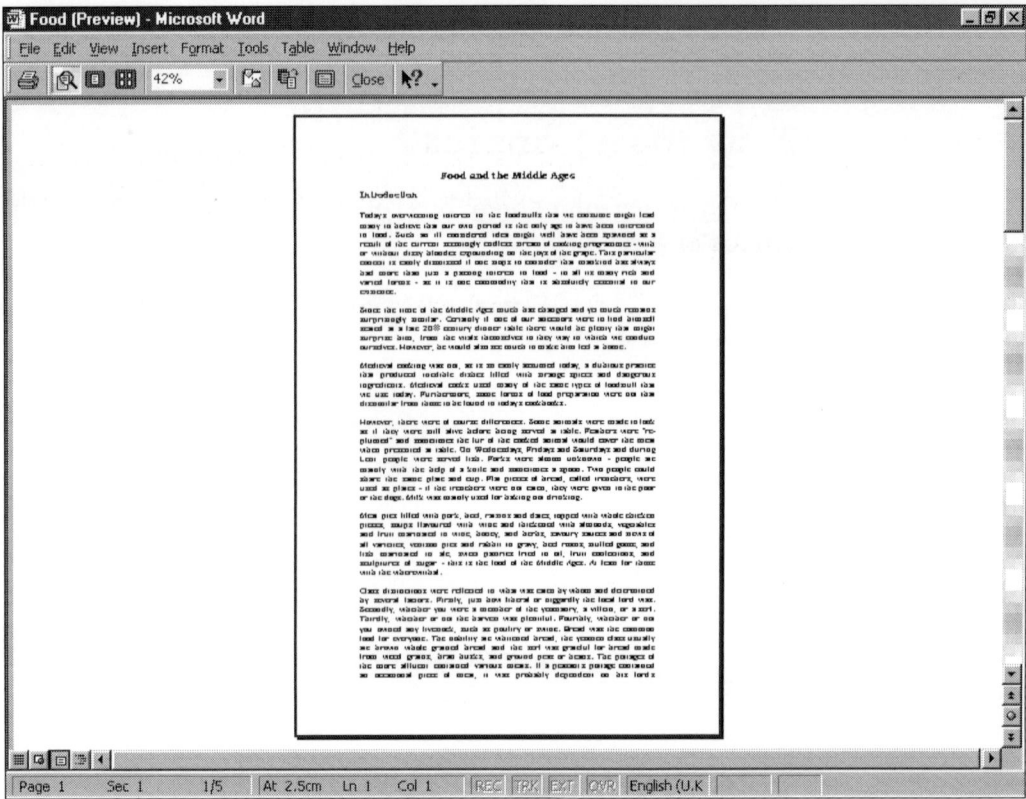

Several options are available including:

- ꙳ If your document runs to several pages, use the **Page Up** and **Page Down** keys to scroll through the document (flip through the different pages)

- ꙳ You can also use the scroll bar to scroll through the document - when you click the scroll box the ScreenTip will tell you which page is displayed

- ꙳ Use the **Multiple Pages** button to view several pages at once and the **One Page** button to view one page at a time

- ꙳ Click anywhere on the document - the mouse pointer changes to a magnifying glass shape - click the document again to enlarge or reduce the display size

- ꙳ To edit the document in Print Preview, zoom in on the document, click the **Magnifier** button so that it is not depressed, then click the appropriate place in the document and make the change(s) you require

✎ To print the document, click the **Print** button in the Print Preview toolbar - Print Preview is closed automatically

✎ If you don't want to print the document, click the **Close Preview** button to close Print Preview

Try out some of these now.

- ```
  Press Page Down and Page Up to move between
  the pages.
  ```

- ```
  Click the Multiple Pages button - a menu of
  pages is displayed.
  ```

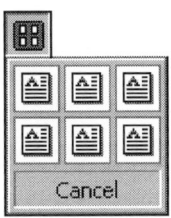

- ```
  Position the mouse pointer over the second
  square in the second row - 2 x 2 pages -
  and then click.
  ```

Four pages are previewed together.

Microsoft Word 2000 ~ Beginners Course **213**
  ```

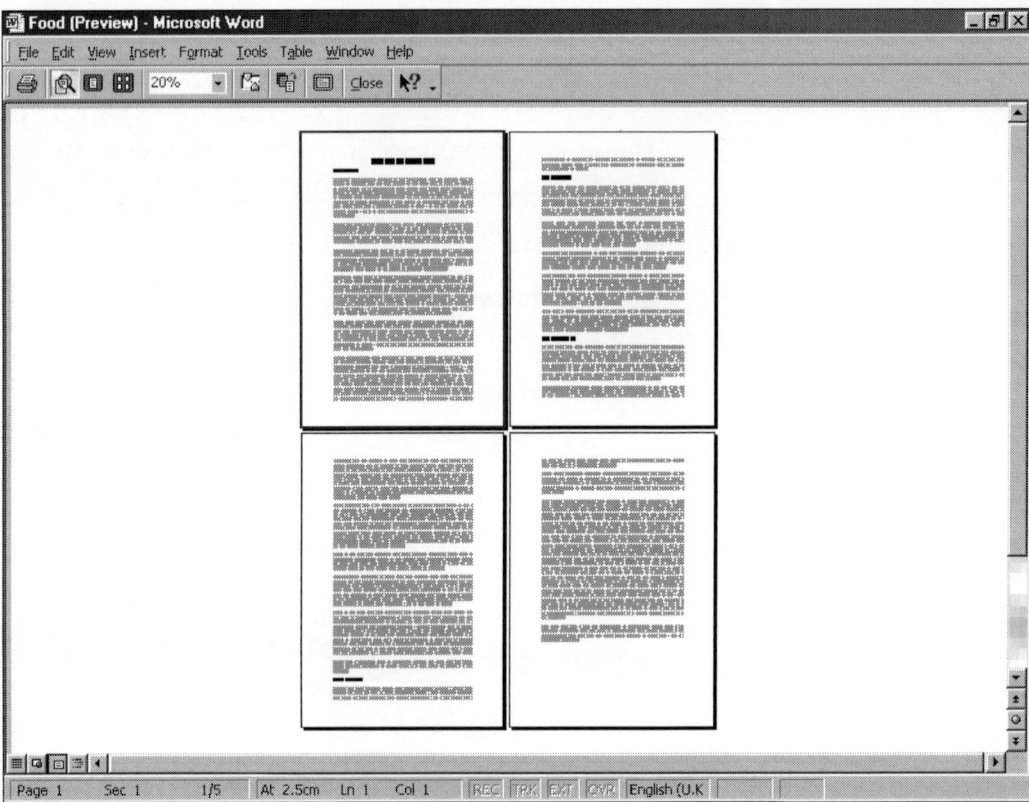

- When you are ready, click the **Close Preview** button to close Print Preview.

Ending the session

You have now completed the tutorial in this chapter. There is an additional exercise that you may wish to do before moving on to the next chapter or exiting Word. First, you should close the current document.

- Open the **File** menu and choose **Close** – choose **No** to avoid saving the changes.

- If you are not continuing directly with the extra exercise or the next chapter, open the **File** menu and choose **Exit** to exit Word.

Exercise 12a

In this exercise you will print a complete document in two stages - printing three pages first and then the remaining pages after.

- Open the **Food** document from your exercise diskette.

- Open the Print dialog box - **File, Print,** or **Ctrl+P**.

- Set up the number of copies and the page range to print **2** copies of pages **1,4,5** - then start the printout.

- Open the Print dialog box and set the options for printing **1** copy of pages **2-3** (you printed a copy of pages 2-3 in the earlier part of this tutorial) - then start the printout.

- Close the document without saving any changes that may have been made - **File, Close**.

The end result will be two complete copies of the document.

Summary ~ Printing & Print Preview

The main options for printing are found in the Print dialog box. There are two ways to open it:

- Open the **File** menu and choose **Print**
- Press **Ctrl+P**

The main options are:

- Which printer?
- What to print?
- How many copies?

The **Print** button in the Standard toolbar prints the document using the current settings in the Print dialog box - these may not always be what you want.

Choosing a printer

To choose a different printer, open the Name list box and choose the printer you require.

Microsoft Word 2000 ~ Beginners Course **215**

Choosing what to print

You can choose to print the whole document, the current page or specific pages. Click your choice and, for specific pages, type in the page numbers. You can also select text and print just the selection.

How many copies?

The number of copies is set in the Number of copies option. Click the up or down arrow to increase or decrease the number of copies required.

Printing

Once you have set the correct values, click **OK** to print the document.

Print Preview

To see what your document will look like, without having to print it out, you can use **Print Preview**. There are two ways to open this view:

> Open the **File** menu and choose **Print Preview**

> In the Standard toolbar, click the **Print Preview** button

Editing in Print Preview

To edit a document in Print Preview, zoom in on the document, click the **Magnifier** button so that it is not depressed, then click the appropriate place in the document and make the change(s) you require

Notes

Use this page to make notes of your own.

Page #   Notes

Notes

Use this page to make notes of your own.

Page #   Notes

_____ _____

_____ _____

_____ _____

_____ _____

_____ _____

_____ _____

_____ _____

_____ _____

_____ _____

_____ _____

_____ _____

_____ _____

_____ _____

Chapter 13 ~ Page Layout

In this chapter you will learn about:

- Page layout in general
- Changing the page margins
- Changing the paper size and orientation
- Forcing page breaks

In addition to using the various font and paragraph formats, you may need to, or simply wish to, make overall adjustments to the size of your page and the margins around it.

Getting started

- If necessary, start Word.
- If the Office Assistant is displayed, right-click it and choose **Hide**.
- Make sure your exercise diskette is in drive A.

- Open the **File** menu and choose **Open**, or click the **Open** button in the Standard toolbar, or just press **Ctrl+O**.

The Open dialog box is displayed.

- In the File name box, type:

    a:Food

- Click **Open**, or press **Enter**.

The Food document is opened.

Microsoft Word 2000 ~ Beginners Course   **219**

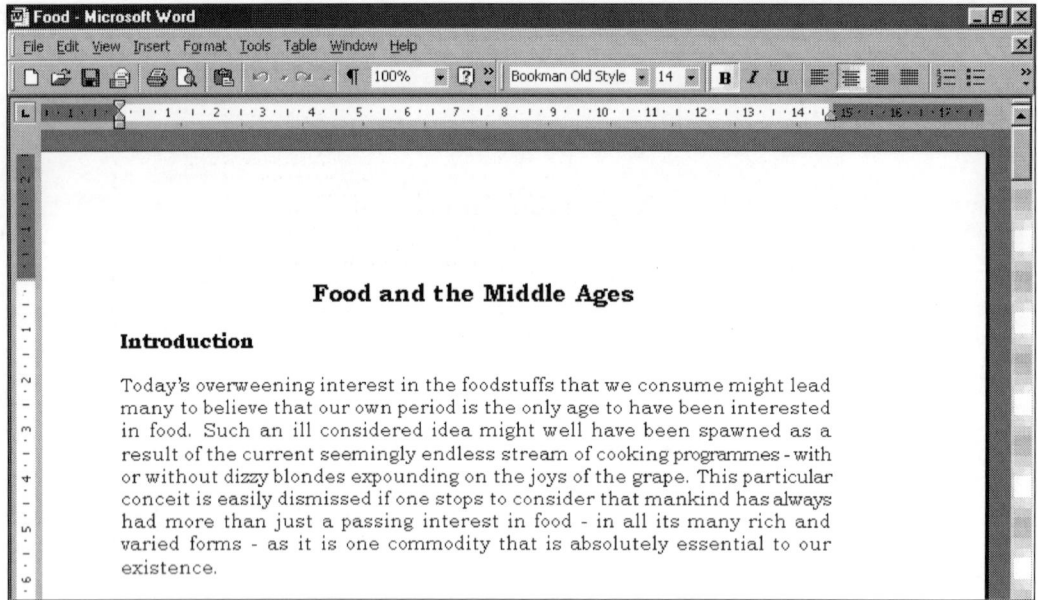

The general layout of the page

The size of the margins, where you position headers and footers, etc., will affect the look of your page quite considerably. It is never a good idea to cram in as much text as possible - white space makes a document much easier to read.

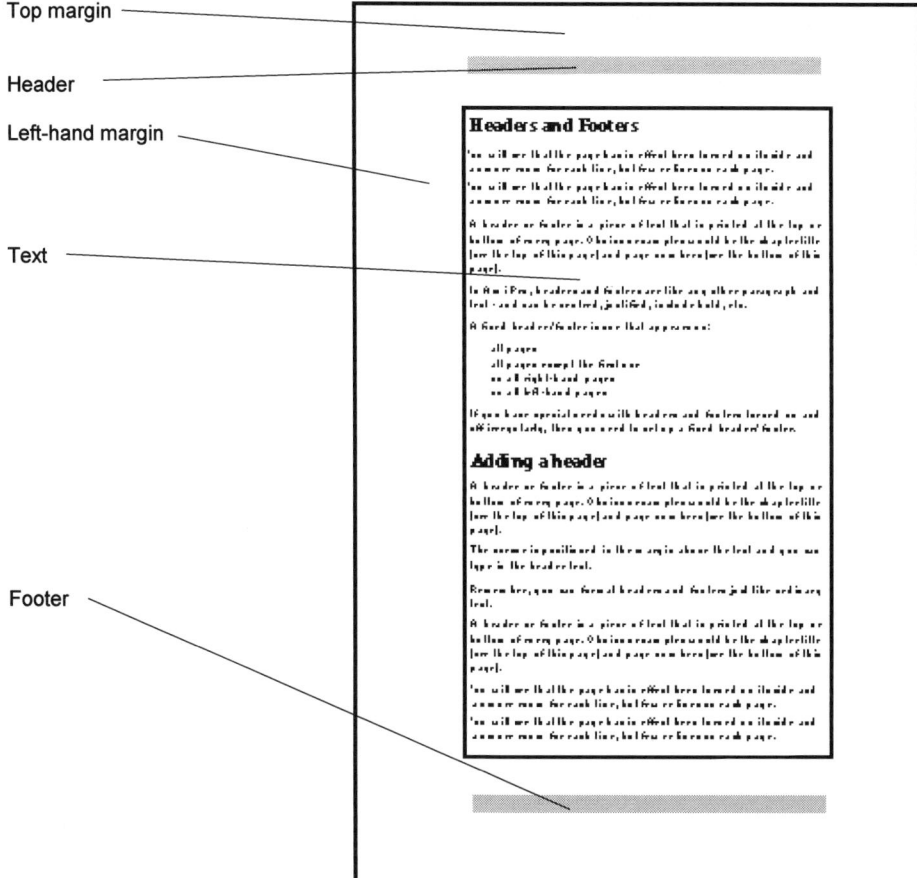

- Unless you have special considerations, a 2.5 cm (1 inch) margin on all sides should be a minimum

- If your documents are going to be hole-punched, then you might need a considerably larger left-hand margin

- If your documents are to be double-sided, you may need to set mirror margins - different margins for the left-hand and right-hand pages

Margins

There are four margins you can set - left, right, top and bottom. Generally speaking about 2.5 cm (1") will look appropriate on A4, 11" or 12" paper, and still leave room for simple headers and footers such as page numbers or chapter titles.

- Open the **File** menu and choose **Page Setup**.

The Page Setup dialog box is displayed.

- If necessary, click the **Margins** tab.

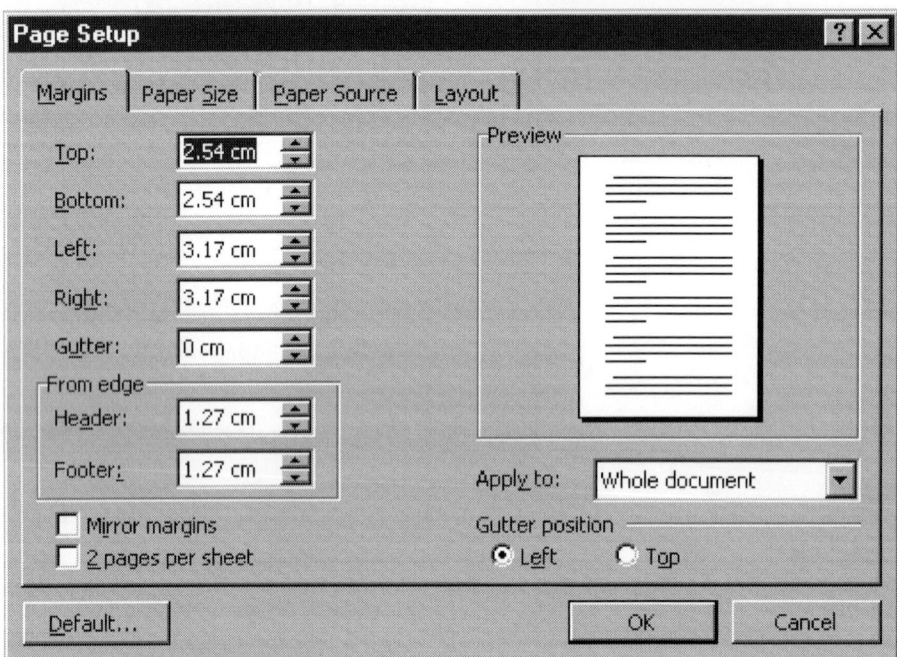

- Enter the following values – use the **Tab** key to move the insertion point to the next input box:

  Top margin   7.5 cm (or 3.0")
  Bottom margin 5.0 cm (or 2.0")
  Left margin   4.0 cm (or 1.5")
  Right margin   4.0 cm (or 1.5")

> ✐ *Note that you can type in inches or centimetres regardless of the current units of measurement. For example, just type 3", 3 in, or 3 cm. The next time you display the **Margins** tab, the measurements will have been automatically converted to the current units.*

- Click **OK**, or press **Enter**.

The text will be adapted to fit the new page size and margins.

> ✍ *If you are viewing the document in Normal view, you may only notice a slight difference in the amount of text that fits in per line. The changes to the top and bottom margins are not shown.*

You can check the effect of changing the margins by using Print Preview.

- Open the **File** menu and choose **Print Preview,** or click the **Print Preview** button in the Standard toolbar.

- If necessary, click the **One Page** button in the Print Preview toolbar to show one page at a time.

- Use **Page Down** to scroll through the pages.

Microsoft Word 2000 ~ Beginners Course

- Use the **Multiple Pages** button in the Print Preview toolbar to view 1 x 2 Pages - click the button and then click the second square in the first row.

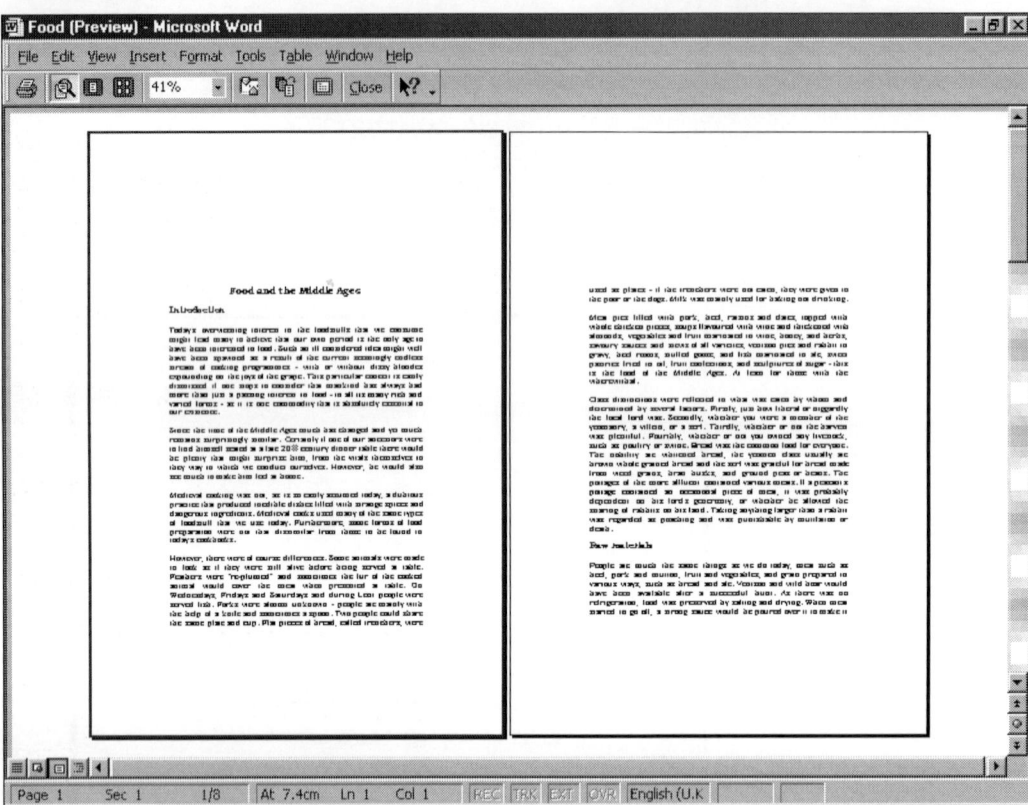

- When you are ready, close Print Preview.

Paper size options

Another set of options that you can control covers paper size.

- Open the **File** menu and choose **Page Setup**.

The Page Setup dialog box is displayed.

- Click the **Paper Size** tab.

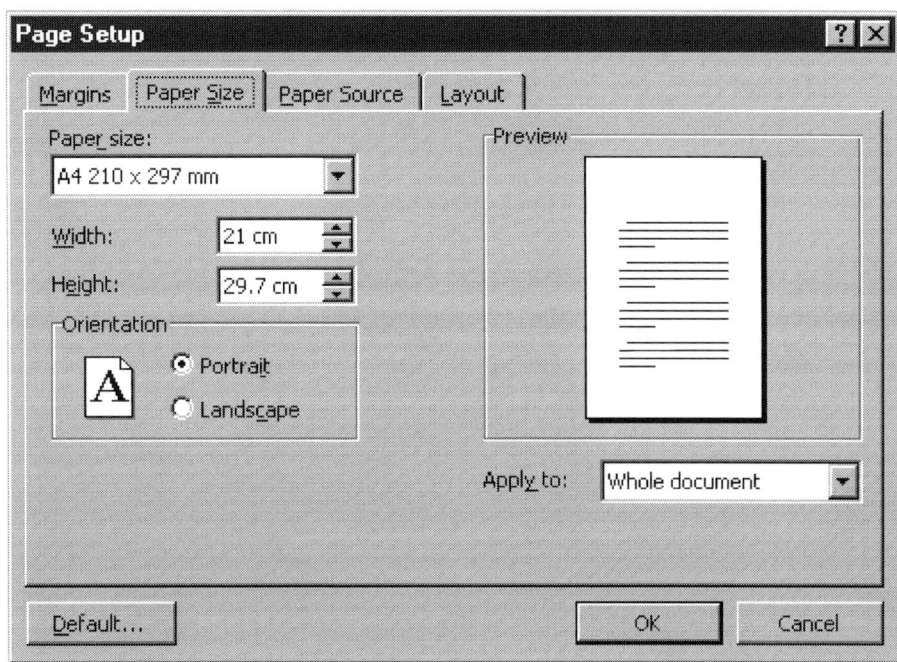

The Paper Size options let you choose a different size and orientation for your paper:

- Portrait - the paper standing on its short side
- Landscape - the paper lying on its long side

Change the orientation to landscape.

- In the Orientation options, click **Landscape** so that it is chosen.
- Click **OK**, or press **Enter**.

The page is now wider and shorter.

- Use Print Preview to check the effects.
- When you are ready, close Print Preview.

Paper source options

If your printer has more than one paper tray, the Paper Source options allow you to choose different paper trays for the first and subsequent pages.

- Open the **File** menu and choose **Page Setup**.

The Page Setup dialog box is displayed.

- Click the **Paper Source** tab.

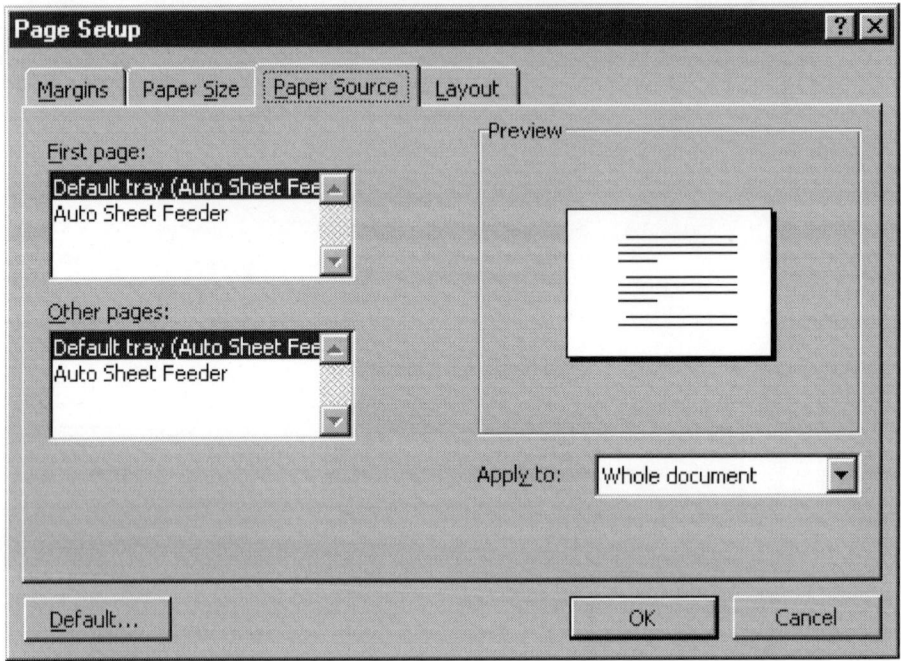

These options are particularly useful if your printer has two paper trays or cassettes - you can use a mixture of letterhead paper and plain paper.

- Click **Cancel**, or press **Esc**, to close the dialog box.

Layout options

- Open the **File** menu and choose **Page Setup**.

The Page Setup dialog box is displayed.

- Click the **Layout** tab.

These options allow you to have a different header or footer on odd and even pages, and also on the first page. This is covered in more detail in the chapter *Headers & Footers*.

The **Line Numbers** button allows you to add or remove line numbers for the section of the document shown in the Apply to box.

The **Borders** button displays the Page Borders tab of the Borders and Shading dialog box, allowing you to apply a border to each page of the document.

- Look at the options in the **Layout** tab without changing any of them.

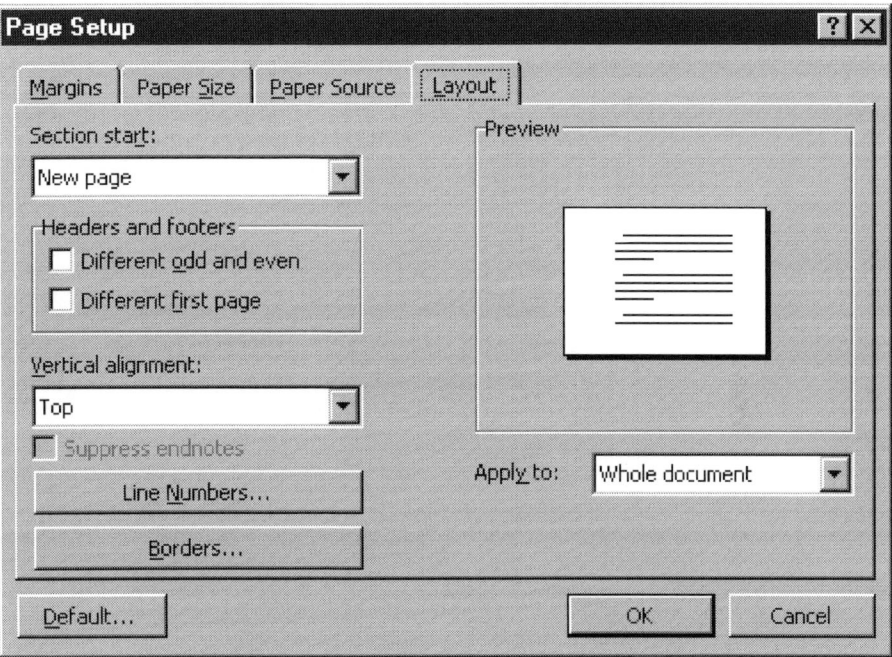

- Click the **Paper Size** tab and reset the page orientation to **Portrait**.

- Click **OK**, or press **Enter**, to close the dialog box.

Inserting manual page breaks

You can insert a page break anywhere in a document by pressing **Ctrl+Enter**.

- Scroll down the document and click immediately before the second heading, Raw Materials.

- Press **Ctrl+Enter**.

A page break is inserted and the heading Raw Materials is moved to the top of the next page.

Microsoft Word 2000 ~ Beginners Course **227**

Page breaks in Normal view

In Normal view, manual page breaks are indicated by a dense dotted line across the page, with the words Page Break in the middle. Automatic page breaks inserted by Word are shown by a lighter dotted line. You may or may not have Normal view displayed just now.

- If necessary, open the **View** menu and choose **Normal**, or click the **Normal View** button.

- Scroll up the document until you can see the page break that you inserted before the Raw Materials heading.

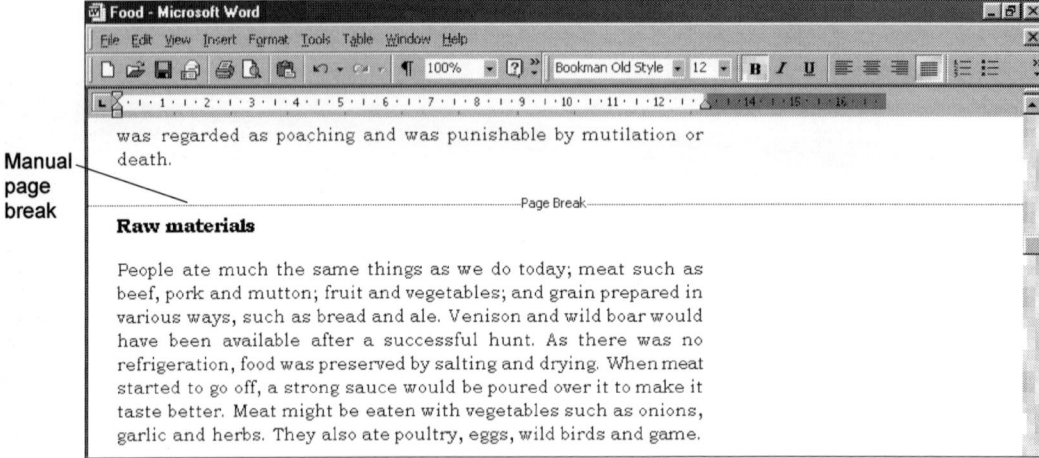

Manual page break

- Use the **Page Up** and **Page Down** keys to scroll through the document again, noting the difference between the automatic and manual page breaks.

You will see that the automatic page breaks do not display the text Page Break. You should have found another manual page break towards the end of the document - just before the recipe.

Ending the session

You have now completed the tutorial in this chapter. There is an additional exercise that you may wish to do before moving on to the next chapter or exiting Word. First, you should close the current document.

- Open the **File** menu and choose **Close** - choose **No** to avoid saving the changes.

- If you are not continuing directly with the extra exercise or the next chapter, open the **File** menu and choose **Exit** to exit Word.

Exercise 13a

In this exercise you will open an existing document and change the page set-up.

- Open the **Information** document from your exercise diskette.

- Before you make any changes, use **File**, **Save As** to save the document on your exercise diskette as **a:Ex13a**.

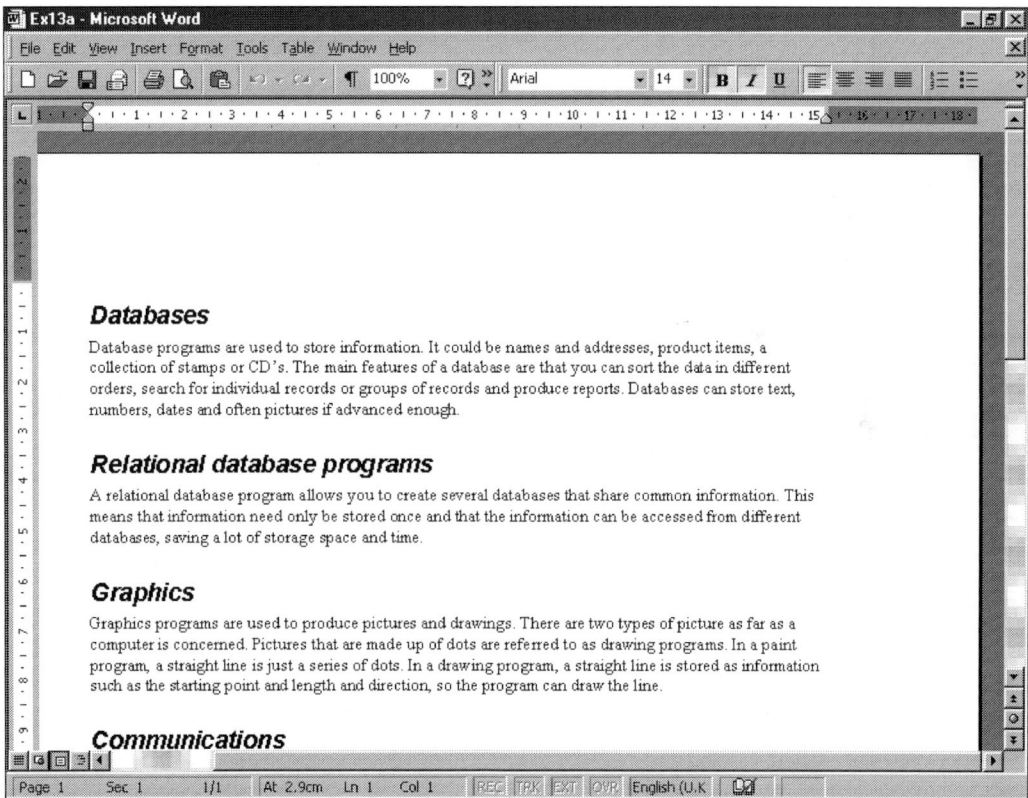

- Open the **File** menu and choose **Page Setup**.

- Click the **Margins** tab.

- Change the Top, Bottom, Left and Right margins to **2 cm (0.8 in)**.

- Click the **Paper Size** tab.

Microsoft Word 2000 ~ Beginners Course

- Change the paper size to **Executive** – or another size of your choice.

- Change the orientation to **Landscape**.

- Click **OK,** or press **Enter,** to close the Page Setup dialog box.

- Insert a manual page break before the heading <u>Communications</u>.

- Save the changes you have made to the **Ex13a** document.

- View the document in Print Preview.

- When you are ready, close the document – **File, Close.**

Summary ~ Page Layout

To produce a document that is clear to read, it is important that you give careful consideration to the page layout. It is never a good idea to cram in as much text as possible – white space makes a document much easier to read.

Page set-up

There are four aspects to setting up a page:

- Margins
- Paper size
- Paper source
- Layout

All the options are available in the Page Setup dialog box – choose **File**, **Page Setup** to display it. The effect of changes to the page set-up can best be viewed in Print Preview – click the **Print Preview** button in the Standard toolbar.

Inserting manual page breaks

You can insert a page break anywhere in a document by pressing **Ctrl+Enter**.

In Normal view, manual page breaks are shown by a dense dotted line across the page with the words Page Break in the middle. Automatic page breaks inserted by Word are shown by a lighter dotted line.

Notes

Use this page to make notes of your own.

Page #   Notes

Chapter 14 ~ Headers & Footers

In this chapter you will learn about:

  ✎ Adding simple headers and footers to a document

  ✎ Setting different headers and footers on odd and even pages

  ✎ Setting different headers and footers on the first page

It is often useful to have a header or a footer that is printed on each page of a document - a page number, date or copyright notice, for example.

Getting started

- If necessary, start Word.

- If the Office Assistant is displayed, right-click it and choose **Hide**.

- Make sure your exercise diskette is in drive A.

- Open the **File** menu and choose **Open,** or click the **Open** button in the Standard toolbar, or just press **Ctrl+O**.

The Open dialog box is displayed.

- In the File name box, type:

  a:Internet Requirements

- Click **Open,** or press **Enter**.

The Internet Requirements document is opened.

Microsoft Word 2000 ~ Beginners Course **233**

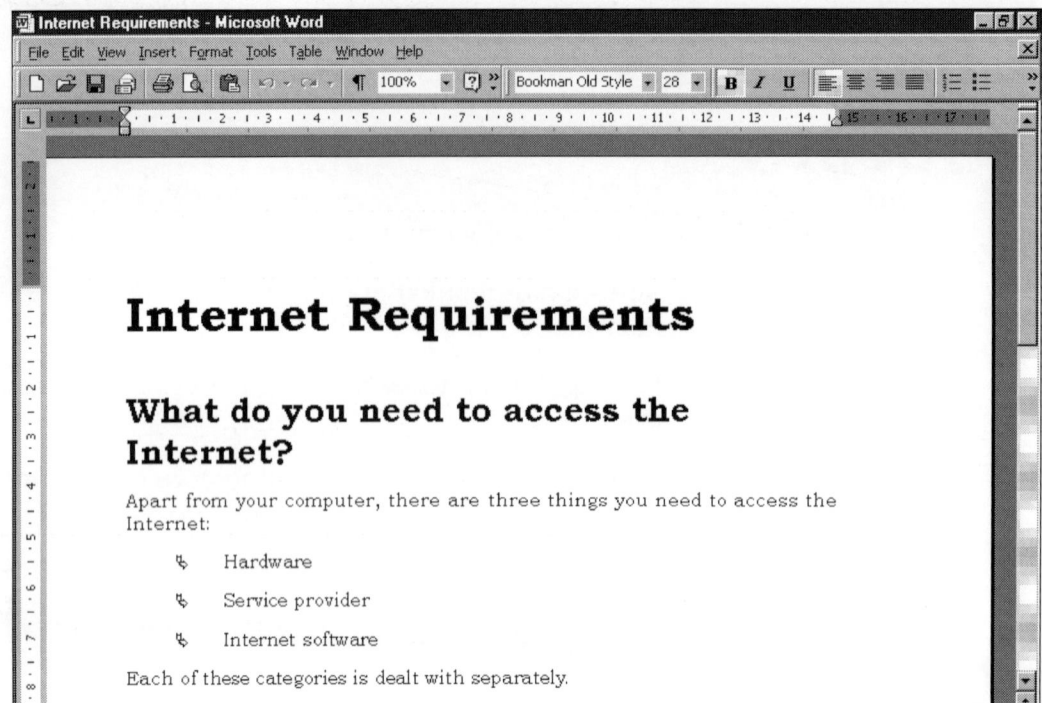

Using headers and footers

A header or footer is a section of text that is printed at the top or bottom of every page. Obvious examples would be page numbers or a company name (see the bottom of this page).

Headers and footers are similar to each other. You can set up different headers and footers on odd and even pages, and can have a different header or footer on the first page - for the title page.

In Word, headers and footers are like any other paragraphs and text, and can be centred, justified, bold, italic, etc.

- Open the **View** menu and choose **Header and Footer**.

A dotted rectangle is outlines the Header area where you can create your header. Note that there are already two tabs set up for you to use - a centre tab in the middle of the page, and a right-aligned tab at the right-hand margin.

The Header and Footer toolbar is also displayed. This has various useful buttons.

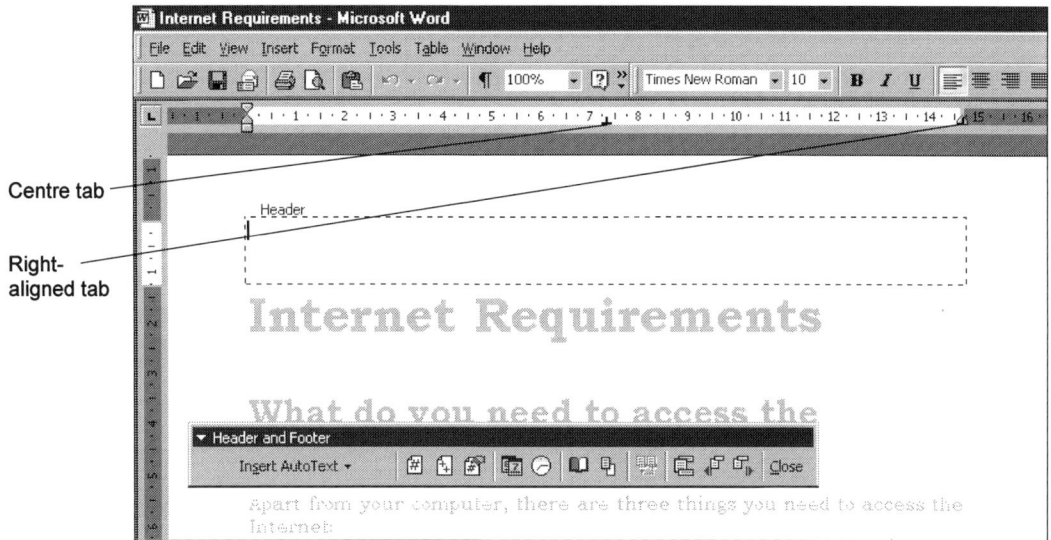

- Move the mouse pointer slowly over the buttons in the Header and Footer toolbar, without clicking them, and read what each button does.

Adding a header

Now add a header in the centre of the top of the page.

- Press **Tab** to move the insertion point to the centre of the current line.

- Type:

    Internet Requirements

Adding a footer

Now create a footer with a page number in the centre.

- Click the **Switch Between Header and Footer** button.

The Footer area at the bottom of the page is now displayed. Note that this also has two pre-set tabs.

Microsoft Word 2000 ~ Beginners Course   **235**

- Press **Tab** to move the insertion point to the centre of the current line.

- Type, with a space at the end:

  Page

Inserting a page number

To insert the current page number, just click the **Insert Page Number** button.

- In the Header and Footer toolbar, click the **Insert Page Number** button.

The header and footer are now complete.

- In the Header and Footer toolbar, click the **Close Header and Footer** button.

Use the Print Layout view to view the document as it will be printed. The document may already be displayed in this view.

- If necessary, open the **View** menu and choose **Print Layout**, or click the **Print Layout View** button.

- Use the **Page Down** key to scroll through the text – you will notice the header and footer in pale grey on each page.

Changing the header and footer

Headers and footers can be edited as normal text – once you have opened the Header and Footer areas.

- Open the **View** menu and choose **Header and Footer**, or double-click anywhere in the Header area.

- Change the header to read:

  All about the Internet

- Click the **Switch Between Header and Footer** button to switch to the footer.

- Move the insertion point to the end of the footer text and press **Enter**.
- Press **Tab** to move the insertion point to the centre of the current line.
- Click the **Insert Date** button.
- Click the **Close Header and Footer** button.

The header and footer have now been revised.

- Using **Page Down** and **Page Up,** scroll through the document to check the header and footer text.

Different on odd and even pages

Word allows you to set a different header or footer on odd and even pages. This is particularly useful when you are using double-sided printing. A sheet of paper might not need the same information on both sides or you might like to align the page numbers to the outer margin.

This is done using the Page Setup dialog box. This can be opened in two ways:

  ✎ Open the **File** menu and choose **Page Setup**

  ✎ In the Header and Footer toolbar, click the **Page Setup** button

The second method displays the Layout tab, which is what you need.

- Move the insertion point to the top of the document - press **Ctrl+Home**.
- Open the **View** menu and choose **Header and Footer,** or double-click anywhere in the Header area.
- In the Header and Footer toolbar, click the **Page Setup** button.

The Page Setup dialog box is opened showing the Layout options.

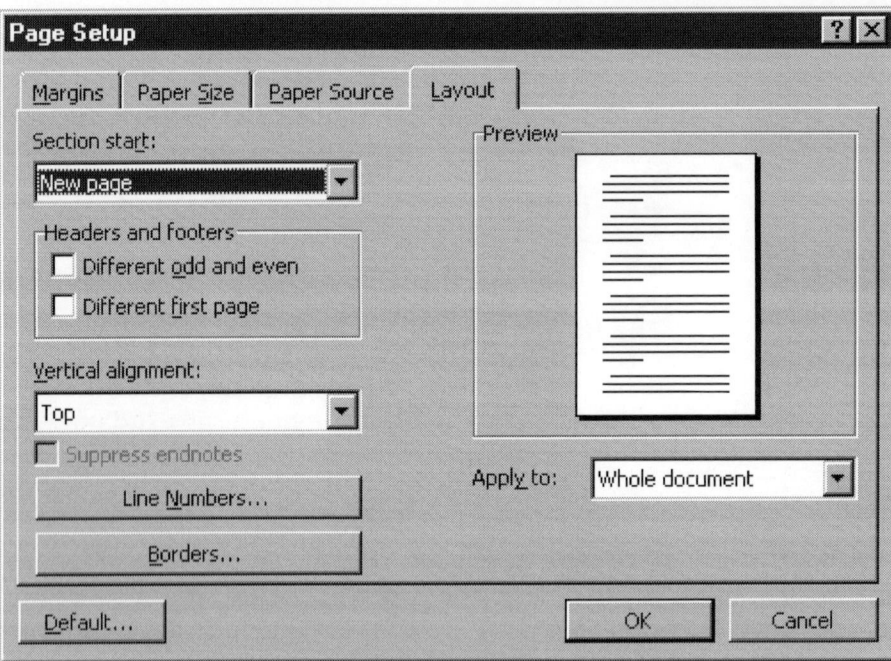

- In the Headers and Footers options, click **Different odd and even** so that it is ticked.

- Click **OK**, or press **Enter**.

You are returned to the first page of your document. The Header area now has the title Odd Page Header.

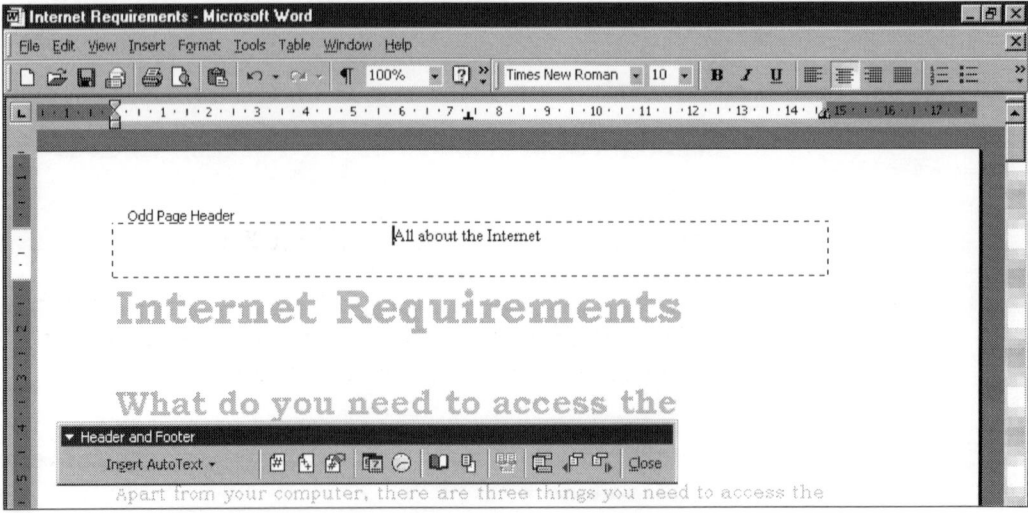

- Change the header text to **Internet Requirements**.

- In the Header and Footer toolbar, click the **Show Next** button.

The second page of the document is now displayed. The Header area has the title <u>Even Page Header</u>.

- Press **Tab** to move the insertion point to the centre of the current line.

- Type a company name:

  World-wide Communications plc

Now return to the first page and set the odd page footer.

- Click the **Show Previous** button.

- Click the **Switch Between Header and Footer** button.

The Footer area has the title <u>Odd Page Footer</u>. You will remove the date and align the page number to the right margin.

- Select the date and delete it.

- Click immediately in front of the word <u>Page</u> and then press **Tab** to move the page number to the right-hand side of the footer.

- Click the **Close Header and Footer** button.

- Use the **Page Down** key to scroll through the document.

Note that the even pages do not have footers - you only set up footers on the odd pages.

Header and footer AutoText

Word stores a list of AutoText phrases - some of which are useful for headers and footers. There are two ways of entering AutoText in a header or a footer:

- Click the **Insert AutoText** button and then choose the text you require from the drop-down list

- Start to type the required phrase - a ScreenTip will appear above the phrase; if you then press **Enter** the AutoText will be inserted and will complete your phrase

Microsoft Word 2000 ~ Beginners Course   **239**

Enter some footer text for the even pages using the **Insert AutoText** button.

- Open the **View** menu and choose **Header and Footer**.

- Switch to the Footer area.

- Click the **Show Next** button to display the Even Page Footer.

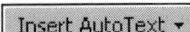
- Click the **Insert AutoText** button.

A list of header and footer AutoText is displayed.

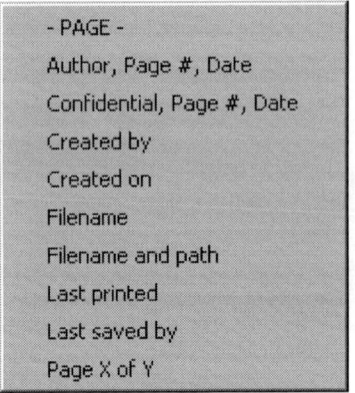

You may have noticed that when you typed Page earlier in this chapter, a ScreenTip appeared above your text showing the text Page X of Y. This was an example of AutoText.

- In the Insert AutoText list, choose **Page X of Y**.

The AutoText, Page 2 of 5, is inserted in your document.

- Click the **Close Header and Footer** button.

- Using **Page Down** and **Page Up**, scroll through the document to compare the header and footer text on odd and even pages.

- Print the third, fourth and fifth pages and notice the differences.

Different on the first page

It is also possible to set the headers and footers on the first page to be different from those in the rest of the document. This is set up in the Page Setup dialog box.

- Use **Ctrl+Home** to move the insertion point to the top of the document.

- Open the **View** menu and choose **Header and Footer**.

- In the Header and Footer toolbar, click the **Page Setup** button.

The Page Setup dialog box is opened showing the Layout options again.

- In the Headers and Footers group of options, click **Different first page** so that it is ticked.

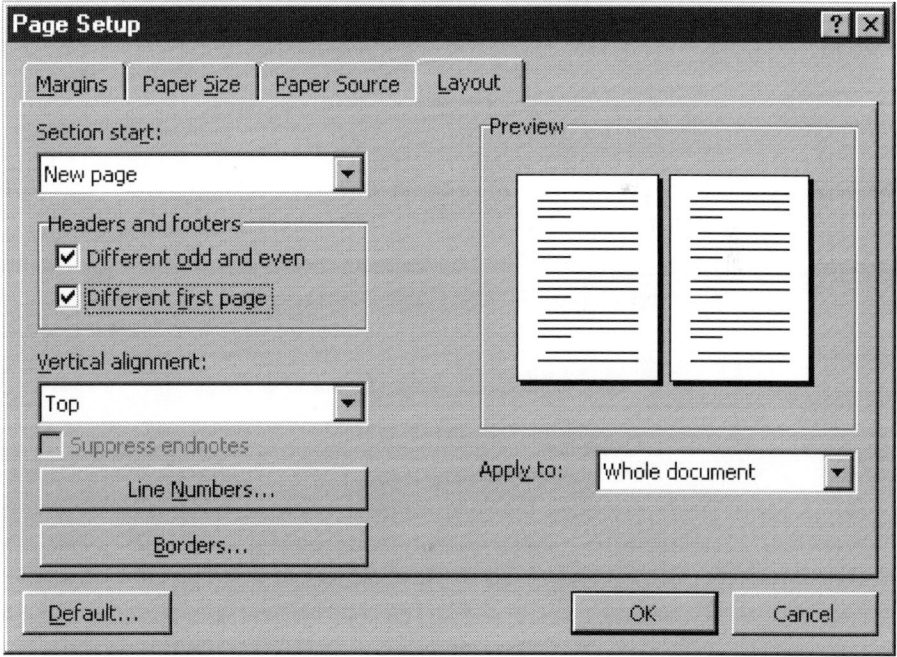

- Click **OK**, or press **Enter**.

You are returned to the first page of your document. The Header area has the title First Page Header.

- Press **Tab** to move the insertion point to the centre of the current line.

- Type:

  Internet Requirements

- Press **Enter**.

- Press **Tab** again.

- Type:

  By W S Hardy

Now move the insertion point to the first page footer and insert the current date.

- Switch to the Footer area.

- Press **Tab** to move the insertion point to the centre of the current line.

- Click the **Insert Date** button.

- Click the **Close Header and Footer** button to return to the document.

Your document will now have a different header and footer on the first page. Print the first two pages to see this.

- Print pages 1 and 2, or use Print Preview if you don't want to print them just now.

Formatting headers and footers

The font or font size of the text in a header or footer can easily be changed. First select the text. Then use the **Font** and **Font Size** list boxes to change the character style. Formatting features, such as bold, italic and underline, can also be applied in the usual manner. To format a header or footer:

- Open the **View** menu and choose **Header and Footer**

- Select the header or footer text you want to format

- Apply the character and formatting features

✎   Close the Header and Footer area

You are left to experiment with this on your own.

Ending the session

You have now completed the tutorial in this chapter. There is an additional exercise that you may wish to do before moving on to the next chapter or exiting Word. First, you should close the current document.

- Open the **File** menu and choose **Close** – choose **No** to avoid saving the changes.

- If you are not continuing directly with the extra exercise or the next chapter, open the **File** menu and choose **Exit** to exit Word.

Exercise 14a

In this exercise you will open an existing document and add headers and footers. Those on the first page will be different from those on subsequent pages.

- Open the **Accounts** document from your exercise diskette.

The margins have already been set for you.

- Open the **View** menu and choose **Header and Footer**.

- In the Header and Footer toolbar, click the **Page Setup** button.

- Click **Different First Page** so that it is ticked

- Click **OK**, or press **Enter**.

Add the first page header and format it.

- Type the header:

  COSTALOT LTD

- Format the header as **48 pt bold, italic, Times New Roman**.

Next, add the first page footer and right-align it.

- Switch to the Footer area.
- Press **Tab** twice to move the insertion point to the right-hand side of the footer.
- Insert the date.

Now add the footer for the subsequent pages.

- Click the **Show Next** button.
- Type:

  Page

- Press **Enter** to accept the AutoText Page X of Y displayed in the ScreenTip above the text.
- Press **Tab** twice to move the insertion point to the right-hand side of the footer.
- Insert the date.

Finally, add the header for the subsequent pages and format it.

- Switch to the Header area.
- Type the header:

  COSTALOT LTD

- Format the header as **24 pt, bold, italic, Times New Roman**.

- Close the Header and Footer area.
- Use Print Preview to view the document, or print it if you wish.
- Close the document without saving the changes.

The first page should resemble the next picture.

Summary ~ Headers & Footers

A header or footer is a section of text that is printed at the top or bottom of every page.

To add a header and a footer

Open the **View** menu and choose **Header and Footer**. Type the header text you require. There are two pre-set tabs in the header and footer areas that you can use for centring or right-aligning the header and footer texts.

To move the insertion point to the footer, click the **Switch Between Header and Footer** button in the Header and Footer toolbar. Then type the footer text you require.

Inserting page numbers or the date

To insert the current page number or the date, position the insertion point where it is required and click the **Insert Page Number** or the **Insert Date** button in the Header and Footer toolbar. You can also click the **Insert AutoText** button and choose a date or page number format from the list of AutoText.

Different on odd and even pages

To have a different header or footer on odd and even pages, choose the **Different odd and even** option in the Layout tab of the Page Setup dialog box - to open the dialog box, click the **Page Setup** button in the Header and Footer toolbar.

Type in the odd and even header and footer texts, using the **Show Next**, **Show Previous** and **Switch Between Header and Footer** buttons in the Header and Footer toolbar to move from one to the other.

Different on the first page

To have a different header or footer on the first page, choose the **Different first page** option in the Layout tab of the Page Setup dialog box - to open the dialog box, click the **Page Setup** button in the Header and Footer toolbar.

Type in the first page header and footer texts, clicking the **Switch Between Header and Footer** button in the Header and Footer toolbar to move from one to the other.

Formatting headers and footers

Headers and footers can be formatted just like normal text. Select the header or footer text and apply the desired font and paragraph formatting features.

Notes

Use this page to make notes of your own.

Page #   Notes

Notes

Use this page to make notes of your own.

Page #   Notes

Chapter 15 ~ Addressing Envelopes & Labels

In this chapter you will learn about:

> Printing an address on an envelope

> Printing an address on a label

It is assumed that:

> You have a printer installed and ready to print

Word provides an easy method of addressing envelopes and labels.

> *You may not wish to follow the instructions in this chapter in their entirety just now, if you don't intend to print an envelope or label.*

Getting started

- If necessary, start Word.

- If the Office Assistant is displayed, right-click it and choose **Hide**.

- Make sure your exercise diskette is in drive A.

- Open the **File** menu and choose **Open**, or click the **Open** button in the Standard toolbar, or just press **Ctrl+O**.

The Open dialog box is displayed.

- In the File name box, type:

    `a:Envelope`

- Click **Open**, or press **Enter**.

The Envelope document is opened.

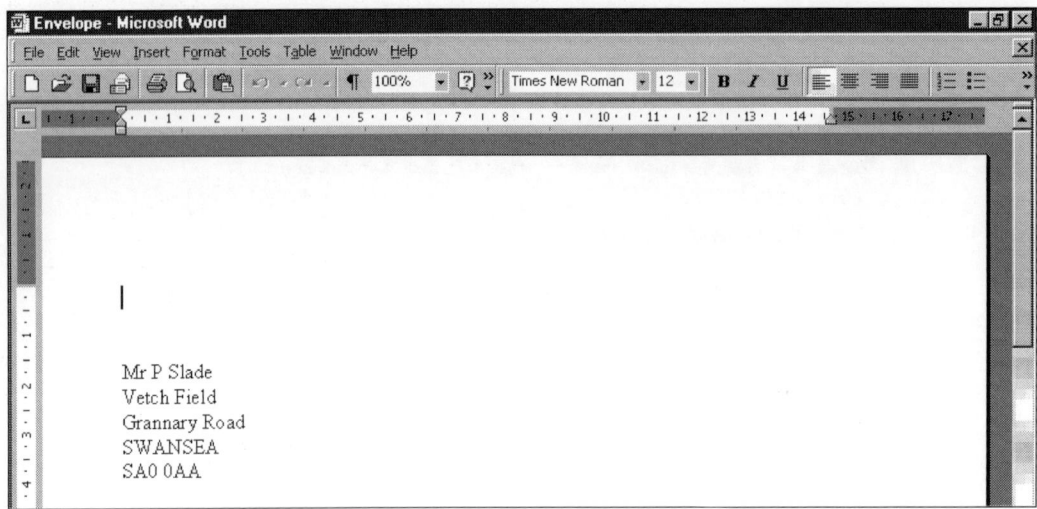

Addressing envelopes

When addressing an envelope, you can simply type in the name and address, or if it already exists in your document, Word can extract it for you.

- Select the name and address at the top of the letter.

- Open the **Tools** menu and choose **Envelopes and Labels**.

The Envelopes and Labels dialog box is opened.

- If necessary, click the **Envelopes** tab.

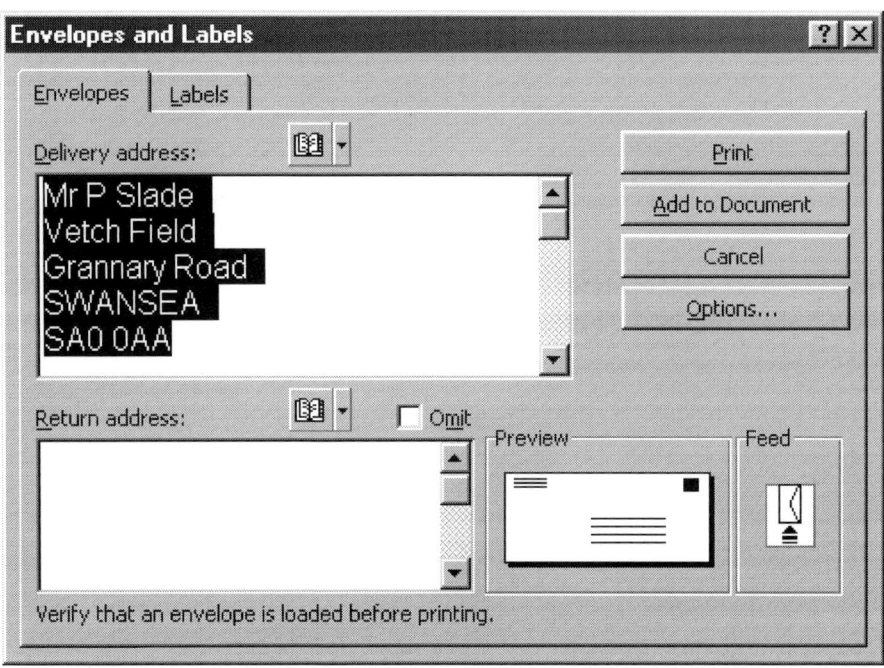

Notice that Word has automatically filled in the address for you. There is also a box for your return address.

Changing the delivery address

You can change the delivery address if you wish. This means that you can use the Envelope feature at any time if you want to address an envelope.

Envelope options

When setting up an address for an envelope, there are two tabs that control the settings:

- **Envelope Options** - where you can choose an envelope type, and position the delivery and return addresses

- **Printing Options** - where you can choose how the envelope is to be fed into your printer

The instructions that follow will act only as a guide, you may have to set the options to suit your own stationery and printer.

- Click the **Options** button.

- If necessary, click the **Envelope Options** tab to show these options.

The Envelope Options are displayed.

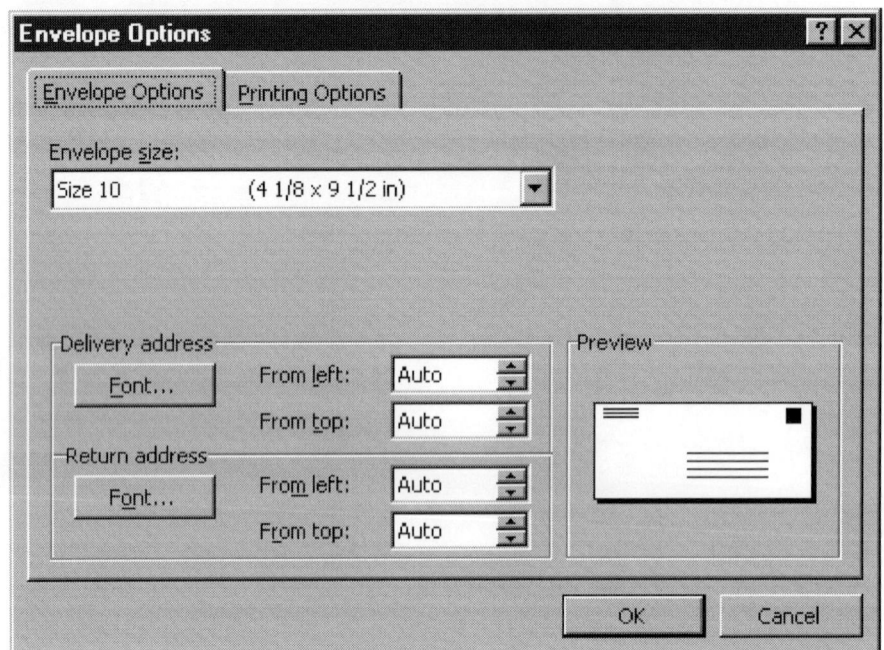

- Make any changes necessary to match your envelopes.

- Click the **Printing Options** tab to show these options.

The Printing Options are displayed.

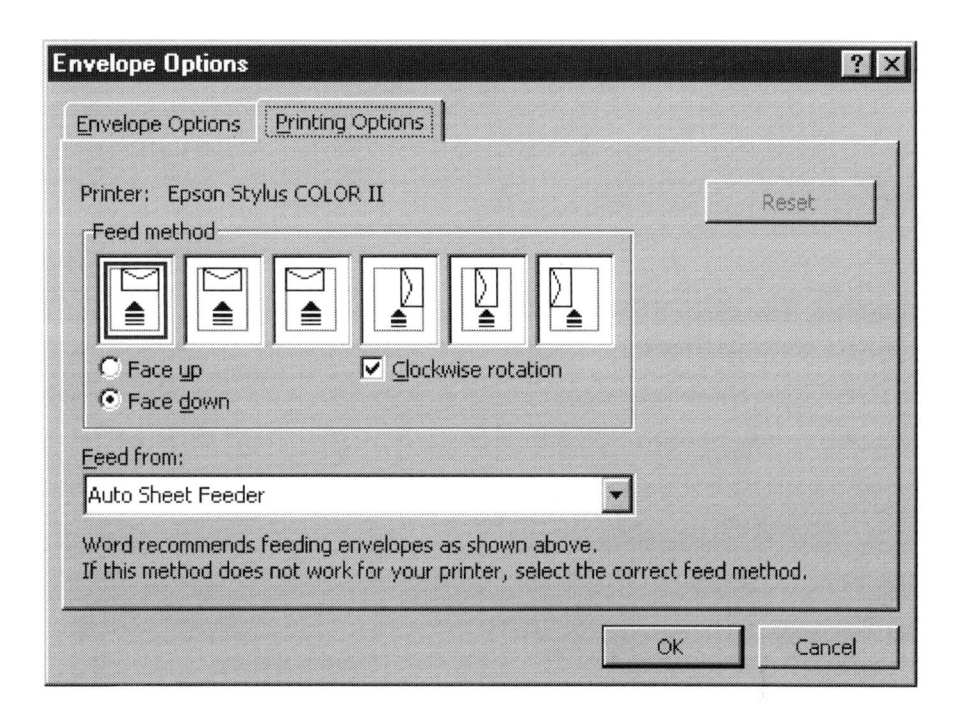

- Make any changes necessary to suit your printer.

- Click **OK**, or press **Enter**.

The return address

You can also add a return address that will be printed on the envelope, or choose to omit it.

- If necessary, click the **Omit** option so that it is not ticked.

- Edit the Return address to whatever you want.

- If you wish to omit the return address, click the **Omit** option so that it is ticked.

Printing the envelope

It is now time to print the envelope.

- Click **Print** to print the envelope or, if you do not want to print it now, click **Add to Document**, then use Print Preview to view the document.

Microsoft Word 2000 ~ Beginners Course **253**

Labels

Address labels can be printed in exactly the same way.

- Make sure the address is still selected.
- Open the **Tools** menu and choose **Envelopes and Labels,** then click the **Labels** tab.

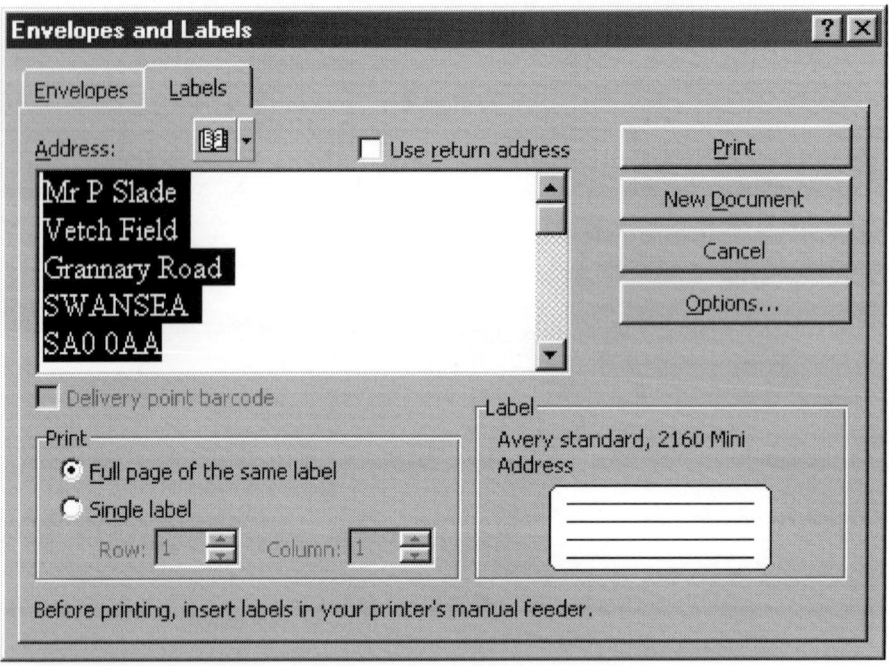

Once again, you can edit the address. You also need to decide whether to print a single label, or a full page of the same label.

- Make any changes necessary to match your requirements.

Label options

Once again there are some options available.

- Click the **Options** button.

The Label Options dialog box is displayed.

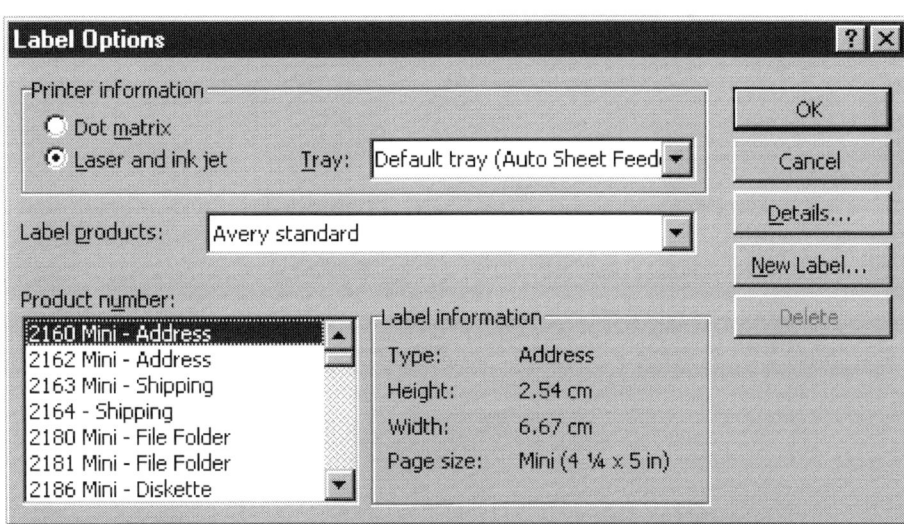

Make any changes necessary to suit your printer and labels.

- Choose **Dot matrix** or **Laser and ink jet** printer.

- Choose the correct Label products option, i.e., the label manufacturer.

- Choose the correct Product number, i.e., the actual label you will be using.

- Click **OK**, or press **Enter**.

You can choose whether to view the labels as a new document or to print them straight away. Do one of the following:

- To view the page of labels first, click **New Document** and use Print Layout view. Then if you want to print them, check you have the right paper loaded and click the **Print** button in the Standard toolbar.

- To print the labels without viewing them first, click **Print** in the Envelopes and Labels dialog box.

- If you don't want to print the labels, click **Cancel** to close the dialog box without printing.

Microsoft Word 2000 ~ Beginners Course **255**

Ending the session

You have now completed the tutorial in this chapter. There are three additional exercises that you may wish to do before moving on to the final chapter or exiting Word. First, you should close the current document.

- Open the **File** menu and choose **Close** – choose **No** to avoid saving the changes.

- If you are not continuing directly with the extra exercises or the next chapter, open the **File** menu and choose **Exit**.

Exercise 15a

In this exercise you will address an envelope.

- Open a new blank document.

- Open the **Tools** menu and choose **Envelopes and Labels**.

- Click the **Envelopes** tab, and then type the following Delivery address:

  Mr J McGray
  The Barn
  Tiswell
  READING
  RD4 6PP

- Click the **Options** button and change the envelope size to **C5**.

The Preview area shows that the address will be printed near the bottom of the envelope. You will change this.

- In the Delivery address options, change the value in the From top box to **7.5 cm**.

Now choose to either print or view the envelope.

- If you want to print an envelope – click the **Printing Options** tab and choose the correct Feed method option – then click **OK** to return to the Envelopes dialog box and click **Print**.

- If you just want to view the envelope, click **OK** to close the Envelope Options dialog box, then click the **Add to Document** button.

- View the document in the Print Layout view.

- Close the document without saving it.

Exercise 15b

In this exercise you will address multiple labels.

- Open a new blank document.

- Open the **Tools** menu and choose **Envelopes and Labels**.

- Click the **Labels** tab, and then type the following Address:

  Mr F Parsons
  12 King Street
  Stratton
  SWINDON
  SN5 3QW

- Choose the **Full page of the same label** option.

- Click the **Options** button and choose suitable options in the Label products and Product number list boxes - if available, try **Avery standard** and a product for **Mini-Shipping**.

- Click **OK**, or press **Enter**, to return to the Envelopes and Labels dialog box.

Now choose to either print or view the labels.

- If you want to print the page of labels, click the **Print** button.

- If you want to view the page of labels, click **New Document** and use the Print Layout view.

- Close the document(s) without saving them.

Exercise 15c

In this exercise you will address a single label.

- Open a new blank document.

- Open the **Tools** menu and choose **Envelopes and Labels**.

- Type the following Address:

  Mr R Stones
  28 Birdwood Close
  Tythe
  WOLVERHAMPTON
  WL7 7JZ

- Choose the **Single label** option.

- Click the **Options** button and choose suitable options in the Label products and Product number list boxes – if available, try **Avery standard** and a product for **Mini-Shipping**.

- Click **Print** to print the label, or **Cancel** to close the dialog box without printing.

- Close the document without saving it.

Summary ~ Addressing Envelopes & Labels

Addressing envelopes

Word can extract an address from a document and position it on an envelope for you:

- Select the address in the document
- Open the **Tools** menu and choose **Envelopes and Labels**
- Click the **Envelopes** tab

The address is inserted in the Envelopes and Labels dialog box together with your return address.

To choose the envelope size and how your printer feeds envelopes:

- Click the **Options** button
- Click the **Envelope Options** tab and set the envelope size
- Click the **Printing Options** tab and choose the feed option
- Click **OK**
- Click **Print** to print the envelope

Labels

Labels can be printed in a similar way by choosing the relevant label options:

- Select the address in the document
- Open the **Tools** menu and choose **Envelopes and Labels**
- Click the **Labels** tab
- Set the options you require

The address is automatically inserted.

To choose the printer type and the type of label you are using:

- Choose to print a full page of labels, or a single label
- Click the **Options** button
- Set the printer type and label type
- Click **OK**
- Click **Print** to print the label

Notes

Use this page to make notes of your own.

Page #   Notes

Chapter 16 ~ A Final Exercise

This last chapter is dedicated to an exercise where you will create a letter with its accompanying envelope. You will use many of the skills you have learnt in this course.

It is assumed that you know how to:

- Create and save a new document
- Create an envelope and add it to a document
- Use various font sizes and styles
- Use default tabs
- Use numbered bullets
- Use the alignment buttons
- Create headers and footers
- Change page margins using Page Setup

The picture on page 262 shows what you are trying to create.

Creating the letter

First of all, open a new document.

- Open a new document by clicking the **New Blank Document** button, or pressing **Ctrl+N**.

Next, set up the page margins.

- Open the **File** menu and choose **Page Setup**.
- If necessary, click the **Margins** tab.
- Set the following margins:

    ```
    Top       5 cm (or 2 in)
    Bottom    4 cm (or 1.5 in)
    Left      2.5 cm (or 1 in)
    Right     2.5 cm (or 1 in)
    ```

- Click **OK**.

Microsoft Word 2000 ~ Beginners Course **261**

PC SUPPLIES LTD

P Archer
Marketing Director
PC Supplies Limited
BRADFORD
LE54 7PS

Today's date

Dear Mr Archer

<u>SUPPLY TOTALS FOR CURRENT QUARTER</u>

Further to our meeting last week, the details of Supply Tools for our primary products have been collated for this quarter as displayed below.

You should note that in addition to this information:

1. Our general performance with regard to supply lead-times has improved by 20%, bringing us to an average lead-time of 4 working days for the majority of consumables.
2. Our quality control has not shown such a marked improvement. Our suppliers have been informed of our dissatisfaction and we are seeking alternative vendors.
3. Our stockholding continues to increase in line with our target to improve on delivery lead-times - this will obviously have to be addressed as it is tying up vital company capital. Any assistance you can offer in this matter would be most appreciated.

<u>Statistics for Major Supply Items</u>

Item	Code	Number Purchased	Number Sold
Floppy Discs	548	1298	1102
Avery Labels	341	900	765
Toner Cartridges	450	400	386
Print Cartridges	430	300	256
Printer Ribbons	420	200	199

I look forward to discussing this information with you at our scheduled meeting next week.

Yours sincerely
R Sommersby
Sales Executive
For and on behalf of PC Supplies Limited (Surrey)

PC Supplies Limited, Middleton, Surrey S54 3LP
Tel:01234-567890 Fax:01234-567891

Adding the header and footer

Now add the company name as a header.

- Open the **View** menu and choose **Header and Footer**.

- Type:

  PC SUPPLIES LTD

- Format the header as **36 pt, bold, italic, Times New Roman**.

Next, add the company name and address as a footer.

- Switch to the Footer area.

- Press **Tab** once to position the insertion point in the centre of the footer.

- Type - pressing **Enter** after the first line:

  PC Supplies Limited, Middleton, SURREY S54 3LP
  Tel:01234-567890 Fax:01234-567891

- Format both lines of the footer as **10 pt, italic, Times New Roman**.

The header and footer are now complete.

- Close the Header and Footer area.

Entering the text

You will now type the main body of text. The font used throughout most of the letter is 10 pt Times New Roman.

- Type the name and address:

  P Archer
  Marketing Director
  PC Supplies Limited
  BRADFORD
  LE54 7PS

- Press **Enter** twice.

- Type today's date and right-align it.

Microsoft Word 2000 ~ Beginners Course **263**

- Press **Enter** three times.
- Type the salutation:

Dear Mr Archer

- Press **Enter** twice to create a blank line.
- Type the title:

SUPPLY TOTALS FOR CURRENT QUARTER

- Select the title and format it as **12 pt**, **bold**, **underlined**, then centre it.

- Press **Enter** twice to create a blank line.

- Make sure the font is set to **10 pt** regular (i.e., not **bold**, not *italic*, not **underlined**).

- Click the **Justify** button to justify remaining text.

- Type the rest of the letter as shown on page 262 keeping the following points in mind:

  - Add blank lines to space out the document

  - Apply numbered bullets for the points in the letter AFTER you have typed the text - don't type the numbers, use the **Numbering** button

  - The title for the list, Statistics for Major Supply Items, should be bold, underlined and centre-aligned

  - Use the default tabs to set up the lists of items

  - The sender's name, **R Sommersby**, should be in bold

Saving the letter

- When you are happy with your letter, save it on your exercise diskette as **a:Ex16a**.

Addressing the envelope

Having created your letter, you will now create an envelope for it.

- In the document, select the recipient's name and address.
- Open the **Tools** menu and choose **Envelopes and Labels**.
- If necessary, click the **Envelopes** tab.

The name and address should be automatically copied to the Delivery address box.

- Click **Add to Document**.

Printing the document

Finally, you can save and print the document.

- Save the document again - **Ctrl+S**.
- When you are ready, print the document and envelope, or use Print Preview to view them.

Ending the session

Congratulations! You have now completed this chapter and the whole of the *Microsoft Word 2000 Beginners Course*. Close the current document and exit Word.

- Open the **File** menu and choose **Close**.
- Open the **File** menu and choose **Exit** to exit Word.

> ☞ *Remember to remove your exercise diskette from the computer.*

Notes

Use this page to make notes of your own.

Page #   Notes

Appendix A ~ Windows Basics

This appendix is mostly about Windows 95 and 98. It will introduce you to some of the most basic concepts. If you have Windows 95 you can follow the instructions in this lesson. You will find that most of the details for Windows 95 also match Windows 98.

> ☝ *The screen shots shown in this appendix are taken from a computer displaying 800 x 600 pixels. The content of some screen shots may not exactly replicate what you see on your screen, but the main details will be alike.*

DOS

From the beginning, computers had DOS (Disk Operative System). The user was presented with a more or less blank screen and had to type in commands for the computer to follow.

A typical blank DOS screen

Common commands included:

- COPY – to copy files from one place to another
- FORMAT – to prepare diskettes for use
- DEL – to delete files

To run a program, you had to type in the name of the program's .EXE file, or .BAT file.

Later versions of DOS had a *DOS Shell* program to make it easier to handle files.

A typical DOS Shell screen

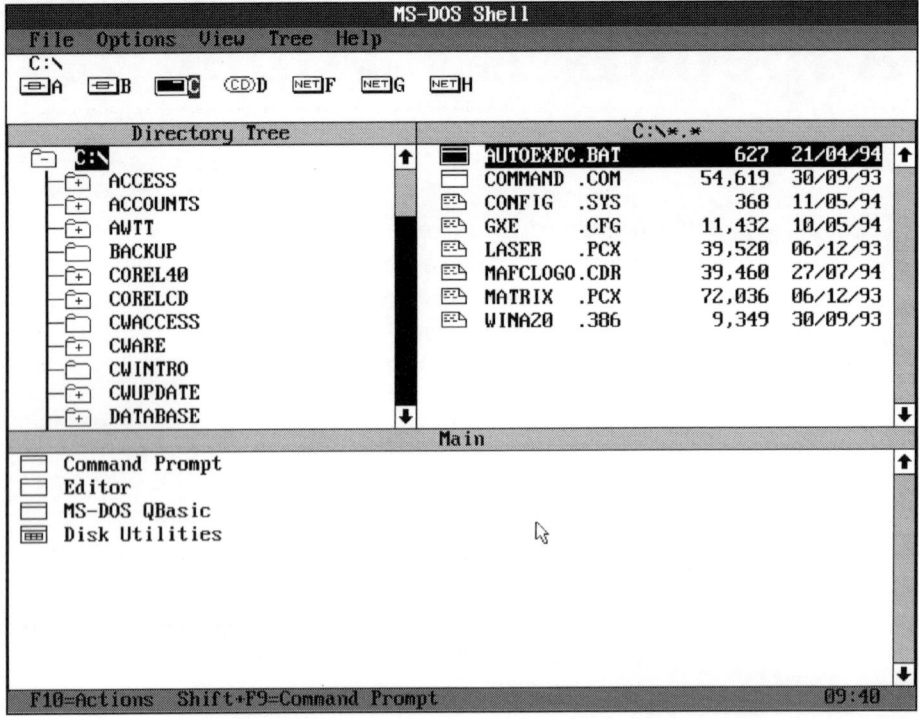

Some modern programs are still based around DOS. For the sake of backward compatibility, all versions of Windows have a DOS mode or DOS window for you to run DOS programs in.

The arrival of Windows

The arrival of Windows heralded a new era in computing. The blank screen and DOS commands were replaced by a *graphical user interface* (GUI). Instead of having to type in commands, you could now use the mouse to point at icons and double-click them to run programs.

A typical blank Windows 3.11 screen

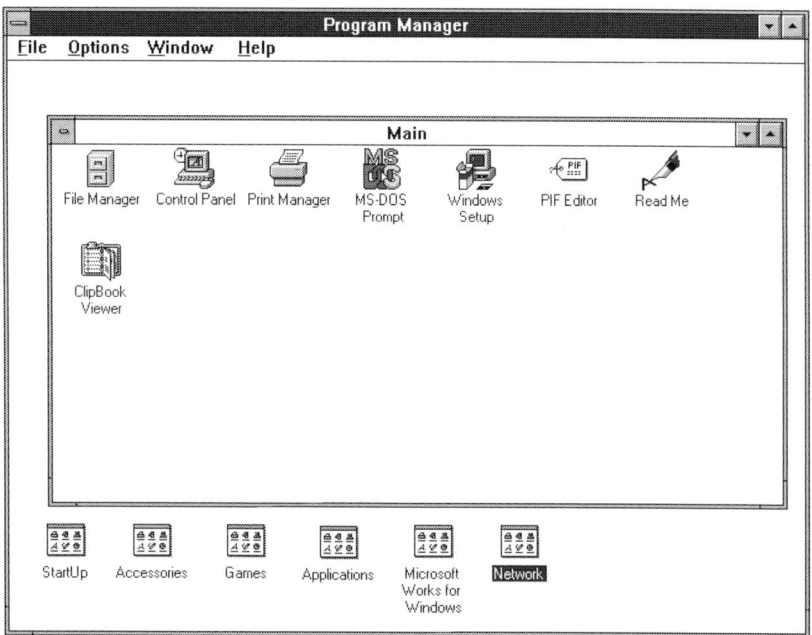

Up to and including Windows 3.11, you still needed to have DOS installed on your computer.

The main problem with Windows was the ever-increasing need for more memory, more storage space and a faster computer. Whereas early versions of DOS ran comfortably on as little as 256 kb of memory, Windows 3.11 required 4 Mb – 16 times as much!

Other problems of compatibility, memory size and storage limits eventually led to the DOS/Windows combination being replaced.

Windows 95 & 98

Windows 95 does not need DOS installed – it has become an operating system in its own right. Many of the problems that arose with the earlier DOS/Windows combinations have been eliminated.

The user interface was changed completely from Windows 3.11 with most operations being simplified.

Some of the main changes include:

> ✎ The introduction of the **Start** button as a simple method of launching programs

Microsoft Word 2000 ~ Beginners Course **269**

- The introductions of the Taskbar at the foot of the screen allowing you to easily swap between open windows and programs that are running

- Pnp – *plug and play* for easy installation of add-in cards and other peripherals

- Long file names

Pnp – plug and play

Installing new peripherals and add-in cards had always been difficult in DOS and Windows. You needed to learn about *interrupt requests* (IRQs) and other technical details. However, with Windows 95 came *plug and play* (pnp) technology.

With pnp, much of the hardware installation process is done automatically for you. If you are installing a pnp network card, Windows will automatically search for and set up IRQs, etc.

Long file names

In DOS and Windows up to version 3.11, the length of filenames was restricted to 8 characters followed by a 3-character extension to identify the type of file it was. While everyone got used to this limit, there is no doubt that if you had hundreds of files, the filenames eventually became more and more cryptic, for example:

- FAX0701.DOC
  LETT3.DOC
  SLSJAN96.XLS

With Windows 95, filenames can be up to 256 characters in length making it very easy to give files meaningful names, for example:

- Fax to J Smith
  Thank you letter
  Sales report Jan-97

Windows 98

In many ways, Windows 98 is just a faster and improved version of Windows 95. Most of the layout and features remain the same. The main difference is the improved connectivity to the Internet.

Starting Windows 95

> *From this point on, the instructions refer to Windows 95, but will work equally well with Windows 98.*

Windows 95 will start automatically when you start your computer.

- `Start your computer.`

Depending on the speed of your computer, it may take quite a while for Windows to start. If it is the first time you are starting Windows after having installed it, there may be an even longer delay.

After a short while, you may get a dialog box called Enter Network Password (see picture below). This is displayed if you are on a network. If you are not on a network and the dialog box is not displayed, you can skip the next section about logging on.

Logging on

If you are on a network, the Enter Network Password dialog box will be displayed.

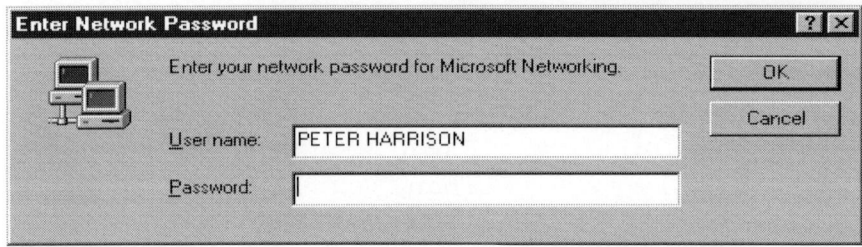

You need to type in your user name and password - the User name box may already have a name in it, but you can change it.

- If you do not want to log on now, click the **Cancel** button - you can then skip the rest of this section.

If you need to change the user name you can click the User name box, delete the current entry using the **Delete** and/or **Backspace** keys, then type in the desired user name.

- If necessary, change the name in the User name box.

- In the Password box, type your password - whatever you type, each character will appear as an asterisk (*).

- Press **Enter**, or click **OK** to continue.

Windows 95 should now be started.

The Welcome screen

The Welcome screen may now be shown. However, it is possible that a previous user may have turned off the Welcome screen, in which case it is not shown.

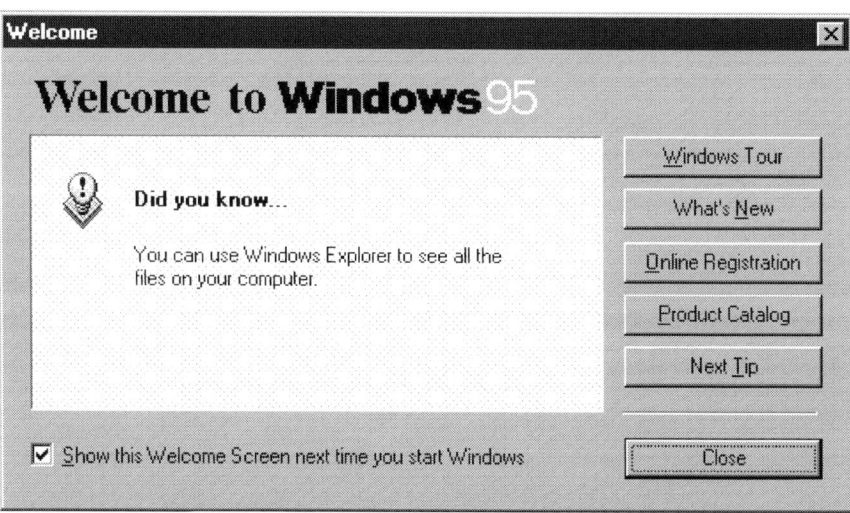

The Welcome screen provides useful tips for beginners. You can also start the Windows Tour (this requires the original Windows CD-ROM) and get other information.

If you want to try the Windows Tour, or any of the other options, you can do so now.

- If you wish to run the Windows Tour, make sure you have your original Windows 95 CD-ROM in your CD-ROM drive, then click the **Windows Tour** button. Follow the instructions on screen.

- If you do not wish to display the Welcome dialog box each time Windows starts up, click the Show this Welcome Screen next time you start Windows option so that it is not ticked.

☑ *Option selected*
☐ *Option not selected*

When you are ready, close the Welcome screen as follows:

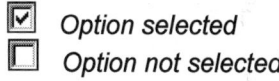
- Click the **Close** button.

The Welcome screen is now closed. You are left with the Windows Desktop.

Microsoft Word 2000 ~ Beginners Course **273**

> ✋ *It is possible that your Windows program has been set up to start in a different way. For example, it may automatically start a particular program. If this happens, you may need to close any opened programs - you may need help to do this.*

The Desktop

The Desktop is the name given to the main screen now displayed:

> ✋ *Remember: Your screen display may not exactly match the next screen shot.*

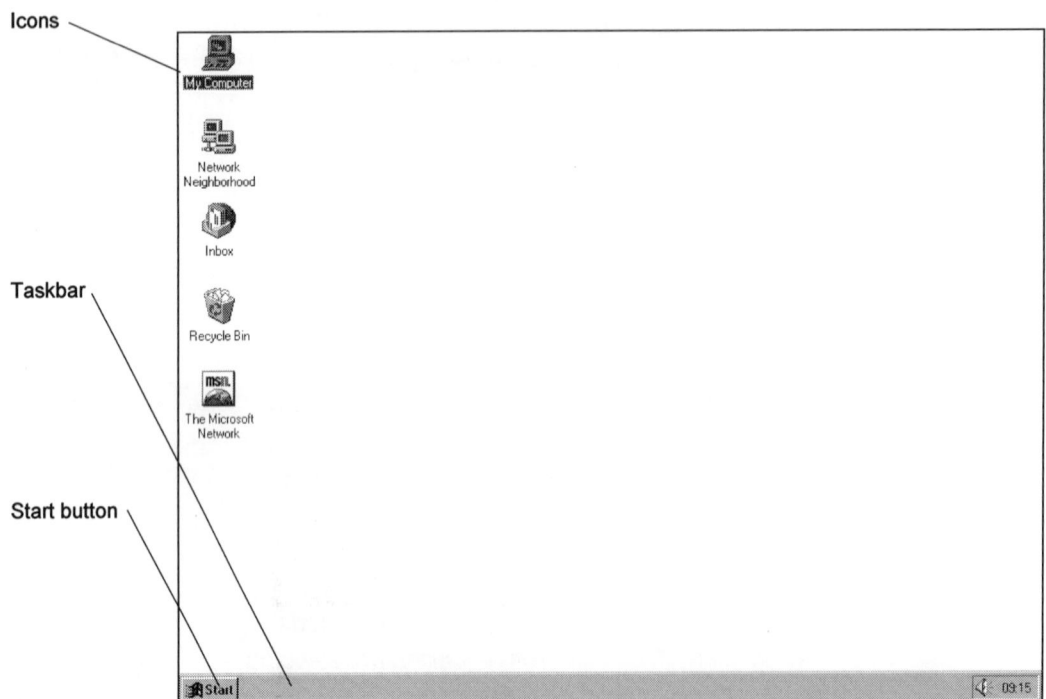

Here is a brief explanation of those items named above:

➢ **The Taskbar**: As you start programs, a button for each started program will appear in the Taskbar. You can then click one of these buttons to swap to that program, just like changing channels on a TV. For Windows 3.x users, this is like the Task List. The right-hand edge of the Taskbar will probably show a clock.

↳ **The Start button**: The **Start** button is used to start programs. Clicking the **Start** button opens a list of menus. You can then work your way through the menu system to find the desired program. For Windows 3.x users, this replaces Program Manager.

↳ **Icons**: Icons on the Desktop can represent folders, programs or documents. Double-click an icon to open the folder, start the program or open the document it represents.

The Start button

The **Start** button is used to launch programs. You will now use it to start the Paint program.

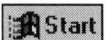

- Click the **Start** button.

The Start menu is displayed.

Notice that some of the options in the Start menu have a small arrow beside them. These are sometimes referred to as *folders*. Choosing such a menu option will open a sub-menu.

To open a folder, or menu, you can:

   ↳ Click the desired option

   ↳ Just point to the desired option

   ↳ Use the **Arrow Up** and **Arrow Down** keys to highlight the desired option, then press the **Arrow Right** key

If you are used to using Windows 3.x, you may find yourself clicking the menu options. That's OK, but you don't have to click!

- `Using the mouse, point to` **Programs**.

The Programs folder is displayed. Again some of the options will be folders.

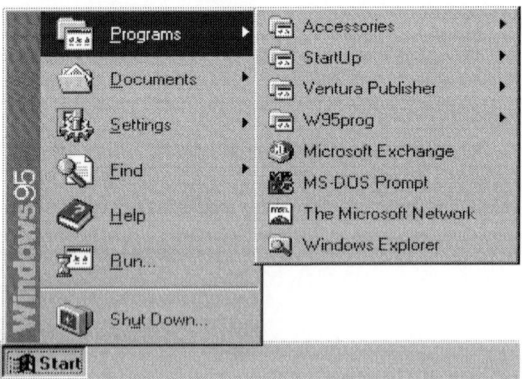

If you let the mouse pointer wander over the menu options, the menus will change, but you can always point to the desired menu option again. The Paint program is in the Accessories menu, so:

- `In the Programs menu, point to` **Accessories**.

The Accessories menu is displayed.

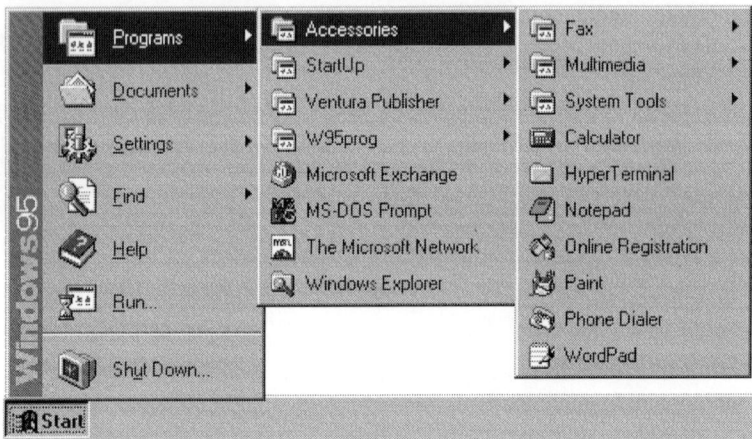

This time the Paint option is in the menu. To start the program you must click **Paint**.

- `Click` **Paint**.

276 Microsoft Word 2000 ~ Beginners Course

The Paint program is started.

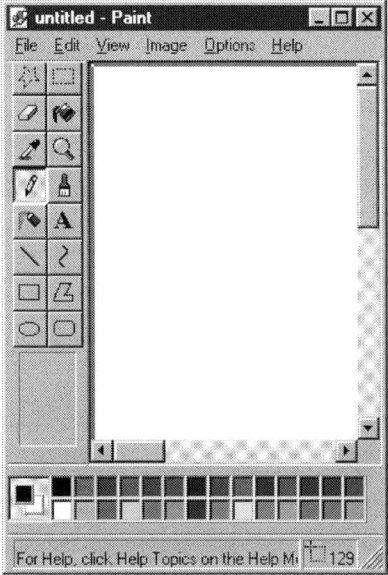

The actual size and position of the Paint program window may vary depending on whether it has been used before or not. It may even fill the complete screen.

In the same way, you will now start the WordPad program:

- Click the **Start** button.

- Point to **Programs**.

- Point to **Accessories**.

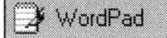
- In the Accessories menu, click **WordPad**.

The WordPad program is started. You now have two programs running at the same time. The next picture shows the two windows open.

The Taskbar

Each time you start a program, a button for that program appears in the Taskbar.

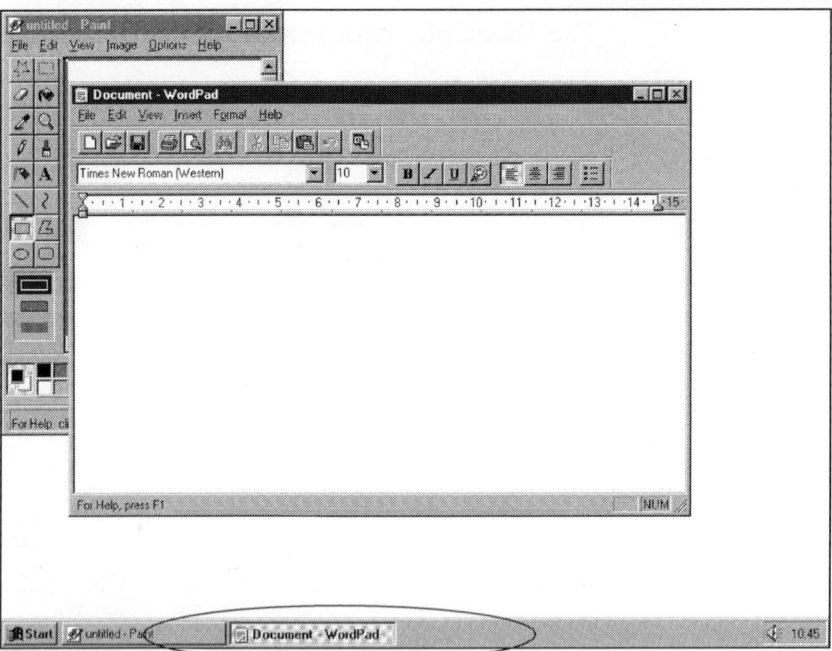

The Taskbar is used to change between programs.

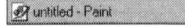

- In the Taskbar, click the **untitled - Paint** button.

The Paint program is displayed on top.

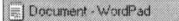

- In the Taskbar, click the **Document - WordPad** button.

The WordPad program is displayed on top.

Closing programs

There are many ways of closing a program. You will now close the Paint and WordPad programs using the simplest method.

- In the top right-hand corner of the WordPad window, click the small **Close** button.

> ♪ *If, for any reason, you have typed something in the document, Windows will show a dialog box asking you if you wish to save the changes made to the document. If this happens, click **No** to continue without saving the document.*

The WordPad program is closed and its button removed from the Taskbar. Now close the Paint program in the same way:

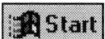
- In the top right-hand corner of the Paint window, click the small **Close** button.

The Paint program is closed and its button removed from the Taskbar.

Shutting Down

When you have finished working with Windows you need to shut it down. It is very important to follow the proper shut-down procedure to make sure Windows can save your work on the hard disk. If you just switch off your computer you could lose or damage files.

Shut down Windows as follows:

- Click the **Start** button.

The Start menu is displayed.

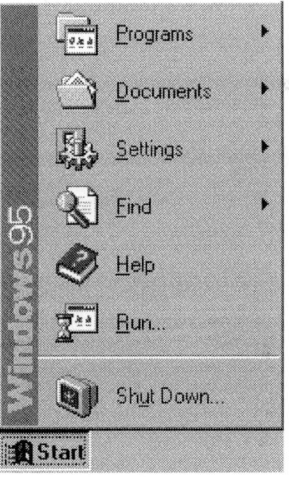

- Click **Shut Down**.

The Shut Down Windows dialog box is displayed.

Microsoft Word 2000 ~ Beginners Course **279**

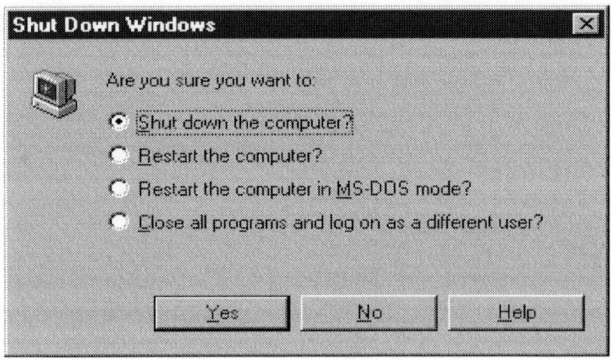

You have several different options. In this case, you want to shut down the computer.

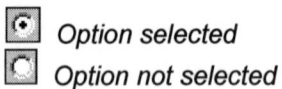

- Make sure the Shut down the computer option is selected - if not, click the Shut down the computer option.

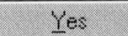

- Click the **Yes** button.

Do not switch off your computer yet.

Windows will show the following messages:

First (if you have a fast computer, this message may just last a second or two):

    ↳ Please wait while your computer shuts down

Then:

    ↳ It's now safe to turn off your computer

When this second message is displayed, you can switch off your computer.

- Switch off your computer now.

Notes

Use this page to make notes of your own.

Page #   Notes

Notes

Use this page to make notes of your own.

Page #   Notes

The PC User Certificate Series

At last you can learn to use a particular software package at home, at work or through a training provider, and then take a short assessment test to gain a certificate that is recognised nationally. Certification normally costs between £20 and £25. For more information contact:

> Phone, normal office hours and ansafone: 01635 529193
> Fax: 01635 46512
> E-mail: kol@newbury-college.ac.uk
> Web site for complete listing of certificate titles, new developments and send-back enquiry form: http://www.newbury-college.ac.uk/kol/pcuser1.htm

The certification process is outlined below.

1. Study the course
Learn your chosen software program using one of *Peter Harrison's PC Training Courseware* packages. This can be done at your own pace, on any PC - at home, at work, or through a training provider.

2. Register for the assessment
Fill in the registration provided and send or fax it together with the *appropriate* fee to the designated assessment centre. You will receive the assessment pack within a few days. To save time, you can register before you have finished studying the course.

3. Do the assessment test
You can do the assessment test on any PC - at home, at work, or through a training provider. You will need to answer some questions on paper and save some practical tasks on disk. The assessment will normally take between 1 and 3 hours to complete.

4. Return the assessment pack
When you have completed the assessment tasks, you should return the required documents and disks to the assessment centre.

5. Get your certificate
You should be notified of your result within 14 days. A Statement of Competence and an official certificate will follow. If you fail, you can retake all or part of the assessment when you are ready.

Q&A about the PC User Certificate series

Who developed the PC User Certificate series?
Newbury College has developed the PC User Certificate series.

Who validates the certificate?
The *Southern Regional Council for Education and Training*, which is recognised as a validating body by the Department for Education and Employment, validates the PC User Certificate series.

What does the qualification lead to?
A PC User Certificate provides you with evidence of competence, which you can use to gain NVQs, thereby increasing your employment opportunities.

Where does the assessment take place and what does it include?
The assessment test can be taken on any computer - at home, at work, or at a training centre. It is based on real tasks and includes a multiple-choice section and practical exercises to be saved on disk.

The PC Crash Course Series

For details about the **PC User Certificate Series**, check the previous page. The ISBN numbers and the titles of books available in the PC Crash Course Series are shown below.

General & Microsoft Windows
187300530X	Computers & the Internet Beginners
1873005318	Microsoft Windows 98 Beginners

Microsoft Office 97
1873005326	Microsoft Word 97 Beginners
1873005334	Microsoft Word 97 Intermediate
1873005342	Microsoft Word 97 Advanced
1873005350	Microsoft Excel 97 Beginners
1873005369	Microsoft Excel 97 Intermediate
1873005377	Microsoft Excel 97 Advanced
1873005385	Microsoft PowerPoint 97 Beginners
1873005393	Microsoft PowerPoint 97 Intermediate
1873005415	Microsoft Access 97 Beginners for Users
1873005423	Microsoft Access 97 Beginners for Developers
1873005431	Microsoft Publisher 98 Beginners

Microsoft Office 2000
1873005695	Microsoft Word 2000 Beginners
1873005709	Microsoft Word 2000 Intermediate
1873005717	Microsoft Word 2000 Advanced
1873005725	Microsoft Excel 2000 Beginners
1873005733	Microsoft Excel 2000 Intermediate
1873005741	Microsoft Excel 2000 Advanced
187300575X	Microsoft PowerPoint 2000 Beginners
1873005768	Microsoft PowerPoint 2000 Intermediate
1873005776	Microsoft Access 2000 Beginners for Users
1873005784	Microsoft Access 2000 Beginners for Developers
1873005792	Microsoft Access 2000 Interm. for Developers
1873005806	Microsoft Outlook 2000 Beginners
1873005814	Microsoft Publisher 2000 Beginners

Microsoft Works v4.5
187300544X	Microsoft Works v4.5 Beginners
1873005458	Microsoft Works v4.5 Word Processing Interm.
1873005466	Microsoft Works v4.5 Spreadsheets Intermediate
1873005474	Microsoft Works v4.5 Databases Intermediate

Sage Accounts
1873005512	Sage Instant Payroll v4 Beginners
1873005822	Sage Instant Payroll v5 Beginners
1873005830	Sage Payroll v5 Beginners
1873005520	Sage Instant Accounting 98 Beginners
1873005849	Sage Instant Accounting 2000 Beginners
1873005539	Sage Line 50 v5 Financial Controller Beginners
1873005547	Sage Line 50 v5 Financial Controller Interm.
1873005555	Sage Line 50 v5 Financial Controller Advanced
1873005563	Sage Line 50 v5 Accountant Plus Beginners
1873005571	Sage Line 50 v5 Accountant Plus Intermediate
187300558X	Sage Line 50 v5 Accountant Beginners

Lotus SmartSuite v9 Millennium Edition
1873005598	Lotus Word Pro v9 Millennium Edition Beginners
1873005601	Lotus Word Pro v9 Millennium Edition Interm.
187300561X	Lotus Word Pro v9 Millennium Edition Advanced
1873005628	Lotus 1-2-3 v9 Millennium Edition Beginners
1873005636	Lotus 1-2-3 v9 Millennium Edition Intermediate
1873005644	Lotus 1-2-3 v9 Millennium Edition Advanced
1873005652	Lotus Freelance Graphics v9 Mill. Ed. Beginners
1873005660	Lotus Freelance Graphics v9 Mill. Ed. Interm.
1873005679	Lotus Approach v9 Millennium Edition Beginners
1873005687	Lotus Approach v9 Millennium Edition Interm.

Corel WordPerfect Suite 8
1873005482	Corel WordPerfect v8 Beginners
1873005490	Corel WordPerfect v8 Intermediate
1873005504	Corel WordPerfect v8 Advanced

Corel WordPerfect Office 2000
1873005857	Corel WordPerfect v9 Beginners
1873005865	Corel WordPerfect v9 Intermediate
1873005873	Corel WordPerfect v9 Advanced

New titles are released regularly. For an up-to-date list, check **www.pcproductions.co.uk**, ask your local supplier for more details, or write to PC Productions Limited – the address can be found on page 2.

The exercise diskette

An exercise diskette accompanies this course. It should be attached to the back cover opposite. If it is missing or damaged, your supplier will be able to obtain a replacement for you.

> ♪ The exercise diskette contains practice files used in the book. There are no programs to install and it has no commercial value.